The Apple //c Book

Bantam Books of Related Interest
Ask your bookseller for the books you have missed

THE COMMODORE 64 SURVIVAL MANUAL
by Winn L. Rosch

THE COMPLETE BUYER'S GUIDE TO PERSONAL COMPUTERS by Tim Hartnell and Stan Veit

THE FRIENDLY COMPUTER BOOK: A SIMPLE GUIDE FOR ADULTS
by Gene Brown

HOW TO GET THE MOST OUT OF COMPUSERVE
by Charles Bowen and David Peyton

THE ILLUSTRATED COMPUTER DICTIONARY
by The Editors of Consumer Guide®

MASTERING YOUR TIMEX SINCLAIR 1000/1500™ PERSONAL COMPUTER by Tim Hartnell and Dilwyn Jones

The Apple® //c Book

Bill O'Brien

A Hard/Soft Press Book

Bantam Books
Toronto • New York • London • Sydney • Auckland

THE APPLE //c BOOK has been written with the knowledge of and some assistance from Apple Computer, Inc. By no means, however, should the reader assume that Apple Computer, Inc. has in any way authorized or endorsed this book, which is the result of the author's own research and analysis.

THE APPLE //c BOOK

A Bantam Book / July 1984

Apple //c is a registered trademark of Apple Computer, Inc. Throughout the book, the trade names and trademarks of many companies and products have been used, and no such uses are intended to convey endorsements of or other affiliations with the book.

Diagrams by Anthony Cinquina.
Photographs courtesy Apple Computer, Inc.
Book designed by Barbara N. Cohen.

ISBN 0-553-34149-9

Published simultaneously in the United States and Canada

Bantam Books are published by Bantam Books, Inc. Its trademark, consisting of the words "Bantam Books" and the portrayal of a rooster, is Registered in U.S. Patent and Trademark Office and in other countries. Marca Registrada. Bantam Books, Inc., 666 Fifth Avenue, New York, New York 10103.

PRINTED IN THE UNITED STATES OF AMERICA

HL 0 9 8 7 6 5 4 3 2 1

This book is dedicated to my Mother and Father, whose genetic code supplied me with my intelligence and wit. If only it had been looks and wealth. . . .

Contents

The Apple //c Book

1

The Apple //c and Its Family Tree

The personal computer industry is still in its infancy. Many of the firms that were tops in the field only a few years ago have vanished without a trace. Others have been swallowed up by big conglomerates or have fallen into the jaws of bankruptcy.

But at least one company has remained consistent in its dedication to personal computers. That company has been producing machines since 1977, and its machines are generally acknowledged to run the greatest variety of software. It's not exactly surprising that the name of that company is Apple Computer, Inc.

Apple Computer began its career with the Apple I, a cassette-based machine that in its day was a marvel of construction. It actually arrived fully assembled, and that alone sufficiently distinguished it from its kit-based rivals to merit a place in posterity.

Looking back at it from today's perspective, that machine wasn't much to brag about. The BASIC programming language it used could only handle integers; dollars-and-cents calculations were out of the question. And the only way you could use it to store information was via tape storage—audio cassette tape, at least, not punched paper tape. Still, other companies tried to get along with even less sophistication.

Apple, on the other hand, decided to improve its product. It wasn't long before the firm introduced the Apple //. And Apple didn't stop there. After that came the Apple //+, with floating-point (decimal) BASIC, the Apple ///, Lisa, the Apple //e, the Macintosh—and now the Apple //c. The mind boggles at the sheer quantity of equipment developed and refined over so short a period of time. Computers aren't just things you can throw together overnight. For each modification of an existing model, as well as for each new model, plans have to be made well in advance.

The Apple // family remains the most successful product the company has ever produced, and Apple remains fully committed to it. Despite all the hoopla over new machines, Apple // machines have stood their ground in the computer marketplace. They're being used in literally millions of American homes and offices for everything you can think of from game playing to controlling sophisticated scientific instruments.

The versatility of Apple // computers is one of the biggest reasons why the machines have been so popular. Another secret of their success is simply Apple's commitment to them. Every time industry pundits begin complaining that the Apple // is an old-fashioned relic (meaning more than a year old), Apple manages to silence their complaints by introducing a new model with features omitted from previous versions. And in doing so, Apple makes sure the new machines are compatible with the old so that they can take advantage of the huge number of software packages already in existence.

Somewhere, someone is trying to make you think you can believe in Apple. It's quite possible they've succeeded. One manufacturer of IBM personal computer products succumbed to Apple's overpowering presence and developed a successful product that in effect turns the much more expensive IBM Personal Computer into a member of the Apple // family. Why would anyone want to go that far? To answer that question, and to explain what's special about the Apple //c, a brief digression is in order.

The Anatomy of a Computer

Computers are simple. They're made up of only three basic components: hardware, software, and firmware. That may seem like a mouthful to you, but it's really easily digestible.

Hardware is the sum total of the electronic and mechanical parts from which the computer system is built. It's the tangible stuff you can see and touch.

Look inside the cabinet of a computer, and you'll see some printed circuit boards, some wires, and some electronic parts known as resistors and capacitors. They help manage the electricity coursing through the machine, but they're not the stars of the show. The leading roles are played by a few black rectangles known as *integrated circuits,* or *chips*. They contain thousands of electrical switches and connections that have been squeezed down into extremely compact size.

The most important of the chips is the *microprocessor*. It does the actual computing: it manipulates data. Two kinds of *memory* chips help it out. *RAM*—random access memory—stores information so that the microprocessor can use it. RAM chips don't change, but the information stored in them does. In fact, if you turn off the machine, the information disappears forever. If you like, you can think of RAM as the computer's workspace. The more of it there is, the more complicated the tasks the computer can perform.

Memory chips, called *ROM* (pronounced "rahm")—read only memory—store information which can't be changed. They store *firmware*—data that tells the computer how to handle its most primitive functions, such as what the machine should do when you turn it on or type your name on the keyboard. What's important about firmware is not how much there is, but what it does.

As a general rule, hardware and firmware are not easily changed. You may be able to augment them, if that has already been planned for in the design of the machine, but the fundamental design will remain what it is forever. And the limitations on the hardware ultimately limit what your computer can do. Think of it in vehicular terms: if you've got a bicycle, you won't be able to make it go 180 miles an hour no matter how hard you try.

Firmware is actually a special type of *software*. Software tells the computer what to do. It may be stored on a disk or a cassette tape, or you may even type it in, but software is simply a set of instructions that make your computer perform a particular task. When you run a program on the computer, you are actually using software. Software is what lets your computer play a game one minute and work on a complicated mathematical model the next. Back to our analogy: even if you've got a car that can go 400 mph, it won't be able to get up to speed until you find a driver who's willing to go that fast. That driver is the software.

The hardware you choose is important because software is *machine-specific;* it will only run on the machine it was designed for. And now you begin to see the beauty of the Apple //c. As part of the august, noble, and long-lived Apple // family, the //c will run virtually all the software developed for this group of computers. And software is what makes a computer perform its magic.

Software and Support

If a computer's going to help make you more productive in your daily life, it must run the software you need. And what the computer industry calls "support"—help when you need it—must be available. Without both, no computer is worth purchasing.

If a computer has been on the market for a long time, you can usually assume you'll have access to a large vault of software for it. Aside from the usual collection of games, there should be word-processing, database, numeric-analysis, telecommunications, and graphics packages all out there waiting to be bundled up in your arms and taken home. With a brand-new model, you usually have to wait for the software to bloom; if sales of the machine turn out to be sluggish, you may just have to wait forever.

By being compatible with the rest of the Apple // family, the Apple //c neatly solves that problem. It's a brand-new machine that just happens to be designed to run literally thousands of programs *already on the market.*

As one of the pioneers in personal computers, Apple has had a major edge on most other companies. That "edge" is important. Since the inception of the Apple //, the quantity of Apple software has grown by leaps and bounds. Because the Apple // family has been in existence for so long, there's a huge library of software for it. With the proper software, you can turn an Apple into a game player, an economic forecaster, a word processor, a musical instrument, a personal tutor, or just about anything else you can think of. In a category like word processing, you can actually choose among dozens of different programs, each with its strengths and weaknesses. Although the IBM family is gaining strength, no other group of computers runs as much different software as the Apple // family. Because the //c runs virtually all of this software, you can use it *now*—not a year from now.

So the Apple //c is definitely a reasonable choice. You can buy it, plunk it down on your desk, and actually get some productivity out of it. People have been doing just that with its older brothers for quite a while now. And the //c comes packed with quite a few goodies that were extra-cost options on those older models.

The Evolution of the Apple // Series

Option	Apple //+	Apple //e	Apple //c
64K Memory	O	I	I
64K Expansion Memory	N/A	O	I
80-Column Output	O	O	I
Uppercase/Lowercase	O	I	I
Serial Printer Port	O	O	I
Serial Modem Port	O	O	I
Disk Drive w/Controller	O	O	I
Game I/O	I	I	I
Mouse I/O	O	O	I
RAM Disk	O	I	N/A
ProDOS Compatible	O	I	I

NOTE: O = Optional, I = Included, N/A = Not Available.

The Portable Dilemma

One day you may wake up and discover that you desperately need a computer. There can be any number of reasons. You've just made a fortune in the stock market and you want to keep track of it. Or maybe you've just lost a fortune (you do have enough left to buy a computer, though) and you want to figure out how it happened. Or you need something to help you write the Great American Novel, and you're aware that typewriters have become all but obsolete.

You buy the computer. After learning how to make it work, you realize you've become dependent on it. You actually use it more than any other tool you've ever owned. And it comes as quite a surprise that you miss it when both of you aren't in the same place at the same time.

What happens when you're away from your desk? Do you suddenly remember what you want to do and have to wait until you get back to your computer to deal with all the things that need to be taken care of? You know, like that $2,100.00 check your client sent you—or was it $2,010.00? Or $2,000.10? What was that great thought you had while you were out of town last week for that sales meeting? If only you could remember it, you just know it would make a big impact on the business.

Having a computer on your desk (or the coffee table, as the case may be) is not always the most practical solution to your needs. Sometimes you'll work with a computer in the office and then remember some small detail you've forgotten—but not until you're home. You can duplicate the setup at home, but what happens if you go on the road? You can't possibly expect to keep or find copies of your computer hardware or software everywhere you might go.

What's Portable, Anyhow?

Look around and you'll notice that a whole new range of computers has recently become available. These machines can be called anything from portables to transportables to lap or notebook computers. The one thing they have in common is that they can be moved from place to place without major complications.

Archimedes claimed he could move the earth if you gave him a long enough lever and a place to stand, and given enough muscle and the right gear, a modern Archimedes could probably move any computer. Both the Apple //e and the Apple /// can be transported in special carrying cases. Some of these cases even have provisions for extra hardware and the video monitors that a computer needs to display its work and yours. There is even a mammoth carrying case that holds the big IBM PC along with its keyboard and monitor. But these machines were never meant to be carried around. If you put four wheels under a barn, that doesn't make it a car.

Likewise, the fact that a computer comes in a snazzy all-in-one case is not really a criterion for calling it portable. The Osborne, Compaq, and Kaypro computers herald themselves as portables, but this nomenclature is dubious. A more accurate term for them is *transportable.* They weigh more than 25 pounds apiece, so they're not items you'd care to heft on a regular basis.

Some lighter models move closer to true portability. Apple's Macintosh weighs in at 21 pounds. A machine called the Hyperion tips the scales at 19 pounds. Both fit into cases that resemble gym bags. And newer machines that bend or fold into suitcase-shaped cases are becoming even lighter.

Lap computers are just that—they fit on your lap and take up about as much room as a three-ring notebook (hence the alternative name "notebook computer"). Usually they have LCD (liquid crystal display) screens that may show as many as 80 columns across (the standard for normal-sized machines), but are seldom more than a few lines high. Their strength, as they currently exist, is in storing information in a special type of memory that can be powered by internal batteries for weeks at a time. But because lap machines can store only relatively small amounts of data, the user will usually want to transfer data to a larger, more powerful machine. Most owners of lap models use them as handy traveling extensions of the bigger computers they already own.

Designing Your Own Machine

But what if you were to design your own portable machine? First of all, it should have a handle. That's not as obvious as it sounds. One major Japanese "portable" computer doesn't have one: it's possible they expect you to tuck it under your arm. And if you're going to carry your computer around, it shouldn't weigh very much. Ten pounds or less doesn't seem an unreasonable burden.

When it comes to keyboards, many computer companies go their own way and introduce supposed "improvements" that can drive good typists crazy. If you know how to type, you won't want to go through a long period of readjustment to a new keyboard. If you don't know how to type, you'll want to learn on something that's standard. Your computer's keyboard should employ the most familiar layout, the one used on the IBM Selectric.

Memory Matters

Memory (RAM) is another important consideration. Computers think in *1*'s and *0*'s. Each of them is called a *bit.* Put eight of them together and you've got a *byte,* which is a lot more useful. A byte is roughly equal to one character (letter, digit, or punctuation mark) in English, although there are

Taking a Byte

One *byte* is equal to eight *bits* of digital data. It's a useful entity because eight bits suffice to code 256 different characters. That's enough to include all the upper- and lowercase letters of the alphabet, all the numbers from zero to nine, and over a hundred special symbols that can be used to control the computer. For most purposes, therefore, each byte corresponds to one character of memory.

times when a computer will use one byte—a single character—to represent a more complex instruction.

Memory is expressed in kilobytes, or "K" for short. One kilobyte is equal to 1,024 bytes, though you can round it off to 1,000 for purposes of comparison. A computer with 16K of RAM, then, has a workspace of about 16,000 characters—or roughly ten double-spaced pages of typed material.

Not long ago, 16K was a common amount of memory supplied with a computer. Though that may seem like a lot at first glance, some rather simple software programs can be eight or nine thousand bytes long. It's not uncommon for software to take fifteen or twenty thousand bytes and more. And data has to squeeze into RAM along with the software. There are ways to do this by swapping portions of programs and data into RAM from somewhere else (such as a disk drive), but such techniques slow down the software.

Though some fancy programs need more than 200K, the Apple // family has traditionally done just fine with 64K. You'll double that to be on the

What's a Kilo?

Anyone who knows anything about the metric system knows that the prefix *kilo-* means "thousand." So why is a kilobyte 1,024 bytes?

Computer engineers count in "base two," dealing in digital "bits," each of which can be either a one or a zero. Rather than using a number system based on tens, where each column of digits represents a power of ten, computer engineers figure in powers of two. The golden number for the "K" of bytes, 1,024, just happens to be an even power of two (2^{10}). The engineers figured it was close enough to exactly one thousand to get away with calling it a "kilo." If you're used to the metric system, look at it this way: you get an extra twenty-four bytes of memory with every K.

safe side and consider allowing memory expansion when higher-capacity chips are available.

Seeing Your Ideas

The computer you're designing would be useless if you couldn't see what it did. Many portables offer only green-on-black or white-on-black displays, but you won't settle for that. Since the kids may want to play games with the machine, and you may want to develop fancy business graphics, you insist on both color and monochrome capability.

Not only that, but the machine should also be able to take the video signal that normally drives a computer monitor and convert it to the special type of signal that a standard TV set can handle. After all, if you're going portable, you may end up in an awful lot of motel rooms that don't have computer monitors but do have color TVs.

The computer must also be capable of displaying 80 columns of characters across a screen. That's the standard for a normal 8½-inch-wide sheet of paper, and there's no reason to settle for less. If it can be asked to display 40 bigger characters on command so that they're readable on a TV screen, so much the better.

Storing What You've Done

There should also be some way to store your information when you turn the power off and everything in RAM suddenly disappears. You could use

An Apple to go.

Apple //c with portable LCD screen (attached), modem (left), mouse (front), carrying case.

audio tape cassettes, but they're not terribly dependable and have no place in the design of a perfect computer. Forget them for now; the industry is certainly trying to.

What you need is at least one disk drive. Two would be nicer, but that would add weight and bulk. You'll settle for one disk drive built into the computer, along with the ability to hook up another one when you settle down for hard work.

Let's not forget that the computer must be compatible with a tremendous selection of software! Everything else would be useless if there were no software to run on your machine. You don't want to go through a waiting period while software is written, tested, and rewritten for a new computer. You want one that will do what you want it to as soon as you get it home.

That's why you'll use the industry-standard 5¼-inch disk drive. The smaller 3½-inch models used on the Macintosh and other machines would certainly save space and weight, but the thousands of programs available on 5¼-inch disks wouldn't fit into them—either electronically or physically.

Hangin' on the Telephone

Although our computer will be as self-sufficient as possible, it shouldn't be forced to fend for itself. Communications facilities would be nice so that our machine could talk with others. We should be able to connect it directly to another computer or let it communicate over the phone lines through a *modem*. That's a MOdulator-DEModulator, a piece of hardware that can translate a computer's electronic signals into special audio tones that can be sent over the phone lines and translate the tones back into signals a computer can understand.

Modems are *serial* devices. They communicate with the world one bit at a time. To do that, they only need one wire for each direction, a ground wire to complete the circuit, and a couple of more wires to do such things as detect that another computer is on the other end of the line.

If you want a modem, you'll need a *serial port* to hook it up to the computer—a jack where the cable hooks up, along with the internal circuitry to make it work. Add the serial port to the specifications for your portable.

Printing and Parallelism

You'll also want to be able to hook up a printer to turn what you see on the screen into *hard copy*—paper output that even people without computers can read.

Printers often communicate with computers in *parallel* fashion. Unlike the one-bit-at-a-time serial method, parallel communication deals with all eight bits of each byte at the same time. To do that, you need eight separate wires to send and eight to receive, a ground wire, and wires to tell each machine that a byte is being sent and wires to let the computer know when the printer is too busy at the moment to receive anything further. It's not hard to make a cable with all those wires, but the connector for it will be big and bulky—and the internal wiring is no picnic, either. It'll take up a lot of space in your little portable machine.

Fortunately, many printers can work in serial mode, one bit at a time, just the way modems do. Solution: add a second serial port so that you can hook up printer and modem at the same time.

Powering Up

For now, adequate battery power is not available for this sort of design. There's just no lightweight, low-cost, self-contained power source that can run the computer you have in mind. Let's stick with wall power for the time being: portability doesn't necessarily mean you should be able to use your machine every moment of your life. At the same time, though, we won't entirely abandon the concept of a battery pack—it's a good idea and technology may soon make it practical. In fact, to allow for the possibility of new power sources and to keep heat from the power supply from shortening the lives of the delicate electronic components in the machine, we'll put the power supply outside in its own separate package.

Welcome to the Orchard

That's some goal you've set for yourself. Will you ever be able to find a computer that matches your specifications—and one that's also compatible with software that runs on Apple // computers?

Of course you will! You either have it in front of you or you're thinking of buying one. Why else would you be reading this book?

If you fall into the latter category, what are you waiting for? Apple's //c meets most of the criteria for your ideal portable computer. And we haven't even begun to mention its dozens of other special features, such as the switch that can change the very way you type or the port that will let you hook up a useful critter called a mouse faster than you can say "cheese." There are very few things you can't do with an Apple //c.

If you're trembling at the awesome prospect of opening the box that houses your brand-new, untouched Apple //c, tremble no more. The Apple //c is a great and wondrous machine, but remember, it's only a tool. Without you, it won't do a thing. You are the driving force behind it. It doesn't have enough innate intelligence to know how to plug itself in—let alone turn itself on!

But together! Together with your guiding hand and the Apple //c's abilities, who's to set limits on what you can accomplish? A disk drive here, a printer there, and a modem for good measure, and the world is at your fingertips. Just sit back. In the following pages you'll learn how far an Apple //c can take you through the new electronic universe.

2

Playing the System

Packed inside the Apple //c box is an exceptionally capable and well-equipped computer. But one visit to the computer store will convince you that well endowed as it is, even an Apple //c computer can't stand alone. To do anything worth mentioning, it has to become the brains of a *computer system.*

There are enough accessories to plug in, shove in, and key in to your machine to keep you in the store for days and put you in the poorhouse for years. If you jump into computing without understanding the "system half" of your computer, you're likely to acquire a lot of equipment that's absolutely useless and miss out on a lot of good stuff you may really need. The trick to your personal survival in the home computer revolution is to understand what a computer system is and know how it works.

Expanding Your Apple's Influence

In the early days of computers, people often referred to them as "electronic brains." When you're considering a computer system, that's not a terrible analogy. Just as no brain can do anything of much use without the help of such items as arms and legs and eyes, no computer can do much of value without the help of such items as monitors and printers.

Although it's filled with hardware power, the Apple //c's greatest strength is not what's inside, but what can be connected to it—the hardware devices that can be added to extend the system's outer edge. By itself the Apple //c is just a box that changes numbers and words into different forms. But when you expand that basic box by connecting the Apple //c to other devices, the system can *do* things: print mailing labels, newsletters,

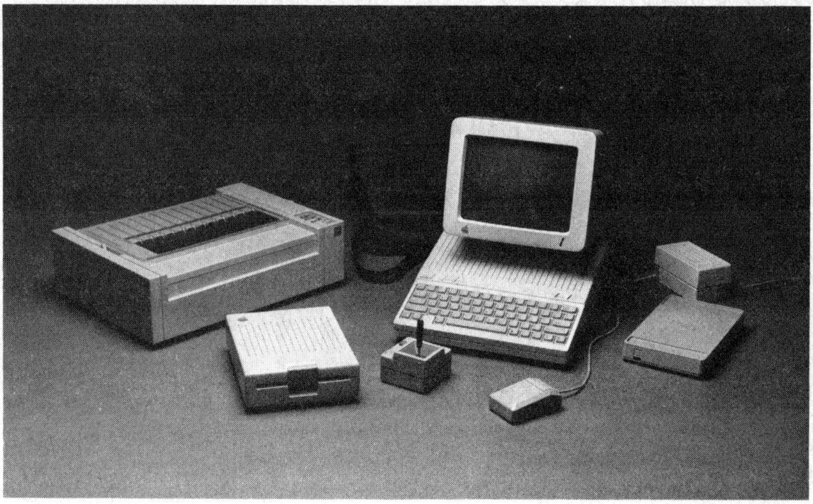

An Apple //c system.

Clockwise from left: Imagewriter printer, computer carrying case, Apple //c and monitor, power supply, modem, mouse, joystick, external disk drive. Some necessary cables are missing from this photograph.

and books, play games on a color video screen, even talk to other computers over telephone lines.

The best way to learn how such a computer system works is to examine its constituent parts, or *peripherals*. In this chapter, we'll look at the hardware—the framework that gives the Apple //c its potential—so you can better appreciate the possibilities locked inside your new computer.

The Brains of the Outfit

The heart of your computer system is the Apple //c itself. You met the fundamental parts of its innards—its microprocessor, RAM, and ROM—in chapter 1. The //c is the central command center of the system.

Next to what's inside it, the most important part of the //c itself is its keyboard. You won't have much trouble finding it, and for good reason: only through the keyboard (or, to a much more limited extent, a joystick, paddle, mouse, or other similar device) can you communicate with the computer system.

Packed in the box with the Apple //c are several important accessories, the major one being the power supply. It's the large cream-colored brick with wires sticking out of either end. You could find it by feel alone: it weighs about 3½ pounds.

Truth to tell, it's not quite the entire power supply. That hefty chunk is actually the transformer that changes the wall voltage into something your Apple //c can use. The electronics used to refine the "transformed" voltage are inside the computer. By doing things this way, much of the weight and a good part of the heat generated by the conversion process are kept outside the computer.

But there are a couple of minor problems with this scheme. When you turn off your machine, the power supply stays on. If you touch it and it's still plugged in, you'll discover it's warm, even if your computer has been turned off for hours. That evidence shows you that even when your computer is switched off, the power supply is still sucking a little electricity from your wall and adding to your electric bill. The power supply has built-in protection against catastrophic effects from its failure, but there is still a possibility that it might get overly warm from an internal malfunction and conceivably start a fire. That possibility is extremely minute, but it should be enough to encourage you to unplug the power supply (or turn off a switchable outlet) anytime you're not using your computer.

Also included in the box with your Apple //c are two cables, a cream-colored switch box, and an *RF converter,* a smallish cream-colored brick with a connector on one end and a hole in the other. You'll need one or more of them to connect your computer to a *video display*—either a television set or a computer monitor.

Picture This: The Display

The keyboard and joystick are your way of communicating to your Apple //c. The display is the Apple //c's way of communicating back. When you use the keyboard, the display will usually show you (or *echo*) every keystroke you type. This tells you that the machine has received all your commands and understood them. The monitor may also give you other information: instructions, status reports, or the results of using a particular program.

You have two choices. You can invest in a "dedicated" monitor, a display device much like a television but without the tuner. They come in monochrome and color in a variety of sizes. But you can get by without a monitor: the RF adapter included with every Apple //c will change the *video* signals a monitor needs into the *radio frequency (RF)* signals a standard TV set demands.

Each choice has its pluses and minuses. The RF adapter will be a godsend when you travel with the computer and don't want to lug a monitor around. With it, you can connect the Apple //c to any handy television set. But TV sets have drawbacks when used with computers.

One measure of the quality of a TV's picture or signal is its *resolution.* Unfortunately, a TV set's resolution is very low compared to the resolution of the signal an Apple //c is capable of generating. Even so, a TV can be used as an inexpensive way to display graphic images (pictures as opposed to text) from the computer. They won't be highly detailed, but if you haven't seen what a color monitor can do, you may never notice.

The video circuitry used in the Apple //c includes a feature called "color burst," which assists it in sending accurate color images to the display device. That's fine for pictures, but unfortunately, the color burst is not turned off when the machine displays text. When you use a color TV with an Apple //c, letters and numbers will have a somewhat smeared or fuzzy appearance that can become irritating to look at after a while. Turning off the TV's color or using a black-and-white set will help.

Video signals—the kinds that monitors use—have several separate parts, roughly corresponding to the brightness and color of the picture, and a synchronizing signal that keeps everything straight. Some monitors use three separate wires to receive signals representing each of the three primary colors of light. Since those colors are red, green, and blue, such monitors are called *RGB* monitors. RGB signals are capable of producing sharper pictures than any others, and they are the choice for exacting video displays. They also require special, expensive cathode ray tubes to display their high quality, which means RGB monitors tend to cost more than other kinds. The signals the Apple //c produces are *not* directly compatible with RGB monitors, but they can be adapted via the video expansion port. If you're thinking about going this route, be sure you have the proper adapter to keep both your Apple and your RGB monitor happy.

The other type of color monitor is known as *composite,* because with it the color, brightness, and synchronizing signals are all combined and sent over one cable. This is the kind the //c requires. Such monitors usually have higher resolution than TV sets, and the pictures they produce are therefore more highly detailed. Text is sharper, too.

The //c can display text 80 columns across. In color, such a display will be uncomfortable to read if not downright unintelligible. Solution? A monochrome (one color, not counting black) monitor with good resolution. Apple Computer offers a brand-new model as a companion for the Apple //c. It uses a green phosphor picture tube, so everything is displayed in green on a black background. But if you prefer one of the increasingly popular amber displays or you already own another monitor, you're not limited to what Apple has to offer. Any standard monochrome monitor will hook up with little trouble. And monochrome monitors are cheap compared to their color cousins. Good ones are available for less than $200.

If you're interested in portability, pay attention to the monitor's size and weight. Apple's new monitor is among the smallest and the lightest available (but still a lot heavier than the new LCD screen), and other companies will undoubtedly release their own lightweights. But if you're going to hook the //c up to TV sets and other monitors in your travels, and your own monitor will stay at home, weight won't matter much.

Just to recap: if you're using the Apple //c primarily for textual work (word processing, spreadsheets, etc.), you will probably want a monochrome monitor. If, on the other hand, your work will be primarily pictorial, either a color TV or color monitor will suffice, with the latter producing the higher quality display.

Progress is blurring the line between television sets and monitors. Many so-called monitors are just television sets with an extra place to plug in a wire to bypass the built-in tuner. A new trend in television called "component video" splits the traditional TV set into two units—one for the screen and one for the tuner.

If money is more of an issue than quality, you can go with a standard TV. But be warned: if you begin by using the wrong display for the type of work you're doing, you'll eventually go out and spend the money on the right one—or you'll become disgusted with your computer. And that would be a shame.

Many companies, including Zenith, Amdek, Taxan, and NEC, manufacture Apple-compatible display devices in both monochrome and color. Try before you buy: your personal preferences may make subtle differences in resolution, color intensity, and monochrome tint more important to you than you might imagine.

Printing the Message

The second item you'll want in your computer system is a *printer*. You need one, although you may not realize it right away. There is not one serious application (aside from some pretty serious games) that does not, at one time or another, require a printer.

A printer turns the electronic thoughts of the Apple //c into hard copy—ink on paper. With hard copy, you can look at what you've done without churning electricity through your computer. You can look at one version of your work on the printed page while you compare it against the version on the screen. And you can rest assured that your work is safely out of the clutches of potential electronic malfunctions.

The most important thing to remember when buying a printer for the Apple //c is that it must be capable of *serial* communications. The Apple //c simply can't communicate with any printer that works only in the parallel mode.

Parallel-only printers do exist, but there are still dozens of other models you can choose from. *Dot-matrix* printers are fast, cheap, and produce characters made up of tiny dots. Some give you text that's downright ugly, but others can produce output that's just short of—but not quite—typewriter quality. As a group, *letter-quality*, or *daisy-wheel*, printers are slower and more expensive, but they work on the same principles as electronic typewriters and can produce text that's typewriter pretty. Which type you need depends on whether you're more intent on using your machine for simple printouts of program listings or for heavy-duty office correspondence.

One excellent possibility is an Apple printer. The dot-matrix Imagewriter offers an attractive combination of low cost and high-resolution output. The Scribe, Apple's recently announced, low-cost, dot-matrix machine, employs an unusual ink-jet design capable of printing in color as well as black-and-white. It could be just the ticket if you're doing a lot of graphics work. Apple also markets an excellent letter-quality machine. Hooking up any of these models to your //c should be a breeze. Get the right cable from your dealer, and you should be in business.

Picking a Printer

Still, you might want to consider a non-Apple printer for a variety of reasons:

- Speed. Some printers can do their work faster than the Apple machines.
- Silence. The Apple printers aren't especially noisy, but they aren't especially quiet, either. Some other printers, particularly ink-jet models, are.
- Quality. The Apple printers give respectable output, but it may not suit your taste. The typefaces you can get from a different machine may be more to your liking.
- Portability. The Apple dot-matrix machines are about as light as such models come, but some ink-jet printers are even more compact. The Apple letter-quality model is designed for heavy-duty office use. If you need a letter-quality machine for the road, you'll want to look elsewhere.
- Use of wider paper. Apple's dot-matrix printers can handle paper no wider than 8½ inches after trimming. Other models can use 14-inch computer paper that's particularly useful for spreadsheets.

Whatever printer you choose, be sure to investigate the availability of service. Printers have parts that do a lot of moving, and sooner or later some of those parts will break down. Convenient locations and procedures for servicing the equipment can help you get up and running in a hurry.

Printers also have a voracious appetite for paper. When you do get your printer, be sure you also buy a sufficient amount of paper to keep it from going hungry for a while.

You'll find a more detailed exploration of printers in chapter 13.

Storing the Masses

A computer is only what a program makes it. Without the program (or software) a computer can do nothing. But how do you get a program into the computer? With the Apple //c, there are two ways: typing programs manually from the keyboard and using diskettes.

The first method has its difficulties. It's a one-way affair. Without something extra, you couldn't preserve your work or your high score when you or your cat or the power company hits the off switch. Entering programs by hand may seem simple, but when the program you want to enter is hundreds of lines long, trying to type all those lines into the machine without making a mistake can be a shortcut to the funny farm.

The built-in disk drive to the rescue! The disk drive lets you buy prefabricated programs on disks and "read" them into your computer. But you can also use disks to store programs that you write yourself *and* any other data that you need. Because they let you record and preserve massive quantities of programs, text, and data, disk drives are often called *mass-storage devices.*

A disk drive combines the best qualities of a tape recorder with the best qualities of a phonograph. Like tapes, a computer's floppy disks can be recorded, played back, and erased magnetically with utmost fidelity. Like records, floppy disks are "random access." Just as you can drop the needle down anywhere you want on a record, your computer can select data from anywhere on a floppy disk. And it can drop its "needle" (actually a moving magnetic head, like the magnetic head of a tape recorder) anywhere for any amount of time and then go on to the next selection. Because of their random-access abilities, disk drives are much faster than the audio tape cassettes early Apple // machines used for mass storage of data. In fact, disks are so superior that the Apple //c has offered no way at all to connect a cassette recorder.

How About Another Disk Drive?

You already know that the Apple //c comes with one disk drive already built in. That's fine. But it's probably not enough. That second drive the salesman may be recommending is definitely a purchase worth careful consideration.

The Apple //c external disk drive.

The slot at lower right lights up when the disk is in motion.

When you take your machine on the road, one drive will suffice. When you get it back to home base, though, you're likely to find working with just one drive an exercise in frustration. Most software will work with just one drive, but you'll often have to swap different disks in and out of the drive in order for a program to work properly. If you want to copy a disk for archival purposes (and you will), you'll have to become adept at performing the disk-drive shuffle—put the first disk in, then take it out, then the second disk in, then do it all again. A second drive eliminates this nuisance. It's the same as with printers: you may not know yet that you need one, but you probably do.

All disk drives may look similar, but you're probably going to have to use Apple's special add-on model with your Apple //c. Although nearly all home computers use the same size floppy disks, 5¼ inches in diameter (inside the black plastic envelope), nearly all machines use different electronic *formats* to record data onto the magnetic surface of the disk.

The format is the particular way the recorded information is stored. In essence, each machine records data on a disk as if the disk were divided into separate concentric bands (called *tracks*), each of which is divided into a number of short lengths (called *sectors*). Different computers use different numbers of tracks and sectors even though they use the same kind of floppy disk. That's why disks *written* (recorded) on one brand of machine will not *read* (play) on another brand. Sometimes disks are incompatible between two different machines from the same company.

Disks produced on and for Apple // computers are generally compatible. Information recorded on an Apple //+, for example, will usually be understandable to your Apple //c. In fact, if you're an experienced electronics tinkerer, you may be able to adapt the interface from an older-model Apple // disk drive to work with the Apple //c. But if you don't have DIN plugs in your soul, Apple's latest model makes it easy to add that second drive to your //c. All you have to do is buy it, bring it home, and plug it in.

Diskette Follies

In its infinite wisdom, Apple does not include any blank diskettes with the machine. The only way you're going to get any information stored away is by using the disk drive, and you'll need diskettes to do it. Be sure to bring home a box of them when you buy your machine.

All 5¼-inch floppy disks are not the same. Disk packages tell the tale in a confusion of terms: data densities (single and double), types of sectors (hard and soft), and numbers of sides (single and double). Actually, all disks are equal "at birth," since all the different varieties can be punched out of a single sheet of the same raw material. The difference is how the individual kinds of disks are tested. The greater the amount, or *density*, of the data to be recorded onto a floppy disk, the more stringent the test made on each disk, and the more disks rejected. Disks designed for greater recording densities are more expensive because more are rejected during testing. The same is true for the number of *sides*. Single-sided disks have magnetic material on both sides, but they are tested only on one side. Double-sided disks are tested on both sides, and that makes them more expensive.

Apple // disk drives are designed to use the least expensive diskettes: *single sided, single density*. That means you can use a disk rated at any density with any number of tested sides, and it should work. However, if you do use disks with extra sides or density, you'll simply be paying for quality that you don't need.

There's one more way in which Apple // drives have a beer-budget appetite. Most floppy disks now available are called *soft sectored*. That means there is a single small hole punched in the disk a short distance from the big center hole. Some disk drives use the smaller hole as a landmark from which to find their place when looking for data on the disk. Hard-sectored disks are generally more expensive and have anywhere from ten to sixteen of these holes. The Apple // doesn't pay any attention to these holes, no matter whether there's one of them or sixteen, so it doesn't matter which type of disks you feed it.

Besides the 5¼-inch variety, disks 8 inches across are readily available, but for obvious reasons they will not fit in your Apple //c disk drive. The newer 3½-inch disks just might, but keep them out of your machine. The size differences are obvious, so you're not likely to make a mistake when you visit your computer store. But if you order disks through the mail, be sure to specify the size you need.

To sum up: when buying floppy disks for your Apple //c, ask for *5¼-inch, single-sided, single-density, soft-sectored* diskettes. They're the cheapest kind on the market.

The Line on Modems

Although there are hundreds of brands of computers and dozens of languages that they speak, enough standards exist that computers can talk among themselves and share information. The primary standard that will soon become extremely familiar to you is called the "American Standard Code for Information Interchange," and is nearly always abbreviated as ASCII (pronounced as-key). This code defines a digital value for each letter of the alphabet, numbers, and special commands. Nearly all communication between computers is done using the ASCII code.

Many large databases (mostly mainframe computers with extremely large memories that are willing to share information with other machines for a price) can be connected to the Apple //c through telephone lines. They provide a wide variety of information and services, from stock quotes to games, electronic mail, and shop-at-home services.

But connecting a computer to a telephone line is not as simple as just plugging it in. Ages ago, telephone lines were designed to carry voice signals, which are completely different from the data signals your computer is comfortable with. For computer signals to be sent over phone wires, the electronic bits of data must first be converted to voicelike frequencies and adapted to the special requirements of the telephone line. The computer on the receiving end must decode the voice signals back into computer language. The voice encoding process is called *modulation,* and the decoding process is called *demodulation.* A device that can convert the signals in either direction, then, would logically be called a "modulator/ demodulator," or *modem* for short.

Most modems are expensive gadgets that sit under telephones and send information from one office of a company to another or let the user hook up to popular database services. Modems range in price from one hundred to thousands of dollars. More money usually buys more speed; premium-priced modems for microcomputers can usually send and receive data four times faster than lower-cost models—but only if another high-speed modem is on the other end of the line. More money may also buy more features; some modems can dial and answer the phone without benefit of human assistance.

With the proper cable, you can plug a wide variety of "outboard" modems right into your Apple //c. Aside from speed and features, the major difference among modems is how you attach them to your phone line. Most modern modems use *direct connection* into the line via a standard "modular jack." Normally, that's the best way to make the connection, but if you're on the road, you may find yourself in a motel room whose phone is wired to the wall to discourage theft. In that case, you'll want a model with an *acoustic coupler,* two rubber cups that hold a standard telephone handset. It's less dependable than a direct-connect type, but in some situations it's the only answer.

Paddles and Joysticks

Before the Apple // series became popular for business applications, quite a few games were available for it. The most famous were modeled on *Space Invaders,* imported straight from the video parlors of Japan. They required moving the small image of a command base back and forth along the bottom of the screen, while firing at the moving aliens above as they dropped spaghettilike bombs.

Using the keyboard to move the command base would have been rather cumbersome. The Apple version of the game would never have caught on if it hadn't been for one small detail: inside the machine was a connector to which you could attach game paddles.

These not-so-successful inventions consisted of a knob and a switch. As you rotated the knob on the paddle, a variable resistor sensed a change in position and moved the command base an appropriate distance. Pressing the switch signaled the game to fire at the aliens.

The paddles tended to wear out, sometimes incredibly quickly. Luckily, they evolved into the joystick, which combined the controls of paddles into one unit that could send left-right *and* up-down movement to a game program. The firing switch was included, too.

Paddles have become yesterday's news, and only a minuscule number of Apple programs require them. If you're serious about playing games, you'll need at least one joystick. The goal of any joystick is to feel as natural and responsive as possible so that you can react and communicate your reactions to your computer as quickly as possible. The shape and feel of the joystick are very important to how well you can play games—how many space monsters you can zap or how many distant worlds you can save from total destruction. Apple offers a modestly priced joystick that is simple and effective, but it just might not match you or your hands properly for top scores.

Fortunately, a wide variety of outside suppliers' joysticks are completely compatible with the Apple //c. However, some that were compatible with older Apple models and some that appear to have compatible connectors may not work at all. Make sure the joystick you buy has a nine-pin connector *and* that it's made specifically for the Apple //c or //e.

Eek—a Mouse!

The *mouse* doesn't have four legs. It's a mechanical device that you roll along a flat surface. A rubber ball inside rolls along with you and moves two sensors. The sensors key an optical device inside the mouse that sends

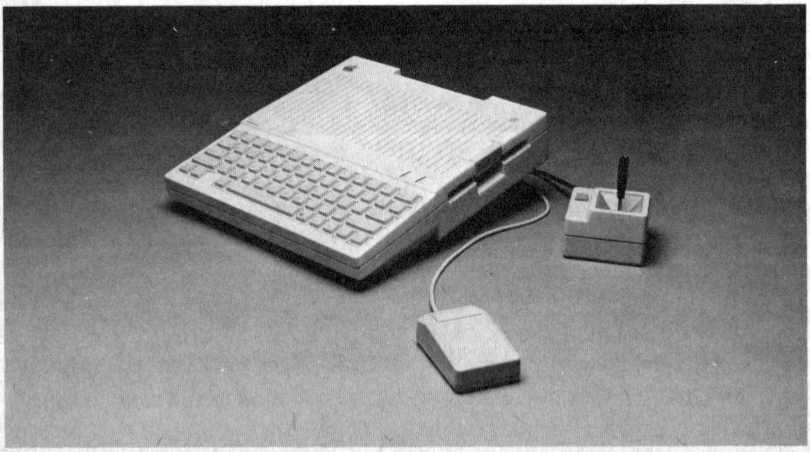

Apple //c with joystick and mouse.

Appearances to the contrary, the joystick and the mouse cannot be connected to the computer at the same time.

signals back to the computer. A program can track the movement of this amazing gadget and provide you with accurate information. The entire mechanism fits in the palm of your hand.

The mouse is a standard feature of Apple's Macintosh, and a worthwhile companion for the //c, particularly for graphics programs, since it makes drawing on the screen a snap. Other companies make mice, but Apple's plugs right into your //c.

Electric Questions

The plug for the Apple //c's power supply has three prongs. One of the two bladelike prongs is for the voltage coming into the machine; the other allows the voltage to return to the wall, completing the electrical path. The blunt, tubular prong is the ground connection. Under most normal conditions, it routes stray electrical signals out and away from fragile computer electronics—as long as you don't defeat it.

If you live or work somewhere that does not support the three-wire system, you should get a three-prong adapter. One side of the adapter accepts a three-prong plug like the one on the power supply; the other will give you two prongs to plug into your wall outlet, along with a metal tab or a wire that takes the place of the third prong. If you want the adapter to do its job, be sure to connect the tab or wire to the center screw of the wall outlet plate. In theory, the metal housing of the outlet should then be grounded and do the rest of the job.

Don't ignore the ground connection. If you do, stray signals may find their way inside your Apple //c and be the cause of its premature failure. Any piece of electronic equipment without a proper ground can be a hazard, both to itself and to you, its user.

Power outlets aren't the most exciting things in the world, but there are a few more things to remember about them. Try to avoid connecting your computer to an outlet shared by a refrigerator, blender, air conditioner, or similar appliance. Such appliances use motors that generate a lot of electrical "noise" which can be transmitted over the power line in the form of large electrical "spikes"—momentary surges of voltage far beyond what the Apple //c can tolerate. Spikes can also obliterate the circuitry in your Apple //c.

If you absolutely have to run your machine from an outlet with "dirty" electricity, all is not lost. You can invest in a *surge suppressor* or *line filter* that will sift out the electrical garbage before it reaches your machine. Such devices usually look like glorified extension cords, so installation is easy. Plug your computer into one end and plug the other end into the wall. You can find surge suppressors at just about any computer store. The salesman who's so eager to sell you the under-$100 device may just be doing you a favor.

You might also want to invest in a multi-outlet *power strip*. These fancy extension cords turn one grounded outlet into three or six, and often include a switch as well. Sooner or later you'll probably find yourself needing one. Some power strips have surge suppressors built in.

If you do need one of these devices or you have to rearrange a few appliances, take care of it before you bring your computer home. When you plug in your Apple //c, you shouldn't have to worry about anything besides making it do what you want it to.

3

The Art of Uncrating Apples

Okay. You've taken our advice and gone out and bought all the peripherals and accessories you need. Now what?

There are three ways to approach any new computer system. You can sit timidly looking at the unopened boxes. You can tear open the box on the floor and scatter everything around, Christmas-style. Or you can really think about what you're doing and plan the actions you're about to take. The last option is, of course, the most logical, but that's not always a point we humans take into consideration.

If you've already opened the box, step back for a moment and get a better perspective. If you've already opened the box and tossed everything around, step back cautiously. You might even consider sitting down.

In many ways a new computer resembles a new child. Until you get to know and understand it, it will spend a great deal of time complaining. The only way to calm it down is often to let it have its own way. You'll also have to give it a comfortable environment and some of the essentials it demands.

Where Do I Put It?

The Apple //c is a portable computer, but that doesn't mean it's indestructible. In fact, a portable like the //c is in some ways more fragile than its desktop cousins. To make a computer portable, everything is packed tightly inside. There is a tough plastic shell around everything, but it won't withstand a whole lot of banging around. Apple itself recommends that you carry the //c in its optional case if the trip is more than a short one.

You can definitely go a long way with the machine, but a little care is in

What you get in the Apple //c box.

Clockwise from lower left: Manuals, stickers, Apple //c, power supply, TV antenna switch box, display cable, RF converter, tutorial disks, registration card.

order. Computers aren't delicate flowers, but they are susceptible to environmental forces. Say you've had a late day at the office. The trip home was murder. You're tired. You put the Apple //c down in a corner, go about your business, and go to sleep. Between the night and the morning, the temperature drops and your heater comes on. The Apple //c gets hit full in the face from your floorboard heater ducts.

The computer won't melt, but it won't take kindly to such treatment. There are just too many possible situations like that for you not to decide on a permanent place for your Apple //c when it's home—a spot where the machine can be safe and you can use it.

Home base for your Apple //c will, more likely than not, be a spot with room for a printer, an additional disk drive, and the monitor. To accommodate all of it, you're going to need a space that's at least 30 inches wide by 24 inches deep. It would be nice if that space wasn't subjected to extremes of heat and cold. Some electrical outlets nearby would be handy. Once you've found that space, you can turn your attention to the Apple //c itself.

Into and Out of the Box

Once you've opened the carton, you'll notice some smaller containers inside. These are your "goodies" boxes. Without them, your Apple //c will make a good piece of furniture, but little else.

One of the boxes holds the power supply. The others hold the RF converter and switch box you'll need if you hook the machine up to a TV set, along with the video cables. Set them all aside for now. We're going for the big stuff—the Apple //c.

Lift the machine out of the box, carefully separating it from its Styrofoam cradle. Take the plastic off and just hold on to your new acquisition for a moment.

Fifteen years ago, the computing power in your hand would have filled half the room you're standing in. Ten years ago, it would have taken up three times the space it does now. Seven years ago it would have been 20% larger and weighed and cost more than twice as much.

It's amazing technology. Let's see what it can do.

Handle with Tricks

You're probably holding the Apple //c by its sides. By doing that, you've probably either closed or opened the disk drive door on the right side of the machine at least once. You'll have to learn to pay that door more respect. As with all of a computer's moving parts, it won't last long if you have a few accidents with it. It's time to learn a new way of hanging on to your new computer.

Your first stop on your tour of the Apple //c is the back of the machine. You don't even need to turn it around. Visible across the top, at the back, is a 4-inch recess. Running across that indentation you'll see what looks like a bar about half an inch from front to back.

That bar has a not-so-secret role. Shift the computer so that one of your hands supports the weight of the machine. Swivel it on your palm so that your other hand now has access to the rear of the computer. Use your thumb to flip down the bar and expose what it's attached to. There's what you should be using to hold it—its handle!

The other purpose for the handle may not be as obvious to you. If you swivel it all the way down so that the grip points toward the bottom of the machine, you'll notice that there is no recess for the handle to fit into. In fact, the entire length of the handle protrudes below the machine. Poor design?

Nope. The Apple //c is a fairly flat machine. Flat's a difficult position from which to type. Could some clever person at Apple Computer have designed the handle to stick out like that? When you place the computer on a flat surface and leave the handle pointing down, the back will be elevated about 2 inches above the surface it rests on. It wouldn't be surprising if the resulting angle gave you a pretty good approach when you began to bang away at the keyboard. Clever, these Apple designers!

A computer with a multifunction handle is a portent of good things to come. Now that you know how to pick it up, hold it, and put it down, pull up a chair and get comfortable. You're about to get familiar with your Apple //c.

Breathing Exercises

If you're sitting in a normal position, you probably won't notice the row of slots at the bottom of the Apple //c, beneath the keyboard. If you tip the machine up a bit, you'll see them. Put the machine back down and look across the top. You won't be able to miss the larger grouping of slots that dominate the rear section. You've got an Apple full of holes.

Do yourself a favor and don't ever block those holes. Apple has yet to use a fan to cool an Apple computer. Its engineers have always relied on a ventilation system called *convection cooling* that takes advantage of the principles that warm air tends to rise, cold air tends to sink, and a vacuum won't remain a vacuum for long.

As the Apple //c operates, the hardware heats up. The air inside starts to get warm and rises. Finding the holes in the top of the machine, it escapes out into the world. And as the air vacates the premises, it tends to leave a vacuum behind in the space it occupied.

The vacuum now needs to be filled. Since the top vents are being used by the warm air that's leaving, the vacuum entices the cold air in through the bottom vents and fills itself. But the cold air doesn't stay that way for long. As it starts to heat up, the cycle begins all over again.

Drama aside, convection is a very efficient method of cooling. It's totally silent and requires no extra equipment to work correctly. The only obstacle to its keeping your computer working forever is you.

In order for the system to work, it needs both sets of vents. So even though space around your desk may be at a premium and even though the flat top of the Apple //c looks like an excellent place to put papers or a book while you're working with the machine—don't do it. And though the space beneath the front ledge of the computer seems tailor-made for spare pencils, pens, and paper clips, don't put them there. If you break the cooling cycle, you'll eventually break the Apple //c. So keep that air flowing.

The World at Your Fingertips

The Apple //c's most obvious feature is its sixty-three-key keyboard, which occupies almost half of the visible surface of the machine. The alphanumeric (letters and numbers) keys are laid out in the traditional QWERTY pattern (sometimes called the Sholes design) familiar to generations of typists.

The //c keyboard also boasts some major improvements over the ones on the original Apple // machines. Like the keyboard on the Apple //e, this one has been designed to conform with the classic Selectric typewriter. That means the quote-and-apostrophe key is where it belongs in relation to the rest of the keys, the *shift* and *return* keys are big enough and in their usual places, and Apple hasn't engaged in any "funny business" with the rest of the keyboard. An especially nice touch on the //c is that the *D* and *K* keys have dimples—raised dots that touch typists can use to reassure themselves that their fingers are on the correct keys without peeking.

If you're not an old hand at computers (and even if you are), many of the keys you see may be unfamiliar to you. You may also wonder what the three switches above the left side of the keyboard do. For now we'll leave you in the dark. The keyboard is so important and so special that we're going to give it much more attention later on.

Seeing the Lights

On the right side of the computer, just above the keyboard, are two slots. All they do is light up. A green light shows through the right-hand slot when the machine is turned on. Many machines, including the expensive IBM PC, don't bother including a power-on signal, but it's invaluable for times when you might want to turn the monitor off to conserve electricity or turn the brightness down to conserve the screen phosphors.

If this green light begins to flash while you are using the computer, *turn the machine off immediately.* The flashing light indicates a possible problem with the power supply. Your failure to react appropriately might result in a lot of damage.

The other slot, to its immediate left, also contains an indicator. This one is red and glows only when the disk drive is being used. Traditionally, disk drives include this light on the front. But since the Apple //c's disk drive is on the side of the machine, such a light would be hard to see. Apple's designers get another point for cleverness!

Speaker of the House

We're not quite done with our tour of the front end of the machine. Run your left hand under the recess on the left side of the keyboard. You'll feel a small rotary switch. Next to it, toward the front, is a small hole in the side of the computer.

The rotary switch is a volume control for the speaker output. Your Apple //c does indeed have a speaker inside, along the front cooling vents. Late at night, when you're doing serious business on your computer (like *Miner 2049er* or some alien shoot-'em-up), you certainly won't want to disturb anyone with bleeps and squawks. By thumbing the volume control you can bring the noise level down from resounding, to low, to nonexistent.

The hole is a connector for an audio miniplug. You can plug in headphones, an external speaker, or your stereo to get a crisper sound than the little 2-inch internal speaker can provide. One inexpensive external speaker that will work is the Radio Shack, number 32-2031—an enclosed bookshelf-sized speaker with a small amplifier and a tone control.

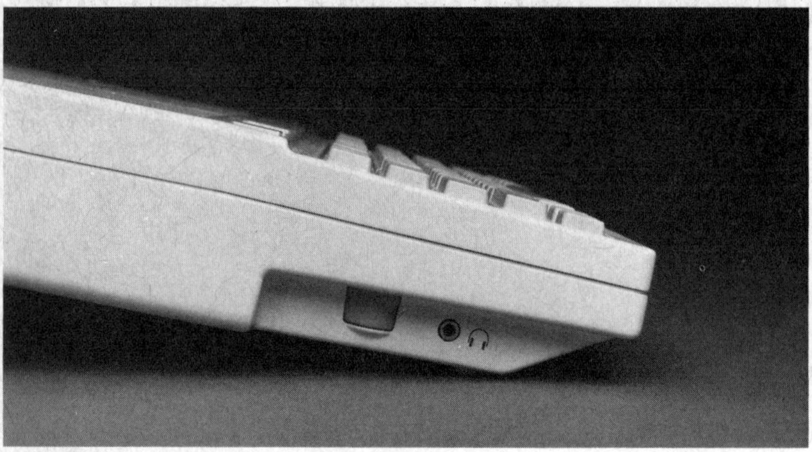

Apple //c volume control knob and audio output jack.

Driving Your Disks

The first Apple computers stored information on audio cassette tapes. Using them was slow, unreliable, and irritating. If the information you needed was at the end of the tape but the tape happened to be wound to the beginning, you had to wind through the whole cassette just to get to work. And getting information to and from the cassette was about as speedy as a lethargic snail.

Today, any serious microcomputer uses *floppy disks*, or *diskettes*, to store information. The //c is no exception. The Apple //c has a single internal disk drive that accepts 5¼-inch disks. You'll find it on the right-hand side of the machine. In order to maintain the Apple //c's compact size and portability, this disk drive is roughly half the height of the original drives used with the Apple // series. Still, the //c is so small that even the half-height drive occupies about a third of the machine's internal volume.

Swivel the machine around so that its right side is facing you. The darker piece that doesn't look as if it has been molded to the computer is the disk-drive door. It performs the dual function of both door and latch so that the disk won't accidentally come out of the drive at an inopportune time.

If the door is not flush with the top of the computer, then it's open. If everything is level, the door is closed.

To open the drive door, press your thumb gently but firmly against the drive latch. Use a horizontal movement as if to push your thumb in through the side of the computer. About halfway in, you'll hear a faint "click." Press in just a little bit further and then use your thumb to swivel the door straight up in one quick upward movement. The latch should follow your thumb with ease. When you open the door with a disk inside, the disk will pop a short way out of the drive.

A Disk by Any Other Name

Let's look at a disk. Each one is made of a flat, round, very thin circular vinyl sheet covered with the same kind of magnetic material as cassette tape. This coating is specially polished to reduce surface imperfections and improve its receptiveness to the electronic signals the drive will be placing on it. Each disk comes in a fairly square, stiff plastic jacket lined with a soft fiber material that keeps the disk clean by wiping it as it turns.

As you can see from the illustration (or from looking at an actual disk), there are several cutouts in the jacket that need some explaining. The big center hole is the most obvious. When you put a disk into a drive and close the door, a circular part called a collet comes down from above and clamps the disk firmly to a hub. When the disk drive is in action, the hub spins, and so does the disk (but not the jacket).

When the disk is rotating on the hub, the drive's sensors can get information from it (*read* from it) or put information onto it (*write* to it) through the oval opening you can see just below the center hole. This is the only place where the disk surface shows through. As the disk spins on the hub, the read-write heads move back and forth along this "slot" in the jacket, with access to the entire surface of the disk. That oval opening in the jacket is duplicated on both sides of the disk. Some machines use both sides of the disk; the Apple //c doesn't, but it's cheaper for the manufacturers to make one type of jacket for all of their disk products.

Disks come in removable protective sleeves that are meant to cover the oval openings, but don't let all that protection mislead you into believing that no harm can come to a disk. Extreme heat, cold, humidity, as well as

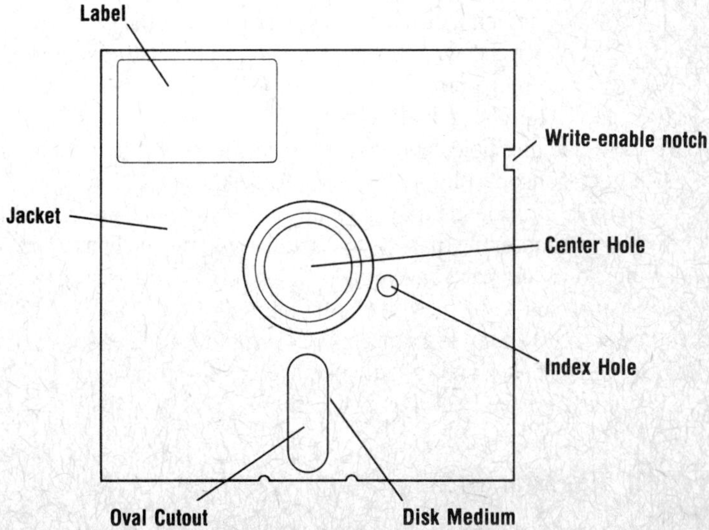

Diskette.

The label should always be the last part of a disk to enter the drive.

magnetism can damage or destroy the information on the disk even though the disk itself can be reused. Folding a disk or poking a hole in it, on the other hand, can destroy both the information and the disk itself. So can writing on the disk jacket or its label with anything but a soft felt-tip pen. A hard writing implement can dent or scratch the disk surface through its jacket. And if peanut butter, jelly, coffee, or any other foreign substance finds its way through the ovals to the surface of the disk, you may well find that the disk isn't much good for anything but the trash.

Even a fingerprint can be a villain. The microscopic quantity of oil your skin secretes can stop a disk cold. Never reach for a disk unless you're looking at it and can see that the access ovals are not about to fall victim to your fingertips.

Protecting Your Information

If you're looking down the top of the disk (the side with the label), you'll notice a small rectangular piece missing from the upper right-hand part of the jacket. This is the write-protect notch.

Dumb as they are, computers blindly follow your instructions and will erase something at your mere suggestion—even if you don't really mean it. There will be times when data you've put on the disk absolutely should not be removed or replaced. That's where the notch comes in handy.

In each box of disks you'll also notice tough little strips of stick-on tape. By folding one over a write-protect notch, you make it impossible for a properly functioning disk drive to alter the contents of that disk. With no tape on the notch, the Apple //c has free rein to follow your commands, no matter how much you regret it later on. By the way, ordinary tape won't do to cover the write-protect notch. Use what comes in the box.

There is one more small hole in the disk jacket, just to the right of the center hole. There's at least one matching hole on the disk as well. It's called the indexing hole, and some disk drives use it in conjunction with a built-in light sensor to keep track of the disk's revolution.

The Apple //c doesn't pay any attention to the indexing hole. As we explained in chapter 2, that means you can use virtually any disk available, including so-called hard-sectored disks, which have a multitude of index holes. But if you're buying disks for yourself, you'll save money by giving the Apple any reputable manufacturer's simplest, cheapest type of disk: single sided, single density, soft sectored. Anything fancier will work, but it's like feeding caviar to your pet gerbil.

Caring for Your Disks

Treat every disk gently. Always insert it with the label facing up and the access slot toward the drive. Don't try to jam it into the drive. It'll slide in fine about nine-tenths of the way, and then you'll feel some resistance. Go just a little further. Now you should not be able to push it any further without bending it. Use your thumb to close the latch and you're home free.

One other thing. The moving parts of the disk drive tend to jiggle around when you move the computer. That's not dangerous for short hauls into the next room. But when you take your computer on trips and it gets bounced by the baggage handlers or it shimmies around in your car, you must protect the innards of the disk drive from unnatural strain.

The door should *not* be left closed when there is no disk in the drive. However, the Apple //c shouldn't be transported with the drive door open. In the open position, there is no tension on the mechanical parts, and they can move around in ways that can throw the drive out of alignment.

Since you're not going to close the drive door without something in there and you're not going to move your Apple //c around unless the drive door is closed, you should delegate one blank disk for survival duty. Whenever you want to travel, just tuck the disk in the drive and close it up to maintain the integrity of the disk mechanics.

Where the Power Goes

Swivel the Apple //c another quarter turn clockwise and behold the wonders of modern technology. Despite all the strange and magnificent things protruding from the back, you won't see one word to describe any of it! English has succumbed to the pressure of international pictograms.

Starting on the right is the on/off switch. It doesn't say "on/off"—hardly any of them do anymore. It says "I/O," but it's an on/off switch all the same. In the "I" position, power goes to the computer; in the "O" position it doesn't. Just think of the "O" as off and don't think about what the "I" is supposed to stand for.

Immediately to the left of that switch is the power connection itself. It's a round receptacle known as a seven-pin DIN-type jack and mates to the

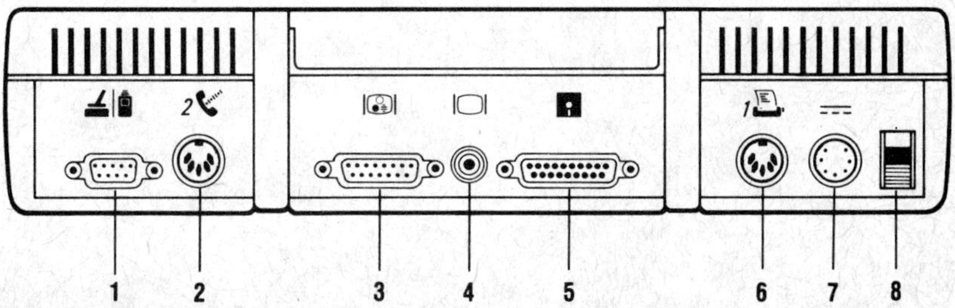

The Apple //c's Back Panel.

1. Mouse, joystick, and paddle connector.
2. Modem connector.
3. Television expansion connector.
4. Video monitor connector.
5. External disk drive connector.
6. Printer/plotter connector.
7. Power supply connector.
8. On/off switch.

connector from the power supply. DIN connectors deserve a little discussion, since three of them reside on the //c's back panel.

DIN connectors can have different numbers of pins, but they're always round and they always have a little bump or ridge at the top. The bumps and ridges serve as "keying" devices that keep you from plugging cables in the wrong way. If you examine the cable, you'll see that there is a corresponding depression in it. You can't possibly get them to go together any way but correctly unless you try to force them—in which case they might just break under the pressure.

Serial Ports

The two other DIN connectors are both five-pin and also keyed, and these, unlike the power connector, are female. That's to keep you from plugging the power line into them and listening to unpleasant sizzles emerging from your machine.

What do they do? The one immediately to the left of the power supply connector is the printer port, as the picture above it might lead you to believe. It supports a serial printer. The five-pin DIN-type connector on

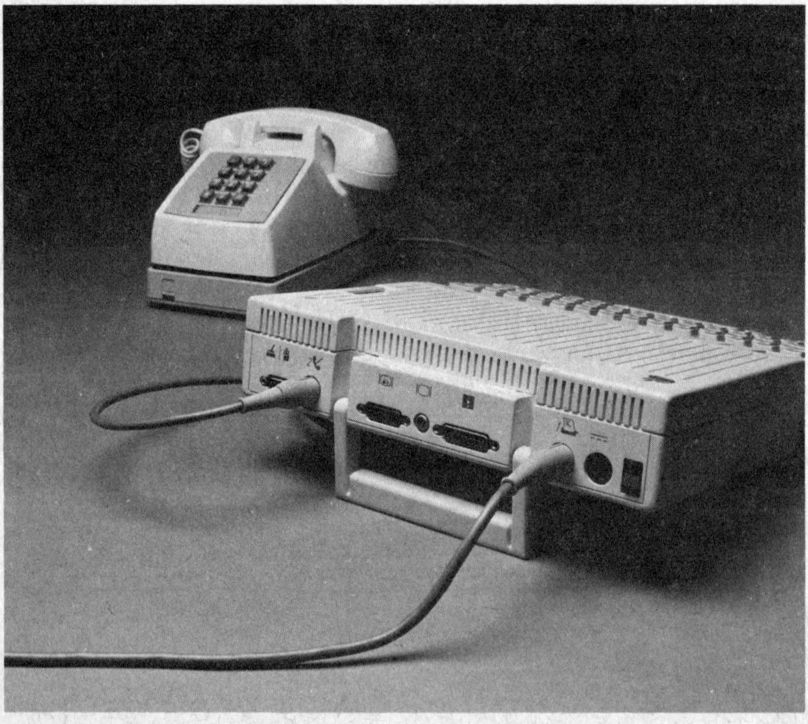

Apple //c with cables attached to serial ports.

The cable on the right connects to an unseen printer. The cable on the left is connected to the modem, which fits neatly beneath a standard telephone.

the other side of the machine beneath the picture of the phone handle is a modem port, also serial.

Both ports can be used simultaneously. Both will support data transfer rates of up to 9,600 baud—a blazing 960 characters per second. *Baud* is a speed rating for data transmission and works out to about one character per 10 baud.

The Handle with Drive

We've discussed the amazing multipurpose handle before. It turns out that the handle has yet another function. The elevation it gives the back panel helps insure that none of the cables connected to the back panel will drag against the surface on which the Apple //c is resting and accidentally pull loose.

To the left of the rightmost leg of the handle is a nineteen-pin D-type connector that's also very difficult to plug together incorrectly. It's used to attach an additional disk drive to the Apple //c. If you're smart, this connector will see a lot of action.

Captains of Video

To the left of the disk drive connector is what's known as an RCA female jack. It supplies the video signal to a monitor. Color information is included in the signal, so monochrome and color monitors both connect to this jack.

Moving down the line, you'll find another D-connector, this one of the fifteen-pin variety. It allows for expansion of the video signals. Today, that's where the RF converter goes to allow TV-set compatibility. It's also where you plug in an RGB color monitor, and where Apple's promised small, slim LCD screen will connect when it becomes available.

Playing Around

You've already seen the modem port, so we'll jump all the way to the left end of the back panel and go on to the next D-connector—a nine-pin job this time. Even with all the symbols, you may not guess what this one's for.

The D-connector on the Apple //c goes the earlier models one better. Not only does it accept game paddles or joysticks whose cables have similar plugs, it also welcomes a newcomer to the hand-operated culture. You can plug Apple's mouse into it.

Making the Connections

Now that you know where everything goes, it's time to hook it all up and turn on the machine. Connecting peripherals to your Apple //c is a simple, painless procedure that's nearly impossible to do wrong—*if you follow two elementary rules:*

> **Never, Never . . .**
>
> 1. Never, *never* plug or unplug anything attached to your Apple //c when the power to either the computer or the attached device is on! That includes any cable or peripheral. Better still, make sure everything is unplugged before making or breaking connections. Disobeying this rule can result in a dead computer. Accidentally crossed connections or surges of power can damage the sensitive internal circuitry of your Apple //c.
> 2. *Never* force a connector into a jack. If it doesn't fit, rotate it or turn it upside down to match its mate. If it *still* doesn't fit, it was probably designed not to fit. Many of the connectors for the //c look the same, but the spacing of the pins or their arrangement might be minutely different. Forcing a cable can result in a broken connector or a broken jack on the computer or peripheral.

Connecting a Monitor

Connecting a composite monitor is about as easy as connections get. The Apple's monitor connector has the exact same RCA male plug—it's got a large central pin surrounded by a thin metal wall—on both ends, so it doesn't matter which end goes into the computer and which end into the monitor.

Be sure the monitor is *off* before you plug one end of the Apple's cable into the RCA female jack on the monitor. Then plug the other end into the monitor jack on the Apple //c's back panel—the round jack beneath the TV-screen pictogram near the middle. That's it.

A similarly simple hookup will get an RGB monitor up and running, but you'll need a special adapter cable with the proper wiring and proper connectors. The adapter doesn't come with your //c, and it's not likely to be supplied with your monitor. You can buy the adapter at a computer store. Once you've got the cable, put its fifteen-pin D-connector into the Apple //c's video expansion port (the bigger of the two connectors beneath pictograms of TV screens). The cable's other end plugs into the monitor.

Connecting a TV Set

If you're using a TV set as a display, things get slightly more complicated. First plug the Apple-supplied RF converter into the fifteen-pin video expansion connector on the //c's back panel. It's the wider of the two connectors beneath pictures of TV screens. Push the same-on-both-ends RCA cable into the RCA female jack on the RF converter and you're nearly halfway done with this connection.

What happens next depends on your TV set. If you have a recent model designed to have a videocassette recorder or videodisc player plugged directly into it, merely plug the cable from the computer where you'd ordinarily plug the other video accessory. The Apple //c will now display its picture exactly as the previously connected video equipment did. Of course, you'll have to play pull-and-plug every time your interest in computing or video wanes and you want to change the source of the TV picture.

Older TV sets usually have screw terminals on the back for attaching antenna wires. Find the terminals marked "VHF" and unscrew the antenna wires. Find the little cream-colored switch box that came with your new computer, and screw the now-loose antenna wires to the screw terminals on the switch box. Use one wire per terminal; which one goes where doesn't

Apple //c connected to TV set.

Squarish RF converter protrudes from rear of computer, light-colored switch box appears above rear of TV set. Neither switch box nor converter is needed for direct connection to a monitor.

matter a bit. Push the RCA plug on the free end of the computer cable into the jack on the switch box.

Now attach the two spade lugs, the metal connectors at the end of the wire dangling from the switch box, to the VHF antenna terminals of your television, exactly where the antenna wires came from. Again, either wire can go to either terminal. If you want, remove the protective paper cover from the sticky tab on the switch box and firmly attach it to the back of your TV set.

The function of this little box should be obvious. It's a special switch to change the input to your television from your antenna to your computer. You will have to switch between antenna and computer, depending on which you'd like to use. For obvious reasons, you cannot use both computer and antenna simultaneously.

If you have both imagination and logic, you can hook up your computer to your television or video system in any of a variety of ways. Because the Apple //c's video signals from the RF adapter are just TV signals, they can be fed directly into your video recorder or routed through any other standard video accessory with little picture degradation. You can send the //c's picture to multiple television sets by using the same kinds of "splitters" used to divide a signal from one antenna or cable among different sets in a house or apartment. Any standard antenna accessory will work with the //c's signals.

The //c's RF adapter gives you a choice of two channels to "broadcast" over your television set: channel 3 or channel 4. To change the channel that your machine uses, merely slide the switch on the converter. To avoid possible interference, it's best to use whichever channel is not used by a television station in your area. If both channel 3 and 4 are free in your area, you can use either. But the best selection should be the channel furthest removed from any stations transmitting in your area.

Connecting a Printer

If you have a printer, make sure its power switch is off, and plug its cable into the printer port jack. The printer port jack is on the right side of the //c's back panel, marked with a number 1 and a picture of a printer.

Don't force the connection. Printer cables aren't standard. If yours doesn't fit easily into the jack, you may need a different cable. Remember, you must use a printer that can accept serial input. Parallel-only printers just won't work. Ask your dealer for advice if necessary.

Connecting a Modem

A modem is next, if you have one. Plug its connector into the communications port—the five-pin DIN connector second from the left on the //c's back panel, marked with the number 2 and a picture of a phone receiver.

Again, don't force anything. Modem cables, alas, aren't standard, either. If you're borrowing one from a friend, you may find yourself going to a friendly computer store in search of one that will fit your machine.

Connecting the External Disk Drive

If you have an external disk drive, now's the time to plug it into the big nineteen-pin D-connector on the back of the //c. Once again, don't force things. If it doesn't go in smoothly, chances are you've got the connector upside down.

Connecting a Joystick, Paddle, or Mouse

Plug the nine-pin D-connector from the joystick, paddle, or mouse into the leftmost port on the back of the //c. Trouble? You've probably got the connector upside down.

Connecting the Power Supply

First, make sure the //c's on/off switch is in the "O"—off—position. Next, make sure the power supply is not plugged into an outlet. Then insert the power supply's seven-pin DIN-type connector into the rightmost jack on the back of the Apple //c. Remember, the bump on the jack must

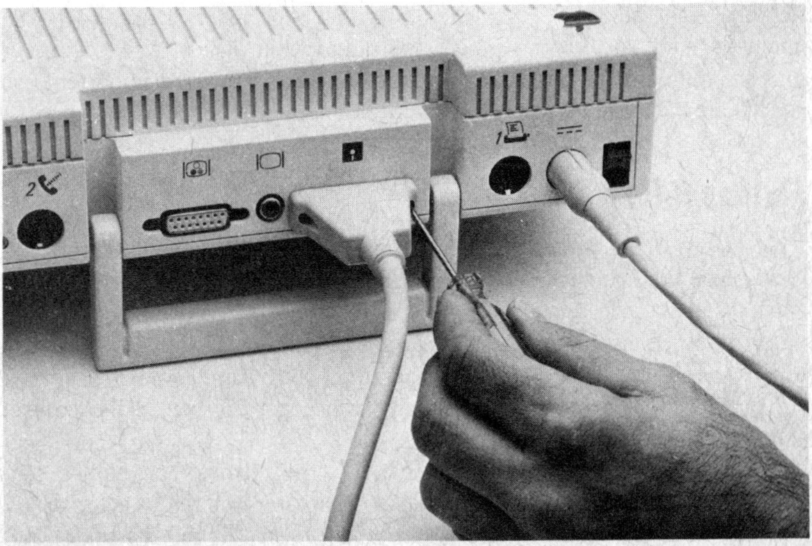

Connecting the external disk drive.

Retaining screws of all D-connectors should be securely fastened to prevent accidental disconnection—and potential disaster.

The Apple //c power supply.

Always make the connection to the computer before inserting the three-prong plug into an outlet.

mate with the depression in the plug; if the plug doesn't go in smoothly, you've probably got it lined up wrong.

Make sure the power switches on *all* the peripherals are in the *off* positions and plug all the power lines into your handy wall socket or multiple-outlet power strip. The next few steps are very important, so read them carefully.

Turning It On

All electrical appliances—computers and computer equipment included—send some voltage back into the electrical line when they're turned on. It can't be prevented; electricity must have a return route to complete its path. Some equipment, like your computer, is more sensitive to this than others. Even though you've taken pains to ground your equipment properly, it's a good idea to get into the habit of turning things on in the correct order to prevent any mishaps.

If you have a printer, turn it on first. It's the "dirtiest" of the accessories you'll ever connect to your Apple //c. Then turn on the monitor or TV set. If you have a modem, and you're going to use it, that's next in line. Guess what that leaves you with? But before you reach for that power switch, make sure you've completed the following Turn-on Checklist. Then proceed to chapter 4.

Turn-on Checklist

1. Unplug computer and peripherals.
2. Make all connections.
3. Make sure computer and peripherals are switched *off.*
4. Plug in computer and peripherals.
5. Turn on printer.
6. Turn on monitor.
7. Turn on other peripherals.
8. Turn on computer.

Turn-off Checklist

1. Save program or text in computer's memory to disk.
2. Remove disk from disk drive.
3. Turn off computer.
4. Turn off all peripherals, including monitor.
5. Unplug computer power supply from outlet (if you don't plan to return to your computer right away).

4

Power Up! Getting Started with Your //c

Normally when you start up your //c, you'll probably use the disk drive. But for now, make sure there's *no* disk in the drive. Just turn the Apple //c's power switch to "I" for "I'm ready to try it!" The green *power* light above the right side of the keyboard should go on.

Unlocking the Magic

Despite the fact that there's no disk in it, the drive will begin to spin. You should see the red *disk-use* light come on and turn off. At the top of your screen you'll be greeted by the computer's logo.

The Apple //c really wants you to put a disk in the drive; without it, you have no way of storing any information. After a few seconds a message will appear at the bottom of your screen, reflecting the machine's anxiety over not finding a disk. It says "CHECK DISK DRIVE."

You could just ignore it. After all, you are the human being and you control the computer. If you don't want to use a disk, you shouldn't be forced to. There's only one problem. In a fit of pique, the Apple //c has locked you out! Go ahead and press any key you want: nothing will happen. Unless you press the correct combination of buttons.

The Art of Reset

On the left side of the machine above the keyboard are three switches. The largest one, all the way to the left, is labeled *reset.* To understand its use, you must first understand a peculiar fact about computer behavior.

Whether from a furious attack of bad software or a spurious burst of static electricity or just ignorance about what should come next (a human programmer forgot to tell it), there are times when your Apple will sit and glare back at you for no discernible reason. Nothing you normally do will have any effect at all. For all practical purposes, your machine has entered the Twilight Zone.

There is always one ultimate way of regaining your control. You can turn the machine off and then on again. That will wipe out everything that's in your machine's RAM memory (which usually includes some important document you're working on).

Still, it's absolutely a last resort. It puts a strain on all of the components and shortens their lifespan. Wouldn't it be nice to have some other way of breaking the Apple //c's mysterious trance?

Most computers, yours included, support two separate functions. One is called *interrupt*, or *break*; the other is *reset*.

An interrupt does just what you'd expect. It interrupts what's going on and brings the machine back to whatever it was doing before it got stuck. If you were locked out of the computer while in the middle of using a program in BASIC, an interrupt would stop the program and take you to the lowest usable level of the BASIC language. You could then run the program again or inspect it to figure out what went wrong, but the program would remain intact. You wouldn't have lost anything except a little time.

To perform an interrupt on the Apple //c, you hold down the key labeled *control* and press and release the *reset* switch. When you use the *control* key as a modifier, the *reset* switch actually becomes an interrupt switch.

How do you make it a *reset* switch? You hold down the *control* key *and* the key with the outline of the apple (called, providentially, the open apple key), and then press and release the *reset* switch. That wipes the Apple //c's slate completely clean. It forgets everything you've told it and anything you were doing. It couldn't care less what it was. You get out of the problem you were in, but in return the machine acts as if you have turned it off and on again.

Older Apple // models let you interrupt the machine by simply pressing a "break" key. After one too many users accidentally bumped that key, Apple decided to make sure you were absolutely positive about performing an interrupt. That's why it takes three keys at once. No one has ever been recorded as accidentally having bumped the *control* and *reset* combination.

Resetting to Square One

So which one do you use to get started with a machine that's insouciantly ignoring your fingers on the keyboard—interrupt or reset? Consider: A full three-key reset would take you back to where you were just after turning on the machine—which is where you are right now.

Try an interrupt. Hold down the *control* key and press and release the *reset* switch. Then let go of the *control* key as well. If all goes according to plan, the internal speaker will make a noise that's known as a "bell" but sounds more like a beep. The screen will clear, and you will see a strange symbol on the lower left-hand corner.

The symbol is a right bracket (])—Applesoft BASIC's *prompt,* its notice to you that it is ready to go. (Exactly what Applesoft BASIC is and where it will take you will be explained soon.) Next to that bracket you see a blinking box. That's the *cursor.*

The cursor is a friendly thing that keeps track of your progress on the screen. It will always be one step ahead of you, marking where the next character you type at the keyboard will appear. Try a little typing. Just press any of the letter or number keys a few times. The cursor is always at the next position.

You can try something else if you'd like. After you've typed a few letters, press the *return* key. Immediately thereafter you will hear the "bell" and a nice comment will appear on the screen: ?SYNTAX ERROR.

Speaking the Language

The ?SYNTAX ERROR message has been an evasive hanger-on in the world of computers. People have tried for years to have it replaced for a very logical reason: while informing you that there *is* a problem, it doesn't tell you how to correct that problem. Unfortunately, there's no simple way to replace it.

What does ?SYNTAX ERROR mean? Well, Applesoft BASIC is a programming *language,* and any language, even English, has rules about grammar and word order. Those rules are called *syntax.*

If someone speaks to you using incorrect syntax, all is not lost. Because you are human, you can usually figure out from the situation and other clues what the speaker is really trying to say. A computer, however, does not perceive. It will follow a series of instructions given to it under the rules and in a format it understands, but it will not make assumptions about any of them. It attempts to act upon each instruction it "sees" quite literally and doesn't even attempt to understand what you *might* mean.

If it finds something it doesn't understand, it becomes confused. There are times when a specific type of error will generate a specific error message, but if your problem was in the construction of the phrase, you'll get a ?SYNTAX ERROR. You won't be told *what* the problem is, just that it exists. Finding the exact nature of the error is called *debugging,* and depends on your knowledge of the language used. With Applesoft, chapter 16 may help. It contains a list of possible error messages and brief explanations of their probable causes.

For now, you're just playing. You'll have to put up with an occasional ?SYNTAX ERROR until you learn a few more things about BASIC.

Apples within Apples

You've already discovered the *control* key and the [open apple] key. We may as well introduce the other apple key. You'll find it on the right side of the space bar, which is the wide key near the front of the computer. It's called the solid apple key.

The [solid apple] key is generally used much the way many of the special keys are: hold it down and press another key at the same time, and what that other key does is transformed into something different from what it usually does. A favorite combination used in many packaged programs is [open apple] and question mark as a request for help. Many programs use [solid apple] key combinations to perform other special functions.

Why All the Keys?

The [open apple] and [solid apple] keys and the *control* key are only the beginning. Since computers can do a lot more than typewriters, computer keyboards have to do a lot more, too. Among other things, they have to be able to send the computer special commands that don't happen to be letters, numbers, or punctuation marks. If there were a special key for each of these commands, the keyboard might well be the size of a large wall. Computer designers decided to do things a different way.

To the computer, each key represents a corresponding value called its ASCII code. ASCII (pronounced as-key) stands for the American Standard Code for Information Interchange. As the name suggests, the code for each key has been standardized among computers.

The keyboard itself is nothing more than a special collection of switches. When you press a key, the Apple //c determines which row and column the key is in. Let's say you hit the key labeled *A* on the Apple //c keyboard. That one's in the third row and second column.

Stored away in the computer's ROM firmware is a table that translates the row-and-column information into ASCII codes. The //c looks the *A* key up and discovers that its value is 97—ASCII code for a lowercase, or unshifted, *a*. More firmware instructions tell the //c to print that character on the screen.

Shifty Characters

But what if you want a capital *A*? Or a character known in the computer world as "Control-A," which will have some very special meaning to your machine? For such purposes, special keys, called modifiers, add or subtract specific amounts to the value found in the internal table. These keys are labeled *shift* and *control*. The way to get them to work is to hold them down while you press the alphanumeric keys.

ASCII Codes and the Characters or Functions They Represent

ASCII Number	Character or Function	ASCII Number	Character or Function
0	Null	29	unprinted
1	Control-A	30	unprinted
2	Control-B	31	reverse linefeed
3	Control-C (program break)	32	space
		33	!
4	Control-D (DOS/ProDOS command character)	34	"
		35	#
5	Control-E	36	$
6	Control-F	37	%
7	Control-G (bell)	38	&
8	Control-H (←)	39	'
9	Control-I (*tab*)	40	(
10	Control-J (↓; line feed)	41	)
11	Control-K (↑)	42	*
12	Control-L	43	+
13	Control-M (*return*)	44	,
14	Control-N	45	-
15	Control-O	46	.
16	Control-P	47	/
17	Control-Q	48	0
18	Control-R	49	1
19	Control-S (stop scroll)	50	2
20	Control-T	51	3
21	Control-U (→)	52	4
22	Control-V	53	5
23	Control-W	54	6
24	Control-X (cancel line)	55	7
25	Control-Y	56	8
26	Control-Z	57	9
27	Escape	58	:
28	unprinted	59	;

(continued)

ASCII Number	Character or Function	ASCII Number	Character or Function
60	<	94	^
61	=	95	_
62	>	96	
63	?	97	a
64	@	98	b
65	A	99	c
66	B	100	d
67	C	101	e
68	D	102	f
69	E	103	g
70	F	104	h
71	G	105	i
72	H	106	j
73	I	107	k
74	J	108	l
75	K	109	m
76	L	110	n
77	M	111	o
78	N	112	p
79	O	113	q
80	P	114	r
81	Q	115	s
82	R	116	t
83	S	117	u
84	T	118	v
85	U	119	w
86	V	120	x
87	W	121	y
88	X	122	z
89	Y	123	{
90	Z	124	| (vert. rule)
91	[	125	}
92	\	126	~
93	]	127	dotted cursor square

If you held down the *shift* key and went through the same procedure you just did, the Apple //c would not only be presented with the key at row 3, column 2, but would also see row 4, column 1 pressed as well. When the firmware found the meaning of this modifier key in its internal table, it would know whatever ASCII value the letter produced, it must subtract 32 from that value. The ASCII code for the capital *A* is 65—the 97 of the lowercase *a* minus 32.

The list of ASCII values should convince you that the *shift* key doesn't always subtract 32 from the unshifted value. For the numeric keys and other keys with two legends, the firmware is smart enough to know that when you hold down *shift*, you want the character on the top of the key, and it adjusts its calculations accordingly.

The *caps lock* key is unlike the rest of the switches that make up the keyboard. It's a switch that you can press and lock in either the on (down) or off (up) positions. Unlike the *shift* key (and unlike the shift lock on typewriters), it affects *only* letter keys, and produces their uppercase versions when it is locked down. The number keys and all the punctuation keys are still interpreted as unshifted when you use *caps lock* unless you also press the *shift* key down.

The *control* key works like *shift*—just hold it down while you press another key—but it's really a special case. As the name implies, it produces "control" values that are used to give the Apple //c some sort of instruction. If you hold down the *control* key and press the *A* key, the computer interprets the combination as the ASCII value 1. What happens next depends on what particular software is running in the machine at the time.

Some *control*-key combinations actually send the computer the same instruction as "dedicated" special-function keys. *Control-I* produces the same ASCII code (9) as the *tab* key. Press *control-M* and you'll get the same code (13) as if you pressed *return*. Try them and see for yourself.

Return to the Keyboard

The key marked *return* is one of the most important on the keyboard. It functions much like the carriage return key on an electric typewriter, moving the cursor from the end of one line to the beginning of the next. If you're using a word-processing program, that's pretty much all it'll do.

But in Applesoft BASIC, where you are right now, it has another important function: it lets BASIC know you're done with the line you're working on and you want it to pay attention to it. Every time you type in a command or a program line, you'll need to hit the *return* key to get BASIC to pay attention. Until you do hit *return*, the program will wait forever for more information.

More Keys

There are still a few keys that may not be familiar to you if you're not an old hand with computers. At the upper right-hand corner is a key marked *delete*. Try it a couple of times.

What you see on the screen is a box that looks suspiciously like your cursor. In Applesoft, putting that cursorlike box up on the screen is all the *delete* key does, and that's pretty useless. But with many programs, the *delete* key will work as a handy *destructive backspace,* moving the cursor one character to the left and wiping out the character that's already there. It's an important principle to understand: A key that performs a particular function in one program may do something very different indeed in another.

The *tab* key is another example. Press it, and you'll see the cursor scoot across the screen eight columns at a time. But in other programs you can choose your own tab stops, much as you can with a typewriter.

The arrow keys at the bottom right of the keyboard will move the cursor around the screen. Try the left and right arrows until you're comfortable with them. Now try the up and down arrows. Surprise! They don't work at all!

That can be remedied. Hit the *esc* (for *escape*) key at the upper left of the keyboard. You'll see the cursor change into a *cross-hair* pattern. Now try the up- and down-arrow keys. They work! So will the left and right arrows. Hit the *esc* key again to get the original cursor back. The up and down arrow keys have died again.

That little demonstration proves once again that keys can operate in different ways in different environments. Sometimes you'll have full access to the arrow keys; sometimes you won't. It all depends on the particular software you're using and the particular point you've reached in it. If a program demands a yes or no answer, for example, it may effectively turn off every key but the *Y* and *N* keys until you come up with a reasonable response.

The Second Column

Immediately to the right of the *reset* switch are two slimmer switches. When they're up, they're off; when they're down, they're on. It's not always easy to tell which position they're in: up, only a tiny nub sticks up through the slot; down, the nub almost disappears into the body of the machine. To change either switch's position, you simply press it down. If it's already "down," it will pop up.

The first skinny switch is marked *80/40*. Your Apple //c can produce a display either 40 or 80 characters wide. Right now you're in 40-column mode. You might be tempted to press the *80/40* switch to see what the 80-column mode can do. Go ahead. Press it.

If nothing happened, don't take your machine back to the dealer. That switch doesn't actually change the display between 40- and 80-column modes. What it does is tell software that has the capability of using both modes (such as some word-processing programs) which one you're interested in. If the switch is on (down), you're telling the software you only want 40 columns across the screen no matter what. If it's off (up), you're telling the software you'll take 80 if the software can give them to you. Not many programs currently available can check the position of the switch, but as more are developed, they'll undoubtedly take advantage of it.

Dvorak's New World

The slender switch marked *keyboard* has a strikingly immediate effect. Press it down (which the designers deliberately made hard to do), and you rearrange the way the Apple //c interprets its keyboard. The standard QWERTY layout is known as Sholes. The *keyboard* switch changes it into another type, called *Dvorak*.

When typewriters were first invented, people could type faster than the primitive mechanisms. The rods and bails and keys would jam, producing general dissatisfaction. A wise man named Sholes came up with an alternative keyboard layout, the one we've used ever since. It put the keys in such odd places that even a practiced typist couldn't type fast enough to jam the early machines. Needless to say, everyone was happy—or at least everyone who made typewriters.

As typewriter mechanisms became more sophisticated, fast typists could no longer jam them, but still the Sholes keyboard prevailed. It was what people learned to type with, and no one wanted to relearn anything else.

There's always an agitator in the crowd. Along came a gentleman named Dvorak who thought people should be able to type as fast as their fingers

Dvorak keyboard layout.

Pressing the Apple //c's keyboard switch down produces this keyboard arrangement for more efficient typing. All vowels fall easily beneath the left hand in the "home row," where the right hand has access to the most common consonants. (Note: The different layout shown in early editions of the Apple //c owner's guide is incorrect.)

could go. He spent a great deal of time watching people type, looking over documents, and developing statistics about which characters were used most frequently. He combined that data with information on the dynamics of hand movements and came up with his own solution. Appropriately, it's called the Dvorak keyboard.

Tests of this new development showed remarkable increases in typing speed. But tradition was tradition. Typewriter manufacturers were geared up to make Sholes keyboards, and changing over would be costly. Typing schools used the typewriters the manufacturers made. Typists, having gone through the horrors of typing school once, did not want to go back again. They were as productive as they thought they could be—so why change?

But the way computer keyboards work makes it easy to change the keyboard layout at the touch of a button. All that's needed is a switch that tells the machine the user wants the Dvorak layout, and ROM firmware that can translate keystrokes with the Dvorak scheme. When the user presses the third key in the second row, the machine simply looks to the Dvorak firmware to come up with the proper ASCII value.

Although not yet overwhelmingly popular, the Dvorak keyboard has received an increasing amount of attention in the last few years. Many novice typists prefer it, and even some veterans have become converts. To try the Dvorak keyboard, just press down the ***keyboard*** switch and start typing.

You'll soon discover one minor problem. If you want the keys to tell what you'll get when you press them, you'll have to gently pry up the keycaps on your Apple //c keyboard and put them back in the Dvorak format. This is not impossible, nor even very difficult as long as you pry in an upward direction, and not to one side. The nylon shafts the keycaps fit on are sturdy, but not indestructible. And consider this: if you break even one shaft, you will void your warranty. You may want to use our chart until you decide whether you're really serious about Dvorak typing, and you may opt to pay a visit to your friendly technician to do the keycap switching if you decide that Dvorak's the best thing since the typewriter.

Capital Compatibility

Now you should be familiar with the keyboard. Before you try giving the machine some genuine commands, find the *caps lock* key. Press it down until you hear it click and then release it. If the keytop is level with all the others, then it's off. If it's slightly depressed, it's on. So what? Glad you asked.

Unlike the Apple //c, the original Apple // and Apple //+ could not produce lowercase letters. If you wanted them, you had to buy an additional piece of hardware or run a wire from the keyboard to another spot inside the machine. Because of this, the Apple //e, your computer's closest ancestor, also needed all uppercase letters to create intelligible commands for many programs (including BASIC and DOS) even though it was capable of producing lowercase letters.

Since the Apple //c was built around the Apple //e, with general Apple // compatibility in mind, you must still use uppercase commands much of the time. Keeping the *caps lock* key down (on) changes the output of the Apple //c's keyboard to all uppercase, befitting the standard. If you press it again, you release the switch (off) and the machine returns to normal dual-case mode. For now, leave it in the "on" position while we deliver a brief but important lecture.

Expansion Slots and Apple Computers

One thing all the //c's ancestors had in common was the presence of expansion capabilities in the main electronic circuit board, the guts of the machine. That large central board, called the *motherboard* because it contains all the chips that do the Apple's computing and remembering, included eight "slots"—eight connectors numbered 0 through 7 into which other pieces of hardware could fit. The Apple did all its communication with the world outside its case via printed circuit cards that fit into the slots and included everything from disk controllers, printer adapters, and serial ports to hardware for controlling scientific instruments. Internal items such as modems and clocks were available as well. Considering the many different kinds of devices in use and those still to be developed over the coming years, the inclusion of slots gave Apple computers unmatched versatility. If there was a particular device you wanted to use with the Apple, you just found the right card and slipped it into the machine.

Board Lore

But a machine that may spend a good part of its life dangling from your hand is not the ideal environment for plug-in cards. Without provisions for bolting it down, an adapter card is likely to find its way *out* of the slot in a portable machine.

There are size considerations as well. The "other" Apple // computers are almost 4 inches tall—and all of that height is used to accommodate the plug-in boards. The Apple //c is, after all, a portable. And it's only 2 inches high.

With earlier models, directing actions to, or in from, any of the cards was as simple as using the correct command. But before a program could use any of the cards, it had to find out which slot the card was in.

This could be a problem. Software checked each slot and looked for a response from the card in question. Sometimes it simply asked the person who was using the program.

Neither of these methods was foolproof. The person using the machine

Card/Slot Assignments for the Apple // Series

Slot #	Usual card	Apple //c Equivalent
0	Language	Display
1	Printer	Serial Printer
2	Communications	Communications
3	80 Column	80 Column
4	Anything	Mouse
5	Anything	
6	Disk Drives	Disk Drives
7	Anything	

didn't always know which card was where, or even what a card or a slot was. Certain cards could be obstinate. They would respond to software queries with a request of their own that the program didn't know how to answer! The card controlled the computer and refused to let go until it got a correct response.

That situation had to be remedied. Apple had always claimed that any card could be used from any slot, with the exception of slot 0, which was sacred to a particular function. However, to avoid conflicts, manufacturers began to standardize their cards' positions within the machine. Even the manuals supplied by Apple for the equipment started to suggest recommended slot assignments. In a moment, you'll find out how they relate to the Apple //c.

Special Places for Special Functions

Slot 0 was reserved for the Apple Language System. For early models with Integer BASIC, the card for slot 0 included Applesoft in ROM, but no RAM at all. For later models, the card was full of memory chips—in fact, it had the exact same amount of usable RAM memory as the Apple // motherboard had ROM (where the machine's firmware was kept).

When you used a disk, Apple arranged for Integer BASIC to be loaded from the disk into the RAM on the card thereby bypassing the Applesoft BASIC in ROM unless you specifically commanded otherwise. That allowed users with old Integer BASIC programs to run them on the newer machines.

Primarily, though, the Language Card was developed because of a programming language called Pascal. In order to run on the Apple //, it needed not only the 48K of RAM on the motherboard, but also an additional 16K—which just happened to be the amount on the Language Card.

Video Idiosyncrasies

Because of limitations built into the video system in order to produce color output, an older Apple could only display 40 characters across the screen of whatever video display it was connected to. This was fine when the machine first came out, since most other personal computers had limitations at least as severe. But as the years went by, other computers switched to an 80-column display—far more convenient, especially for word processing, since it matched the number of typewritten characters that could fit across an 8½ × 11-inch sheet of paper.

Because of the popularity of the machine, several manufacturers developed plug-in boards that would increase the Apple's display capacity to 80 columns on demand. Such cards were usually plugged into slot 3.

Shuffling the Cards

Each disk card could handle two of the Apple's disk drives. The position for the card that controlled the first pair of drives was always slot 6. If you wanted to increase that number to a maximum of four, you could add a card to one of the unused slots.

Apple originally offered two printer cards, one parallel, the other serial. Either could go into slot 1. They were eventually replaced with the Apple PIC (Parallel Interface Card) and SSC (Super Serial Card). The Apple //c does not offer a way of using parallel communications.

Slot 2 was the home of the Apple Communications Card, a serial output device used for hooking up modems. It, too, was replaced by the SSC.

The Next Generation

Next came the Apple //e, and things changed a little for the // series. The motherboard changed for the better. Taking advantage of advancements in technology, it used fewer, more powerful chips. Instead of having three rows of RAM chips totaling 48K, it had one row of newer chips that packed a full 64K of memory. That removed the need for the Language Card.

The //e still had eight slots, but they were arranged a little differently. Only seven of them were numbered, and the eighth was labeled AUX CON (AUXiliary CONnector). Apple released its own 80-column display card, along with an extended version that also included an additional 64K of memory, all on one board. Either of these new devices went into the AUX CON slot; the model with memory brought an Apple // machine's official memory count up to 128K for the first time.

Small but Powerful

Which brings us to the Apple //c. The Apple //c motherboard incorporates the latest technology. In that tiny package is all the hardware needed to duplicate the Apple //e without the use of slots and plug-in cards.

The motherboard contains sixteen high-capacity RAM chips, giving you a total of 128K of memory. Applesoft BASIC is a permanent fixture in ROM. Video-controller electronics permit either 40- or 80-column display widths. Special chips feed the two serial ports, and others provide for both the internal disk drive and an additional drive connected externally. It's all there. The question is, how do you use it? Let's find out.

Addressing Mythical Slots

For reasons of compatibility, when you turn on the Apple //c, its display width—the maximum number of letters, numbers, or symbols that will be visible across the face of your monitor or television—is 40. On an Apple //e, that situation can be rectified by inserting a special card into the AUX CON slot. But 80-column capability is built right into the Apple //c. We already know that the *80/40* switch doesn't get at it. What does?

As shown earlier, 80-column adapter cards originally went into slot 3 of Apple // computers. To turn on 80 columns with the Applesoft BASIC prompt and cursor visible, you would address slot 3 by typing PR#3 from the keyboard and then pressing the *return* key.

This command syntax followed through to the Apple //e and likewise onto your own powerful pippin.

Try it. Simply type:

```
PR#3
```

and hit the key marked *return*.

Three things happen. Your screen clears; the Applesoft BASIC prompt reappears in the upper left-hand corner, but smaller; and the cursor changes shape. Rather than the dotted rectangular pattern, the cursor is now a solid rectangle. This is the Apple //c's signal that you have activated the 80-column mode. Try typing more characters and you'll discover the new approach the Apple //c has taken to showing you what you type.

This example gives you the secret of using Applesoft BASIC to gain access to your computer's capabilities. The Apple //c simulates the slot environment of its relatives. There are no physical slots, so when you give a PR# command, the firmware routes your output to a theoretical "slot" and "card" controlled by the Apple //c's built-in hardware. From then on, all output goes through that "slot" until you tell the machine otherwise. And when we say *all,* we mean it. Unless you issue special echo commands (which we'll explain in the printer and modem chapters), the screen won't even display what you type.

PR#3 sends information to the 80-column card. PR#1 gets you the serial printer port, and PR#6 starts the disk drive spinning in search of information.

If you're using a modem attached to the Apple //c, you might assume that you'd access it by issuing a PR#2 command. Almost, but not quite. A modem is a bidirectional device that can send and receive information.

The complement to the PR# command is IN#. With it, you direct information from the card *into* the computer. IN#2 lets you use the Apple //c as a transmitting *and* receiving device that can communicate over the phone to another computer or a large computer network.

In this mode, without any additional software to control it, the Apple //c will emulate what's known as a dumb terminal. It can do communications, but that's about it; features like transmitting stored information or saving what you're receiving aren't available.

To stop the computer from using any of these devices, you can use either the PR#0 or IN#0 commands. Both of these direct input and output through the slot 0, which the computer recognizes as itself. Only the 80-column mode will be unaffected by these two commands. Remember, you may have to type these commands "blind"—without benefit of seeing your keystrokes on the screen.

Back to 40 Columns

How do you go back to 40 columns? One way is to reset the machine. It's not the recommended way, nor the only way, but reset does restore everything on the machine to the way it was when you first powered it on.

Try a reset. Hold down the *control* key, then hold down the key, and while holding them down, press the switch marked *reset*—then release them all. You'll get the same screen display, including the disk message, that you saw when you originally turned the machine on. You'll have to go through the interrupt procedure again by holding down *control* and pressing *reset*. Release all the keys.

Now you're back at the Applesoft BASIC prompt (]) and the dotted cursor of the 40-column mode—just where you wanted to be. But that's only a quick bail-out procedure and wouldn't do you much good if you wanted to switch from 80 to 40 columns without wiping out everything in the computer's memory.

Instead of PR#3 this time, press and release the key labeled *esc*. Just like the last time you used the *esc* key, your cursor changes to a solid white box with a cross through it. The *esc* key is also a modifier, but somewhat different from the ones we've already mentioned. It produces an ASCII code of 27, which a program can check for, but when it's pressed with just the Applesoft BASIC prompt showing, the Apple //c uses it for its own purposes. The cross hairs in the cursor show you that. With the cross hairs showing, press the number *8*. Two of the three things that happened when you entered PR#3 have happened again. The screen didn't clear, but everything on it has now become slightly smaller to accommodate the new width, and the cursor is now solid again.

If the key sequence *esc-8* put you into 80-column mode, will *esc-4* return you to 40 columns? Try it. Look: the cursor didn't return to the dotted rectangle. It's still a solid block!

That's because the 80-column electronics are still active. You've turned them off temporarily, but the Apple //c still knows they're there. If you don't go one step further, you can get your machine thoroughly confused, to your everlasting chagrin. Press and release the *esc* key and the cross hairs will return. Then hold down *control* and press the *Q* (for Quit) key. Release them both.

A lot of things happen. Everything reverts to 40 columns. The Applesoft BASIC prompt appears in the lower left-hand corner of the screen. A "\" appears on the screen line directly above it. Finally, the cursor is back to being the dotted rectangle signifying 40 columns. It all lets you know the 80-column card has been deactivated.

There is no *esc-control* sequence to turn off the other slots. If you've directed output to the printer, for example, the only way to turn it off is to direct it back to the Apple //c by typing PR#0 or IN#0. Then, when you hit the *return* key and the machine accepts the command, it shuts down any slot assignment (with the exception of the 80-column mode) and routes all material back to the video electronics and onto the screen. It doesn't affect the display characteristics, because it's entirely possible that you'd want to remain in the current display mode even though you no longer want information going somewhere other than the screen.

5

Applesoft: The Basics

Sooner or later, you're going to want to tell your computer to do something special just for you. If you're an old-fashioned hacker who's been around since the days of room-sized computers, you may insist on using nothing but strings of ones and zeros to communicate in *binary code*. If you're a more modern programmer and you care more about how fast your programs run than how long it takes you to write them, you may enjoy working with terms like "LDA," "5BH," and "NOP" that are common in assembly language.

In the early days of computer history, those methods were virtually the only ways for humans to communicate with computers. But as computers evolved, experts got the bright idea of inventing *high-level* languages—ways of instructing computers in terms that at least superficially resemble human languages more than the strings of ones and zeros that computers use to do their thinking.

Over the years, dozens of these languages (with weird acronymic names like ALGOL, FORTRAN, COBOL) sprouted up and evolved. The one that became the most popular for microcomputers was the one called BASIC—which stands for Beginner's All-purpose Symbolic Instruction Code. Although you can communicate with your Apple //c in other languages, BASIC comes free and built into each and every one, so it's probably the one you'll use first and most.

Basically Speaking

There are good reasons for BASIC's popularity besides the fact that you don't have to pay extra to use it. The COBOLs and FORTRANs of this world are *compiled* languages. Once you've written a program in a compiled language, you have to use a program called a *compiler* to convert it to information the computer can understand. Only then can you run the program. If there are any errors in it (and you can bet there will be), you have to correct them and run the program through the compiler again. After the fiftieth time you've done it, you may well give up all hope of ever getting your program to work properly.

BASIC, on the other hand, is an *interpreted* language. With an interpreted language, the computer does its translation of the program while the program is actually running. Interpreted languages tend to do things more slowly than compiled ones, but they're suitable for many uses, and they're very simple to learn. If you make a mistake, an interpreted language will let you know about it so that you can fix it in a matter of seconds.

BASIC comes in a variety of "dialects" that differ from machine to machine. With its very first version of the Apple //, Apple Computer provided Integer BASIC. It was a limited system that dealt, as you can imagine, only with nondecimal numbers and was aimed at the original Apple's primary storage device, the cassette tape. It does not see very much use today. However, to provide continuity among its machines and to cope with those few Integer BASIC programs still around, Apple continues to provide the language for its current computers. Because it is fading from the memory of computerdom, we won't be dealing with it here.

The Orchard Blooms

The most widely used versions of BASIC come from a company called Microsoft. The Apple //c has its own version of Microsoft BASIC. It's called Applesoft BASIC and is simple to learn, but like all languages, it has certain rules and regulations that govern how it can be used. English, French, Spanish, and the other languages of the world all have certain syntax and structure requirements. BASIC has no less.

In English, you begin each sentence with a capital letter and end it with a period. In BASIC (and since we're talking about the Apple //c, we'll refer to it from now on as Applesoft BASIC) you use line numbers, in ascending order, to indicate the beginning of each instruction you enter. To indicate the end of a line of instruction, you press the key on the keyboard marked *return.* It's as easy as that. Well, almost.

Getting Started

First you've got to get the Apple //c up and running. Again, you're going to ignore the fact that your computer has that funny slot in its side. That slot and its fancy sliding door are part of the built-in disk drive, and you'll learn all about them soon. For now, just turn on the Apple //c.

Once more you'll be told to check your disk drive, but you know you can get around that by holding down the key labeled *control* while pressing and releasing the *reset* switch just above and to the left of the keyboard. You've done it before, and it's no different now. Once you've pressed the *reset* switch, release them both.

With the hard part out of the way, you'll be greeted by the Applesoft BASIC prompt—the right bracket (]) you met once before. Make sure the *caps lock* switch is down, because you're about to try some programming.

Solving a Problem

The main reason to write a computer program is to get the computer to help you solve a problem. So let's decide on a problem and figure out how to get the computer to help us solve it.

If you earn $15,000 a year (or more, or less), many, many little hands manage to snatch pieces of it. Suppose you lose 20% to taxes and whatever. If you were to turn it into a formula, it would be:

SALARY – DEDUCTIONS = REMAINDER

The remainder should tell you how much you have left over for luxuries like food, rent, and clothing. But that formula still doesn't tell you how much the deductions are. Since they're 20% of your income, it's simple enough to figure.

SALARY × PERCENTAGE = DEDUCTIONS

You know the salary already, and you know what percentage is removed. It's simply a matter of doing the math. You could dig out the old and dusty calculator, but as long as you have the Apple //c sitting there, why not try a short computer program to figure it out for you?

A Program to Solve the Problem

Let's tackle the deductions first. Type the following line in from the keyboard exactly as you see it here. When you're finished, hit *return*. That's how the Apple //c knows you're done with the line.

```
100 PRINT 15000*.20
```

All of a sudden you're staring at the screen and saying "What?" But it's easy once you get the hang of it.

First, you have to start with a line number. In this case it's 100. You could have started with any number from 1 to a maximum of 63999, but it's a good idea to leave yourself room on both sides, in case you change your mind later on and decide you want the computer to do something before or after it performs this calculation.

PRINT does pretty much what you might expect. Here, it prints on the screen whatever follows it. The 15000, obviously, is your salary, and .20 is 20% expressed as a decimal number. But what is that asterisk in between?

You've probably guessed already. Traditionally, multiplication has been indicated by a crossed pair of lines that look very much like the letter *X*. On calculators that's no problem, since they deal only with numbers and their keyboards have no letters to worry about. But on a computer's keyboard, *X* could stand for either the first letter in "Xmas" or the commonly accepted multiplication sign. To avoid confusion, BASIC uses an asterisk to indicate multiplication. Division, by the way, requires a slash: 10/2 = 5. Exponentiation requires a caret: 2^3 = 8. And BASIC has a very definite idea of the proper order in which to do arithmetic.

Okay. You're all set. You have a line number, a command following it, and you've pressed the *return* key to tell the Apple //c there are no more instructions on that line. The one thing you don't have is an answer. Why not?

Rules of Arithmetic Precedence in BASIC

In doing arithmetic operations, BASIC follows an order of precedence in evaluating what is to be done first. From highest to lowest, that order is:

( )	sets off operation within
^	exponential
* /	multiplication and division
+ −	addition and subtraction

Operations with equal precedence on the same program line are performed at the same time.

An expression such as:

(3*2)/5^2+12

would be worked out as:

3*2	= 6
5^2	= 25
6/25	= .24
.24+12	= 12.24

RUN—Now Do It!

The Apple //c has accepted your instructions, but now it's waiting for you to tell it to do something with them. You must understand—computers, as a breed, have absolutely no initiative. They only do what you say, exactly what you say, when you tell them to do it.

Type the word RUN, press *return,* and watch what happens. On the next available screen line you should see the answer. It's 3000.

RUN is a command that BASIC understands to mean "Perform all of the instructions I've given you, starting with the line with the lowest number, and working up from there." Once Applesoft gets through all the lines you've entered, it lets you know you're back in control again by displaying the right-bracket prompt.

Back to our problem. We've got the amount of the deductions. Now we need to find out what's left. Try this:

```
120 PRINT 15000-3000
```

By this time you know that after every line of computer programming (and that's what using Applesoft BASIC in this way is called), you should press the *return* key to indicate its end. If the line you're typing exceeds the physical space afforded on one screen line and tumbles to the next (in-the-know computer folks call it "wrapping")—don't worry. Applesoft BASIC handles it automatically. Just use the *return* key when you reach the *conceptual* end of the line—the point at which you want it to stop.

You also realize that to see any results, you've got to type the word RUN and press *return*. That's what you should do from now on when you're told to "run the program." Well, run the program!

Numbers should appear on two lines of the screen. One should show 3000, the deduction; the other will show 12000, the amount you have left. If not, you've probably typed something in wrong. No problem: just retype the offending lines in any order. When you instruct the program to run, Applesoft will sort through the line numbers and figure out which comes first.

Hurry Up and Wait—BASIC's Two Modes

Think about what you did. You entered something to be used at a later time, and then you told your computer to do something right away. On the Apple //c, or any computer, these two distinct approaches are called *modes of operation.*

When you entered the program lines, you were using what Apple calls the *deferred* mode and some people call the *program* mode. Your lines contained instructions that would have to wait to be done.

When you entered the word RUN, you used what Apple calls the *immediate* mode and some people call the *direct* mode. You told the Apple //c to do it—and do it now.

All programming occurs in the deferred mode. It's the nature of a program that it doesn't do anything until you tell it to. But to do something you don't always need to write a program. You could very well type:

```
PRINT 15000*.20
```

When you press the *return* key, the Apple //c will notice that this command has no line number in front of it and will immediately execute the instruction. You could then use the answer in another line:

```
PRINT 15000-3000
```

This would give you the final amount. You can use the Apple //c as a calculator in this mode. Try it!

How about another immediate command? Type in the word LIST (and, of course, press *return*). Below it on the screen should appear the following:

```
100 PRINT 15000*.20
120 PRINT 15000-3000
```

It's a LISTing of the two program lines you wrote. Try RUNning the program again. It should still work fine.

Try one more immediate command. Type NEW and hit the *return* key. Nothing much seems to happen. But now run your program. Nothing. Nada. Zilch.

NEW wipes out the program currently in memory and does it for keeps. The only way to resurrect your old program is to type it in again. Moral: use it with care.

It's good practice to type NEW before entering any new program. Otherwise lines from an old program may turn up in the new one and produce undesirable effects that can be excruciatingly difficult to find and eliminate.

In case you're wondering, you've seen the immediate mode before. That's precisely what you were using when you experimented with PR# commands in the last chapter. You'll use many of the Apple's commands in just that mode.

Variations on a Theme—Applesoft Variables

That first program would work fine as long as your salary or rate of deductions remained the same. But if they went up (they certainly won't go down), you'd have to change both lines to reflect the new numbers.

That's an awful lot of work to go through, but BASIC has ways to let you avoid it.

Remember all the hypothetical situations you'd invent to get around asking questions that you needed answers for? You know, the type that began "I have a friend who has a rather unsettling disease and I was wondering . . ."

What you did was use an abstract reference (usually "a friend") to avoid using a specific reference (usually yourself) in case the answer you expected wasn't the one you received, or in case the circumstances changed. By using the abstract "someone" you allowed for making adjustments.

Computers can imitate life. In BASIC there are also abstract values. They're called *variables* because what they are can (and usually does) vary. Enter this simple program and see for yourself.

```
10 A=1
20 PRINT A
30 A=2
40 PRINT A
```

RUN the program. Even though the command in line 20 is exactly the same as the one in line 40, you should see two different numbers, *1* and *2,* on your screen right underneath each other.

How come the same command gave different results? Because the value of A changed. In line 10, the value of A was 1 and that's what line 20 printed out. But in line 30, A became 2, and that's what line 40 obediently sent to the screen. The value of A could vary because A, in that little program, is a variable.

The Three Flavors of Variables

There are three primary types of information these variables can represent: integer, real, and string. Variables therefore come in three flavors.

Integer variables represent "whole numbers" like the ones you use to count with. They can be positive or negative in value, but they cannot contain decimal points or fractions: 1, –2, 87, and 31,024 are all integers, while 1.2, 3/5, and 49.7878787 are not.

Real variables (no, there are no unreal variables) also represent numbers, and can be either positive or negative. However, they may also contain decimal points.

String variables simply represent collections of numbers, letters, and characters in a "what you see is what you get" way. The number 47 as a number (integer or real) stands for the *value* 47. You can add it, subtract it, multiply it, or divide it. The number 47 as a string stands for two characters "4" and "7," right next to each other. The way you tell your computer the difference is by enclosing it in quotes.

Still confused? How about some examples?

Describing the Unknown

As long as the first (or only) character is a letter, you can use any 1- or 2-character combination to identify a variable. Applesoft BASIC will actually let you use a variable name that's up to 238 characters long, but it ignores anything after the second character. For instance:

```
SOMEVARIABLESLOOKLIKETHIS%=123
```

is the same as

```
SO%=123
```

In both cases, the additional "%" (*percent sign*) is used to inform Applesoft BASIC that this is, indeed, an integer variable. The number assigned to it cannot be greater than 32767 or smaller than –32767.

Real numbers just use the variable name with no specifier suffixed to them.

```
THISISAREALVARIABLE=12.098
```

Or, as you just saw,

```
TH=12.098
```

The largest real number Applesoft BASIC can deal with is 1E38, the smallest, –1E38. The use of E here is called exponential (or scientific) notation. The number to the left of the E is multiplied by 10 raised to the power indicated by the number at the right of the E. Thus, 4E10 could also be written $4*10^{10}$. The Apple will only display nine digits of a number and uses scientific notation to display the rest of it.

Strings are easy. As mentioned, they are any characters enclosed in quotes and can be as long as 255 characters.

```
THISISASTRING$="HI THERE!"
THISISASTRINGALSO$="123838"
T$="SO'S THIS"
```

The dollar sign tells the Apple //c that it's using a string variable. Even though the second example includes only numbers, the fact that they're enclosed in quotation marks negates any value they have other than being the characters 1,2,3,8,3, and 8 "strung" together.

When dealing with variables, you must continue to use them as you've originally defined them. The variables G$, G%, and G are all separate and distinct as far as your Apple //c is concerned. You can't make G (a real variable) equal to "Joe's Bar"; you can make G$ equal to 475 only by putting quotation marks around the number. If you don't, you'll get a ?TYPE MISMATCH error message.

Defining What's Left

Let's type in a new program. Type NEW, hit *return*, and then type in these lines exactly as they appear here:

```
50 SALARY=15000
60 PERCENTAGE=.20
70 MESSAGE$="ALL THAT'S LEFT IS "
100 DEDUCT=SALARY*PERCENTAGE
120 INCOME=SALARY-DEDUCT
130 PRINT MESSAGE$
140 PRINT INCOME
```

Very ancient versions of BASIC will not accept variable definitions as you've used them here. These relics of a time long gone require a command to actually define them. Line 50, in such a system, would have to read:

```
50 LET SALARY=15000
```

One reason for this kind of syntax is that it avoids such mind-boggling but perfectly legal statements as

```
1999 A=A+1
```

by insisting on the theoretically clearer

```
1999 LET A=A+1
```

Applesoft BASIC *never* requires the LET type of construction, although it will accept it. It's mentioned here just so no one will ever throw you a curve with it.

You'll also notice that you've used a shortened form of the word "deductions"—DEDUCT. Applesoft BASIC gives you a lot of freedom, but some responsibilities go hand in hand with it. Certain combinations of letters are reserved for special commands. The ON in DEDUCTIONS is one of those combinations, and would cause quite a bit of confusion. Right now we'll just avoid the problem; later on we'll explain it in more detail.

Back to the program. It's getting fancy. You've defined two real variables, SALARY and PERCENTAGE, in the lines numbered 50 and 60. Likewise, you've set up a string variable, MESSAGE$, in line 70. Your old line 100 has been replaced by a new one that shows you that a variable can become the result of the interaction of two other variables.

DEDUCT is a result of calculating SALARY times PERCENTAGE. DEDUCT, and INCOME in the next line, are special cases. They were not defined until they were used. Before that, in case you were wondering, they were equal to zero. If your program consisted of only lines 130 and 140, two zeros would appear when you ran it. Applesoft BASIC initially sets all undefined variables equal to zero (or, in the case of strings, to "", which is a null, a string with nothing in it at all—not even a blank space).

Finally, INCOME, in line 120, is the result of subtracting DEDUCT from SALARY. When the calculations have been made, your heartfelt message is printed followed by the value of INCOME. With the exception of MESSAGE$ (read as "message string"), all of the variables you've used are real. Although it might not be readily apparent, they must be. SALARY can have a decimal point, as does DEDUCT, as can INCOME.

Finally, note that none of the variables you used shared the same two first letters. That's good. If they did, the last one you defined would cancel the value of the one before it. When naming variables, it's important to bear this in mind: keep *GO*LD and *GO*RP out of the same program.

RUN the program. Not bad, but not beautiful, either. It looks like this:

```
ALL THAT'S LEFT IS
12000
```

It's time to learn about *delimiters*—little extra things you can add to a PRINT statement to make what you print look more presentable.

Looking Good—Basic Screen Formatting

Delimiters come in two types: commas and semicolons. Each performs a worthwhile and different function. Let's see how they work.

This time don't type NEW. Let's get rid of line 140. Enter this line:

```
140
```

Anytime you enter a new line that begins with a number, it replaces the one that formerly existed with that number. As soon as you hit the *return* key, your old line 140 will be gone for good. Since new line 140 has nothing in it, Applesoft simply discards it.

Now let's change line 130 to:

```
130 PRINT MESSAGE$, INCOME
```

All you have to do is type it in. The old version of line 130 goes to program line heaven.

Now run the program. Your final output (which, in this case, is technese for "what you're printing") should look like this:

```
ALL THAT'S LEFT IS   12000
```

That's an improvement over what came out before. The comma you added to the line told the Apple //c to go to the next tab position after the MESSAGE$ was printed and then print the value of INCOME.

Put It on the TAB

"What's a tab position?" is a reasonable question, and it deserves a reasonable answer. Just like a typewriter, your Apple //c has tab positions, natural spots where it can stop when you tell it to. These are found at columns 1, 17, and 33. The comma tells BASIC to travel to the next available tab position and deposit whatever else is to be printed at that spot.

Let's rewrite line 130 one more time (you're certainly getting a lot of mileage out of that line, aren't you?). This time change it to read:

```
130 PRINT MESSAGE$;INCOME
```

Now run the program. The output reads:

```
ALL THAT'S LEFT IS         12000
```

That looks a heck of a lot better.

The semicolon, like the comma, tells the computer where to print what follows it. It places the next printed item on the same line as the last, and immediately after it. It does *not* insert a space. Where did the space between the IS and the 12000 come from?

LIST your program. If you typed it in exactly the way it appears in the book, you typed an additional space in line 70 before you added the final quotation mark. If you didn't, just retype the line and put it in.

You also have a couple of other useful commands at your fingertips. SPC(n) tells the //c to insert n spaces before PRINTing the next character. TAB(n) is an order to PRINT the next character in column n. Try these samples to see the difference:

```
PRINT "WHERE?"; SPC(20) "HERE!"
PRINT "WHERE?"; TAB(20) "HERE!"
```

But back to our friend line 130.

Even with all this professional formatting, there's still something missing from that final line. It would be nice to know what the 12000 is. Is it 12000 geese, or 12000 artichokes? You know what it is, but you never know when someone else might want to understand what you're doing. It's time, then, to introduce you to another concept, called the *literal.*

Literally Speaking—A Not-So-Variable String

If the word *literal* looks a little strange to you, or you think it's some more strange computer jargon, you're not approaching this from a human point of view. Literally, it means . . . well, that's *precisely* what it means. You want to make a literal statement, and Applesoft will let you do it. Literals, by the way, may be either uppercase or lowercase—it doesn't matter.

Let's redo line 130 one more time:

```
130 PRINT MESSAGE$;INCOME;" DOLLARS"
```

Run the program, and you'll get:

```
ALL THAT'S LEFT IS 12000 DOLLARS
```

You added the literal string " DOLLARS" and used the space in front of the word to make up for the fact that the semicolon causes printing to be done in the next available position. The space-plus-word combination is still a string, because it's a value enclosed in quotation marks. It's a *literal* string because you're using it for itself, without defining it as a variable.

If you think your program's complete, think again. This is a computer you're dealing with. It's there to work for you. Why should you have to rewrite the program and manually change the value of SALARY or DEDUCT just because one of them changes? Let's see a few more of the tricks Applesoft BASIC has in store for you.

Getting the Information In

So far in your program you've dealt with output—what the program prints on the screen. There must be a corresponding alternative to it. There is. It's called, naturally, *input.*

Let's do some more rewriting and see how it works.

```
50 INPUT SALARY
60 INPUT DEDUCT
```

It doesn't look like much, but it does a lot. Run the program. A question mark will appear on the screen, and all action will halt until you supply a number for SALARY and press the *return* key. Once you've done that, you'll get another question mark. This time you'll have to enter another number, the value of DEDUCT.

INPUT knows it should be getting numbers because you've specified real variables. Either time, if you try to type a nonnumeric value, like a string, you'll be chastised by a cryptic notation: ?REENTER. INPUT knows you did wrong and is giving you another chance. Still, what appears on the screen does not make life as easy as possible. Here's what should have happened when you ran the program. Your responses will be shown in boldface.

```
?15000
? .20
ALL THAT'S LEFT IS 12000 DOLLARS
```

The question mark is INPUT's way of telling you it's waiting for a response. Now, you may know what responses it wants, but what if your cousin Sally wanted to use your program? Who's to say she'd know what in the world was going on?

Remember the PRINT statement? How about using it together with a literal to put a message on the screen? Try entering this:

```
50 PRINT "ENTER YOUR GROSS SALARY ";:INPUT SALARY
```

Something new has been added: the colon. In English, when you finish a sentence and you want to start another thought, you place a period where the first thought ends. In Applesoft BASIC, when you finish one command and want to put another on the same line, you have to tell it so. You do it by separating the commands with colons. What you're saying to the Apple //c, through Applesoft, is "Print this message. Get this information."

Better Input with Prompts

Since you do have a computer, you almost certainly want to use it to get more work done in less time. Why, then, use two commands when you only need one? INPUT has another format that will help. Back to the keyboard. Type in:

```
50 INPUT "ENTER YOUR GROSS SALARY: ";SALARY
60 INPUT "ENTER YOUR DEDUCTIONS AS A DECIMAL: ";
   DEDUCT
```

What good would a question be if there was no way to state what type of answer was required? The question mark offered by the bare INPUT statement was certainly not sufficient by itself, since it didn't provide enough information. Now it does. When you run the program, it will look like this:

```
ENTER YOUR GROSS SALARY: 15000
ENTER YOUR DEDUCTIONS AS A DECIMAL: .20
ALL THAT'S LEFT IS 12000 DOLLARS
```

When you use a *prompt* (which is what the literal string is) in an INPUT command, INPUT dispenses with its usual question mark. To make up for that here, you've put a colon within the literal. If you had asked WHAT IS YOUR GROSS SALARY, you could have included a question mark.

One thing you can't do is use a delimiter (a comma or a semicolon) when you answer an individual INPUT statement. INPUT reads an answer with a delimiter in the middle as if it were two separate answers. For example, you could use the line:

```
INPUT "HOW DO YOU FEEL?";A$
```

If you answered:

```
NOT REALLY BAD
```

everything would be fine.

On the other hand, if you answered:

```
NOT BAD, I GUESS
```

A$ would become NOT BAD. Seeing characters after the comma, Applesoft would triumphantly announce ?EXTRA IGNORED, the program would continue, and I GUESS would vanish forever as "extra" material to the right of the comma which, as far as Applesoft is concerned, has no business being there.

Conditionals

Taking all of the changes together like this shows a much neater and more informative use of the Apple //c. Are you satisfied? Of course not. You paid big U.S. dollars for your computer and you want the most out of it! Fine. Let's add three more lines:

```
55 IF SALARY=0 THEN 200
140 GOTO 50
200 END
```

Now LIST the entire program. You should see:

```
50 INPUT "ENTER YOUR GROSS SALARY: ";SALARY
55 IF SALARY=0 THEN 200
60 INPUT "ENTER YOUR DEDUCTIONS AS A DECIMAL:
   ";DEDUCT
```

```
70 MESSAGE$="ALL THAT'S LEFT IS "
100 DEDUCT=SALARY*PERCENTAGE
120 INCOME=SALARY-DEDUCT
130 PRINT MESSAGE$;INCOME;" DOLLARS"
140 GOTO 50
200 END
```

As promised, all of the lines you've added have been inserted in their proper places automatically by Applesoft BASIC. It's a very nice feature, and saves a lot of extra work. The other thing you may have noticed is that you've just used three new features of the language.

The first, in line 55, is called, understandably, an IF . . . THEN clause. It's a conditional statement that uses the results of the first half, the IF part, to determine whether or not the THEN part occurs. It's obvious that you're checking to see if SALARY equals zero, but why would you want to do it? To understand that, and what's going to happen if your condition is met, go to line 140 for a moment.

Branching

Do you see what you just did? When you read the last sentence of the last paragraph and saw the instruction that said "go to line 140" you went there. Line 140 is a way of giving the computer that same type of instruction. You've told it that when it reaches that line, no matter what else is happening, it should GOTO line number 50—which starts the program over again. When it's used this way, it's called an *unconditional* branch. There's no choice in the matter.

That will help you understand the second half of line 55. You can assume that you want the program to go to a line number *if* the condition is met (which is why it's called a *conditional* branch). The problem is there's no GOTO in that half, it's just THEN 200. There doesn't have to be. When you're using an IF . . . THEN clause that incorporates conditional branching, the GOTO is understood without explicitly stating it. In other words, line 55 actually reads:

```
55 IF SALARY=0 THEN GOTO 200
```

In fact, you can type it in that way and it'll work just fine. But since computers are supposed to save time, when you can leave something out, you should.

There's something else you should know about an IF . . . THEN statement. Just as you've used two statements in other Applesoft lines (separated by a colon, remember), you could do the same here. Only one problem arises. When the IF section of your condition *isn't* true, Applesoft ignores everything else on the line. It will never get to the second statement.

In some older versions of BASIC, this is not the case, and the second (and any following) statements are executed no matter what the result of the condition. This is *never* the case with the Apple //c and Applesoft, but you should keep that in mind if you're looking at someone else's programs written on a different machine.

Two Ways to Stop

Let's GOTO line 200 and see what the big deal is all about. All it says is END—and it's a good thing it does. If there were no line 200, when your condition was met in line 55 you'd have been told "?UNDEF'D STATEMENT ERROR IN 55." That's one of the ways Applesoft thumbs its nose at you (you'll see more later) when you make a mistake. But you did include line 200 and BASIC expects to find additional instructions there.

In effect, line 200 says, "Drop all the variables you're playing with, and stop. This is The End." In older versions of BASIC, all programs had to have an END statement. Applesoft has no such rule. We're using it here to make the program quit whenever someone enters 0 as a salary. It's a convenient way to stop the program from cycling through to line 140 and beginning over again.

There's another way to stop your program. To illustrate it, add one more line:

```
10 PRINT "HA":GOTO 10
```

RUN it. You're now stuck in an *endless loop*. To break out of it, you could perform an interrupt. But there's an easier way. Hold down the *control* key and press *C*. You'll stop the program cold and get your Applesoft prompt back again. *Control-C* is absolutely essential, because it interrupts your *program* but not your machine.

Type:

```
10
```

This will get rid of that dumb program line.

Now LIST the program, but as soon as you hit the *return* key, hold down *control* and press *S*. If you're quick with the trigger finger, the listing stops. Press any letter key, and the listing begins again. It's nice to be able to slow down long lists.

That's your first program, from start to END. But there's so much more that Applesoft has to offer. For instance, what do you do with your program now that you've written it? To find out, move on to the next chapter. If you want to save yourself some typing, don't type NEW and don't turn your computer off.

6

Applesoft: A Bit More Intense

If you've still got your program from the last chapter in your machine, great! If not, type it in now.

Now what? You could make the program safe and sound for the ages by saving it to disk. Unfortunately, we're saving the method for doing that until you learn about disks and DOS.

You've seen what LIST can do. It prints a list of your program lines on the screen. But suppose you want to show this wonderful invention of yours to Uncle Godot? If he's standing there looking over your shoulder, you'll have no problem. If you've got to phone him to come look at the screen, you may have a long wait before he arrives—and while you're waiting there's nothing else you can do with the computer. That's decidedly unproductive.

If you had a printer, you could print a listing of the program and show it around wherever you wanted. All you'd need to know is how to get your information to that other piece of hardware. Unfortunately, typing LIST just puts information on the screen. So does the PRINT statement. There must be another way—and there is.

If you have a printer, read on. If you don't, either go out and buy one or skip the next section.

Hard Copy

Printing is just a matter of getting what's in the machine out onto paper. To do that you'll need a printer that's hooked up to the //c's printer port, properly loaded with paper and ribbon, turned on, and turned "on-line."

If the printer has met all those conditions, it *may* be all set for the big step. But it may require that you first perform some arcane procedures including the one known as "setting the baud rate." You'll find the information about it in chapter 13.

Once the printer's set, you must open a channel to the printer. That channel, as we've seen, is through port #1. Type PR#1, followed by the *return* key.

You have now established a link to the Apple //c's serial interface section and all the way to the printer. Now tell the Apple to LIST your program. Does it cascade down the screen? It does not!

But your printer is sure making a racket! In the coming days you will begin to hate the noise a printer makes when it's doing its job. Right now that clatter is probably the best sound you've ever heard. When the printing is done and you've listed the program as many times as you can stand it, type:

```
PR#0
```

That closes the channel to the printer. If you LIST your program now, you'll see it on your screen.

That's all there is to it—if all you want to do is LIST! But sometimes you may want to use your program to send information to the printer. To do that, Applesoft requires a little adjustment in the type and content of the command you give it, and you'll see exactly how when you learn about DOS.

Selective Program Destruction

Okay. You can't rest on your laurels now. Time to move on. NEW would give you a clean slate. But let's learn another way.

If you want to get rid of a whole bunch of program lines, you can use the DELete command. Try:

```
DEL 140
```

Now LIST the program. Line 140 is gone. Let's get more dramatic. Type:

```
DEL 70, 120
```

If you LIST the program, you'll discover that lines 70 through 120 have disappeared.

The program's a wreck now, but what if you just want to see a little of it? LIST, followed by a line number, will do the job:

```
LIST 130
```

This puts line 130 up on the screen.

```
LIST 55, 130
```

puts lines 55 through 130 up on the screen. And

```
LIST 55,
```

shows you all the lines from 55 on up.

There's one more thing to know. The command LIST ,100 will operate on all the lines up to and including the number following the comma.

Out with the Old and In with the New

Type NEW anytime you begin working on a new program.

Still, that doesn't do anything about the mess on your screen. You've listed the program a few times and have run it as well. The results are littering the display. So let's clean it up.

Type HOME (and don't forget to press the *return* key to let Applesoft know you're done with the line; henceforth, we won't remind you). First your program vanished; now everything on your screen disappears as well! You're a pretty good magician. Before you hurt yourself patting your own back, keep in mind that without the correct tools, even Houdini couldn't always get the stunt right. Applesoft recognizes the HOME command as a signal to clear the screen. You can use it in immediate mode to get rid of a confused mess, or you can use it in a program to start off with a nice clear screen.

In fact, we'll do it that way in a brand-new program. Type this in for openers:

```
10 HOME
50 INPUT "HOW MANY TIMES SHOULD I REPEAT IT? ";T
60 FOR N=1 TO T
70 PRINT "I MUST BE A GOOD APPLE //C"
80 NEXT N
90 PRINT
100 PRINT "DO IT AGAIN (Y/N)? ";
110 GET A$
120 IF A$<>"Y" AND A$<>"N" THEN 110
130 IF A$="N" THEN 150
140 GOTO 10
150 END
```

Looping with FOR and NEXT

Now, that's a program! You should understand the first two lines by now, so let's go straight to line 60. That line begins what's known as a FOR . . . NEXT *loop* that ends at line 80. It's all here:

```
60 FOR N=1 TO T
70 PRINT "I MUST BE A GOOD APPLE //C"
80 NEXT N
```

FOR . . . NEXT loops are terrific tools for repetitive tasks. Using them, you make the program repeat whatever instructions are contained between the FOR and the NEXT. In our program, the variable N keeps track of how many times you've gone through the loop. It begins with a value of 1, a convenient starting point. The program performs the action in line 70, then goes to line 80, and sees the NEXT N statement. When it gets there, it adds 1 to the value of N. Then it loops back to line 60 and goes around again—until N becomes greater than T (which comes from the user's INPUT in line 50). At that point, Applesoft knows it's done enough and jumps to the line immediately after the NEXT statement. It all happens automatically.

Aesthetics and GETting

The PRINT command will display any variable that follows it or any literal in quotes. If you use it all by itself, as in line 90, it simply prints a blank line. Every once in a while aesthetics should play a part in programming.

Now, here's something new:

```
100 PRINT "DO IT AGAIN (Y/N)? ";
110 GET A$
120 IF A$<>"Y" AND A$<>"N" THEN 110
130 IF A$="N" THEN 150
140 GOTO 10
150 END
```

Line 110 seems as though it should do something interesting. It does. On the Apple //c, GETting a variable halts all other operations. Your Apple //c will sit there patiently waiting for you to press one of the keys on the keyboard. Here we're using it much like INPUT. But unlike INPUT, GET doesn't wait for you to press the *return* key. When it senses that you've pressed down a key, it assigns the value of that key to the string variable you designated—A$ in this example.

When Things Don't Equal

What we're trying to do in line 120 is check for a "Y" or "N" answer to the question posed in line 100 and ignore anything else.

```
120 IF A$<>"Y" AND A$<>"N" THEN 110
```

While the conditional IF here may be familiar to you, the two symbols "<" and ">", used as they are here, may not be. From mathematics, you

Symbols used in Basic to compare quantities and strings include:

=	equals	>	is greater than
<	is less than	=>	is greater than or equal to
<=	is less than or equal to	<>	does not equal

will know them as the "less than" and "greater than" symbols, and that's the way Applesoft interprets them when they're used alone. (Or with an equals sign: >= means "greater than or equal to" and <= means "less than or equal to.") Together, though, as in line 120, they mean "is not equal to," equivalent to the mathematical symbol "≠".

The AND is called a Boolean operator in honor of George Boole, a nineteenth-century mathematician who described a system of logical relationships. OR and NOT are two other operators you can use. For example, line 110 could also be worded:

```
120 IF A$="Y" OR A$="N" THEN 130
```

It'd be clumsier, though. You'd need an extra line for the cases when neither "Y" nor "N" were entered:

```
125 GOTO 110
```

Be careful when using Boolean operators. As you've seen, using OR here meant adding an extra line, which takes up extra memory and means more work for you and for the computer. Avoid accidentally combining Boolean operators in such a way that *no* condition you're testing for will ever be true. It's a great way to cause a program to "hang" and refuse to do anything.

Branching Backward

If neither a capital *Y* nor a capital *N* is pressed, the operation branches back to the GET statement. When you want to accept only specific one-character answers (GET won't wait around for a second character) or you want to screen each character entered in an answer, GET is the command to use.

```
130 IF A$="N" THEN 150
140 GOTO 10
150 END
```

The rest of the program is really simple and contains things you've seen before. Line 130 is another conditional branch that depends on the answer to your question. If the response is "N," the program goes to line 150 where it ENDs. If it's "Y," the program goes back to the beginning and starts all over again.

Prince VAL and Princess STR$

Type NEW, then type in this program:

```
10 HOME
20 PRINT "CHOOSE A NUMBER BETWEEN 0 and 9 ";
30 GET N$
40 IF VAL(N$)=0 AND N$<>"0" THEN 30
50 PRINT
60 PRINT "YOU CHOSE THE NUMBER ";N$
70 PRINT
80 PRINT "ANOTHER? "
90 GET A$:IF A$<>"Y" AND A$<>"N" THEN 90
100 IF A$="Y" THEN 10
110 END
```

There's only one new concept waiting for you here. It's in line 40. To Applesoft, all characters have ASCII values, but only numbers can express quantities. In line 30, you'd like to GET a quantity. Unfortunately, GET only handles strings without hazard.

Well, maybe not quite unfortunately. Since they have no quantity associated with them, letters and other nonnumeric characters are considered to have a quantity of zero. And the VAL function comes to the rescue. VAL (N$) examines the variable to determine the quantity associated with it. When a letter is assigned to N$, VAL(N$) will be zero. This is a good way to check for a letter. But the number 0 also represents a quantity of zero. That's why you added the second half of the Boolean comparison. It checks to make sure N$ isn't 0.

You can also use VAL to change the nature of a variable. By using the form A=VAL(A$), you can assign the quantity associated with the value A$ to the variable A. If A$ is composed of letters, then A will equal zero. But if A$ is numeric, A will take on the quantity represented by the string.

```
X$="VARIETIES": X=VAL(X$): PRINT X
```

will put 0 up on the screen.

```
Y$="57": Y=VAL(Y$): PRINT Y
```

will show you the number 57.

The complementary command is STR$, and it's used in the form

A$ = STR$(A). If the value of A was 145.35, A$ would equal "145.35". It's even simpler than the VAL function, since A can only be a number.

You've just seen something that you can expand into a general Applesoft rule. Commands that include a "$" character produce strings as their result. Commands that don't include the $ give you numeric results.

ASC for the CHR$

Remember the ASCII values from chapter 4? There are times when they can come in handy in programming. The two commands that help you with them are ASC and CHR$.

ASC works on single characters. To find the ASCII value of the uppercase *G*, all you need to enter is:

```
PRINT ASC("G")
```

The number 71, which happens to be the ASCII code for G, should appear on the screen.

CHR$ translates in the other direction. Try:

```
PRINT CHR$(71)
```

You should see the letter G magically appear.

The CHR$ function is particularly useful for dealing with control codes. Try:

```
PRINT CHR$(7)
```

Do you hear a "bell"?

Stringing Along

LEN is the simplest *string function,* but it doesn't include a $. Does it return a number? Let's see. Type this in:

```
A$="DAYTIME": PRINT LEN(A$)
```

You should get the result 7. Count the letters in DAYTIME. LEN(A$) produces a number that's equal to the number of characters in the string variable.

Applesoft has three other string-handling commands: LEFT$, RIGHT$, and MID$. You can tell that they produce letters as their result. But how?

As far as Applesoft is concerned, A$ still equals "DAYTIME," and it will until you change it, reset the machine, or run a program. Type:

```
PRINT LEFT$(A$,3)
```

You should see DAY. LEFT$(A$,n) asks Applesoft for the leftmost *n* characters of A$.

And RIGHT$? You've probably guessed. Type:

```
PRINT RIGHT$(A$,4)
```

You should see the rightmost 4 characters of DAYTIME.

MID$ is not as simple. Type:

```
PRINT MID$(A$,4,3)
```

Your friend TIM appears. The 4 in the expression tells Applesoft to start with the fourth character in the variable A$. The 3 tells it to give you that character and two more—3 in all. MID$(A$,X,Y) starts at *X* and gives you *Y* characters.

Playing with strings can be fun. Type NEW and then this program:

```
10 A$="STARBRIGHTLIGHT"
20 PRINT LEFT$(A$,4);" ";RIGHT$(A$,5);", ";
30 PRINT LEFT$(A$,4);" ";MID$(A$,5,6)
```

Run the program, and you'll see:

```
STAR LIGHT, STAR BRIGHT
```

Line 20 prints the first four letters of the variable, a space, the last five letters, a comma, and a space. (Although commas have special meaning in several situations, they're just normal characters within strings.) The line ends with a semicolon so that the next PRINT statement will start at the next screen position without moving down a line. Line 30 prints the first four letters again, a space, and then the six characters it finds beginning at the fifth letter of A$. When it comes to programming, there's always another way. Type these lines:

```
20 B$=LEFT$(A$,4):C$=RIGHT$(A$,5)
30 D$=MID$(A$,5,6)
40 PRINT B$;" ";C$;", ";
50 PRINT B$;" ";D$
```

To do what we're doing here, this method is not very efficient, since it requires more memory. But memory isn't the only consideration. If we were planning to use STAR, LIGHT, and BRIGHT later in the program, storing them as variables might save us a lot of work when we got there.

Type NEW after you've finished with this program, and we'll proceed.

Subroutine Warfare

Type this program in for something new:

```
10 HOME
20 PRINT "PICK A NUMBER FROM 1 TO 3: ";
30 GET A$
40 IF VAL(A$)<1 OR VAL(A$)>3 THEN 30
50 A%=VAL(A$)
60 ON A% GOSUB 200, 300, 400
70 PRINT
80 PRINT "ANOTHER TIME? ";
90 GET A$
100 IF A$<>"Y" AND A$<>"N" THEN 90
110 IF A$="Y" THEN 10
120 GOTO 500
200 PRINT "ONE IS THE LONELIEST NUMBER"
210 RETURN
300 PRINT "TWO CAN LIVE AS CHEAP AS ONE"
310 RETURN
400 PRINT "THREE'S A CROWD"
410 RETURN
500 END
```

If you've zeroed in on line 60 as the main source of your next bit of information, you're right. Let's try rewriting it in English. "ON determining the value of A%, use it to GO to the SUBroutine at either line 200, 300, or 400 depending on the value of A%." If A% equals 1, the program will GO to the SUBroutine at the first line number in the list. If 2, it will go to the second, and so on.

But what's a subroutine? In a sense it's "a program's program," a miniature program all its own. Programs perform repetitive tasks for humans; subroutines perform repetitive tasks for programs. In this program, we have three subroutines, and we've given them separate line number groupings—200s, 300s, and 400s—just to keep them straight in our minds.

Why didn't we use GOTO to get to them? GOTO works in one direction only. There's no automatic way to get it to return to the spot in the program you left when you used it. Line 60 could indeed have been written:

```
60 ON A% GOTO 200, 300, 400
```

but we'd need three extra GOTO statements to get back from each of the subroutines. And since those extra GOTOs would each send you back to a specific line number, you couldn't use these subroutines from any other part of the program.

With GOSUB, the program *flow* jumps to the correct subroutine, performs whatever functions it finds there, and when it comes across a RETURN statement, goes back to the statement that immediately follows the GOSUB that sent it there. Since there is no other statement on line 60, the program flow continues at line 70. You don't have to worry about sending the program back to where it came from. It remembers that for you.

Arrays of Light

All the programs we've written so far have been pretty useless. But computers really are terrific at handling information. Our next program will almost have some marginal utility.

Let's assume you have fifteen friends and you want to keep track of them. Type this one in:

```
10 HOME
20 DIM F$(15)
30 FOR N=1 TO 15
40 READ F$ (N)
50 NEXT N
60 PRINT "NOW I KNOW ALL YOUR FRIENDS!"
70 PRINT
80 INPUT "WHICH ONE DO YOU WANT TO SEE (1-15)? ";N
90 IF N<1 OR N>15 THEN GOSUB 500:GOTO 80
100 PRINT F$(N)
110 PRINT "ANOTHER?";
120 GET A$
130 IF A$<>"Y" AND A$<>"N" THEN 120
140 IF A$="N" THEN 200
150 HOME:GOTO 80
200 END
500 IF N>15 THEN 550
510 PRINT "YOU HAVE MORE FRIENDS THAN THAT -"
520 GOTO 560
550 PRINT "YOU DON'T HAVE THAT MANY FRIENDS -"
560 PRINT "PRESS ANY KEY TO TRY AGAIN"
570 GET A$
580 HOME
590 RETURN
600 DATA "FRED", "HARRY","GEORGE","SAM","DAVE",
    "DEAN","TIM"
610 DATA MARK,BARNEY,TOM,TED,ALAN,JETHRO,BOB,JOE
```

Whenever you deal with information, it's a good idea to keep it organized. Organization doesn't necessarily mean it has to be arranged in any particular way, shape, or form—the computer can do that for you later on—but you should know where your information is at any given time.

The Apple //c's memory can give you incredibly fast access to information once you've organized it in some way or another. One good way is to use an *array*. An array is Applesoft's analogy to this situation. It's a group of fillable spaces or pigeonholes, and you defined it in line 20:

```
20 DIM F$(15)
```

The DIM command sets up the DIMensions of the array you want to use. In this case you've created an array called F$ with fifteen slots to fill. It's the same as having fifteen mailboxes, numbered consecutively, stacked one on top of another. Only one item will fit in each of your computerized pigeonholes. Actually, there are 16 slots here. DIM gives you a slot called F$(0). We're not using it here, but it's there if we wanted to.

Filling the Array

You're already familiar with the FOR . . . NEXT principle in lines 30 to 50:

```
30 FOR N=1 TO 15
40 READ F$(N)
50 NEXT N
```

Here, you're incrementing N from an initial value of 1 to a maximum of 15. And in line 40 you're giving your pigeonholes numbers: F$(1) through F$(15). You're also putting values in those pigeonholes by using the READ command.

Where do you READ those values from? Look all the way down to the last two lines of the program:

```
600 DATA "FRED","HARRY","GEORGE","SAM","DAVE",
    "DEAN","TIM"
610 DATA MARK,BARNEY,TOM,TED,ALAN,JETHRO,BOB,JOE
```

What better place to READ information from than a spot marked DATA? If you count the number of literals on both lines, you will notice that there just happen to be fifteen of them. It's a very nice coincidence.

But why are the literals in line 600 enclosed in quotes and the ones in line 610 absolutely naked? To illustrate a point. In one of its weirder exceptions, BASIC does not require you to enclose literals in quotes when they appear in DATA statements. Our guess is that the folks who invented the language got sick and tired of hitting the *shift* key.

To use a READ statement as you've used it here, the program must include DATA statements that have at least as many elements in them as you want to read. In DATA statements, commas serve as delimiters. If you want to put more than one element in an individual DATA statement, you must separate them with commas.

The DATA elements can be strings or numbers, but if you ask for fifteen of them, at least fifteen had better be there. If not, your program will grind to a halt and an ?OUT OF DATA ERROR IN <line number of READ statement> will appear on the screen.

When it encounters a READ statement, Applesoft searches out the first unused piece of data in a DATA statement. It does all the reading you ask for and leaves a little mental note to itself to remind it where it left off. The next time it has to READ, it picks up where it left off.

One nice thing is that BASIC doesn't care where DATA statements are, as long as they're in the proper order. They don't have to be at the end, they don't have to be at the beginning, or even the middle. You can put a DATA statement *anywhere* in the program you want. In this program, lines 600 and 610 would work just fine if they were numbered 1 and 2, 75 and 85, or 107 and 506. The reason most programmers put them at the end where they stick out like a sore thumb is that they're easy to find in case of a missing comma or a missing piece of data.

Back to the array. Once it's filled with all fifteen names, you're ready to use it.

```
80 INPUT "WHICH ONE DO YOU WANT TO SEE (1-15)? ";N
90 IF N<1 OR N>15 THEN GOSUB 500:GOTO 80
100 PRINT F$(N)
```

Line 80 lets you input the number of the friend you want to see. Line 90 checks to see that you've entered a legal value and sends you to the subroutine at line 500 if you haven't. Line 100 uses the proper element of the array to print out the name you're looking for.

And the rest of the program? Most of it does what's known as *exception processing* to insure that the user can't do anything that will make the program "crash." The program would work fine if you left it all out—until someone accidentally entered a value of sixteen or more.

Rows of Arrays

Arrays in Applesoft can get even fancier and more useful. So far, we've seen that an array can include a whole mess of pigeonholes where we can stick information. But conceptually those pigeonholes work in only one dimension. So far, the mailboxes have to be stacked one atop another.

But you can also define something called a matrix, which lets you work in two dimensions at once. In a sense it's really an array of arrays, and the most useful way to think of it is as a grid. Let's add two stacks of fifteen mailboxes side by side with the ones we've got, for a total of three. The way to do that is to try:

```
DIM A$(14,2)
```

Why 14 and 2? Didn't we say we wanted *3* columns of *15* mailboxes? Yup. But when you DIMension an array, remember, the elements begin with 0.

If all you wanted to track was fifteen friends with three pieces of information about each—say name, age, and phone number—you'd need a matrix this size: F$(14,2). Your first friend would fit in like this:

```
F$(0,0)="FRED"              (the friend's name)
F$(0,1)="27"                (Fred's age)
F$(0,2)="(212) 555-1234"    (Fred's phone number)
```

To print the name and statistics of any friend, you'd include a program line that read:

```
PRINT F$(<row>,<column>)
```

where <row> is a number from 0 to 14, and <column> is a number from 0 to 2. In fact, since ROW and COLUMN are valid variable names, you could write a FOR . . . NEXT loop to print out your whole address book. After you DIMensioned your matrix and put information into it via INPUT or READ statements, you'd include a section like this:

```
1000 FOR ROW=0 TO 14
1100 FOR COLUMN=0 TO 2
1200 PRINT F$(ROW,COLUMN)
1300 NEXT COLUMN
1400 NEXT ROW
```

For Applesoft to increment the ROW number, it must first cycle through all of the COLUMN numbers. NEXT COLUMN comes before NEXT ROW to make sure of this. Using combinations of FOR . . . NEXT loops this way is called *nesting.*

You now have most of the essentials you need to write reasonable Applesoft programs. You still haven't learned anything about graphics or about how to use your disk drive. And there are a few tricks that may come in handy.

7

BASIC Tricks and Tips

Mistakes somehow manage to pop up into programs when you least expect them and can least afford them. They can work tragic results on the most carefully thought out Applesoft program. The best way to avoid them is to know some of the pitfalls in advance.

If your //c is on, type NEW and make sure you're in 40-column mode. If you've turned off the machine, turn it back on, but don't use a disk (all in good time . . .). Go through the *control-reset* sequence and bring up the Applesoft prompt and cursor. Stay in the 40-column mode for this little exercise.

Variations on Variables

You have a lot of flexibility in choosing variable names in Applesoft, but that can be a trap. Remember our first example, in which we wanted to represent deductions from income. If you recall, the actual variable name we used was DEDUCT. Try it in the long form:

```
10 DEDUCTIONS=.20
```

Although it's only one line, it's still a program. But in fact it won't do anything—not even assign the value correctly. LIST it. You should be a little surprised by what you see:

```
10 DEDUCTI ON S = .20
```

Unexpected, to say the least. Applesoft ignores spaces in program lines. It can afford to do this because it can (and will, as you've seen) insert its own if it thinks one is needed.

The word ON is a *reserved word* that Applesoft uses for program control. So are AND, OR, GOTO, and others you've met already. You can find them in the chart on the facing page. As Applesoft examines or *parses* the program line, it assumes reserved words are being used the way Applesoft intended and assigns spaces accordingly. RUN your one-line program. Because of the way Applesoft divided your variable into three parts, you'll see ?SYNTAX ERROR IN 10.

How about the extended variable name IGOTONE? Try entering:

```
10 IGOTONE=1
```

Even before you LIST it, you probably know what you'll see when you do:

```
10 I GOTO NE = 1
```

It doesn't matter where in a variable name the reserved word is. Applesoft will ferret it out and totally disrupt what you're doing. SCORE often seems a particularly good name in games, but it doesn't work, since it contains the reserved word OR. Moral: either stick to one- and two-letter variable names or become familiar with the list of Applesoft reserved words. It'll save you a lot of grief later.

Editing: Making Amends

What happens when you type in a line and decide to change it? How about:

```
100 IF X<>30 THEN PRINT "SORRY, JIM IS 30 YEARS OLD"
```

Obviously, that line will print a message if the value of the variable X does not meet your expectations. But what if you later discover that old Jim is actually 28?

As you know, you could retype the line in its entirety. Retyping a line using an existing line number erases the old line and replaces it with the new one. But that's very time-consuming for long program lines. The Apple //c has a solution—complete with its own potential hazards.

Escaping Again!

You put your fingers on the esc key when you learned to switch back and forth between a 40- and 80-column screen display. Whenever you press it, the Apple //c thinks that what's next is special.

Type NEW to get rid of any old stuff, then type in line 100 as it appears above. Now LIST the line. You'll see that Apple's penchant for parsing and rearranging produces something that looks like the line at the top of page 90.

Reserved Words Used by Applesoft, DOS, and/or ProDOS

The following words are used by your computer for its own functions. If any one appears within a variable name, the //c will attempt to split the variable name and extract the reserved word, usually leading to a ?SYNTAX ERROR or, worse, a program problem that may be extremely difficult to ferret out.

ABS
AND
APPEND
ASC
AT
ATN

BLOAD
BRUN
BSAVE

CALL
CAT
CATALOG
CHAIN
CHR$
CLEAR
CLOSE
COLOR
CONT
COS
CREATE

DATA
DEF
DEL
DELETE
DIM
DRAW

END
EXEC
EXP

FLASH
FLUSH
FN
FOR
FP
FRE

GET
GOSUB
GOTO
GR

HCOLOR
HGR
HGR2
HIMEM
HLIN
HOME
HPLOT
HTAB

IF
IN#
INPUT
INT
INVERSE

LEFT$
LEN
LIST
LOAD
LOCK
LOG
LOMEM

MID$

NEW
NEXT
NORMAL
NOT
NOTRACE

ON
ONERR
OPEN
OR

PEEK
PEL
PLOT
POKE
POP
POS
POSITION
PREFIX
PRINT
PR#

READ
RECALL
REM
RENAME
RESTORE
RESUME
RETURN
RIGHT$
RND
ROT
RUN

SAVE
SCALE
SCRN
SHLOAD
SIN
SPC
SPEED
SQR
STEP
STOP
STORE
STR$

TAB
TAN
TEXT
THEN
TO
TRACE

UNLOCK
USR

VAL
VLIN
VTAB

WAIT
WRITE

XDRAW
XPLOT

```
100 IF X < > 30 THEN PRINT "J
    IM IS 30 YEARS OLD"
```

Worry not. It may look different, but it's the same as what you typed in. Applesoft always starts the text portion of a program line on the third space to the right of the last character in the line number. When a line exceeds the screen width, Applesoft continues it on the next line, with the first character indented seven character positions from the left of the display.

The Arrow Keys

You're lucky. The original Apples only had left and right arrows. In fact, if you try all four keys now, you'll discover the left and right arrows are the only ones that work.

Remember the *esc* key? Press it. The cursor will change to a solid block and the cross hairs will appear. The Apple //c is waiting.

Using the ↑, bring the cursor up until it rests on top of the *1* in 100. Press *esc* again. The cursor will return to its blinking dotted rectangle (unless you've activated the 80-column video section—in which case, the *1* will appear in black surrounded by a solid box). You're about to do some editing.

What are you going to change? There are two places in the line where Jim's age is referred to as 30. Using the right arrow, move the cursor along until it's directly over the first *3*. Press the *2* key. A *2* replaces the *3* and the cursor moves forward one position. Now press *8*. You've corrected one of the entries. Correcting the other seems like a snap—just move the cursor along until it reaches the next *3*, right?

Well, not quite. Use the right-arrow key to move the cursor until it rests on top of the *J* in JIM. Then hold on. When it's used to edit a program line, the cursor acts like flypaper. It collects everything it passes over as part of that line—which is why you started with the line number itself. If you were to continue with it past the *J* in JIM, you would add all of the intervening spaces between the letter *J* and the continuation of the name on the next line. JIM would become J   IM, and that won't do at all.

The answer is to press the *esc* key yet again. When it's in the escape mode, the cursor ignores any characters it passes over. With the cross hairs again visible, use the arrow key to move the cursor to the next line until it rests on top of the *I*. Press *esc* one more time. Now all you have to do is bring the cursor up to the *3* the way you did before and change the *30* to *28*. But once you've done that, you're still not through.

Normally when you've finished putting everything into a line of programming, you press *return* to signal Applesoft that you're done. As far as you're concerned you're done, but if you press *return* now, you'll cut off everything beyond the cursor's current position. You'd have to go back up and reedit the line, adding what you deleted.

Instead, just use the → key to bring the cursor one position beyond the last character in the line. At that point you can press *return* and Applesoft will accept the whole line, just as you intended. You've just done your first editing job.

Control-X

What if you start editing a line, then recoil in horror when you realize you didn't want to make the changes you just made and you can't quite remember what the original line looked like? Don't panic, and *don't* press the *return* key. Instead, hold down the *control* key and hit the letter *X*. You'll see a backslash on the screen, the cursor will jump down one line, and Applesoft will forget all the editorial changes you've made. You can LIST the original line to prove it's still intact.

How about another use for your newfound editorial talents? Press *esc*, then use the ↑ to get to the *1* in the line number. Press *esc* again to get the normal cursor back. Now change the *1* to a *2* and use the → key to get to the end of the program line, remembering how to get around that gap between the letters *J* and *I*. Once you're done, LIST what you've got:

```
100 IF X < > 28 THEN PRINT "J
   IM IS 28 YEARS OLD"
200 IF X < > 28 THEN PRINT "J
   IM IS 28 YEARS OLD"
```

This time you didn't replace the line in the Apple's memory. Instead, you added a line! It's not just a nice parlor trick. There will be times when you'll want to duplicate some of the lines in a program, or change only a character in them. The *esc* and arrow-key sequences let you do it with a minimum of effort.

As we noted, older Apple // computers did not have four arrow keys. To edit program lines with them, you *esc*aped into an editing mode. But in that mode, even the ← and → keys didn't work. Instead, you had to use the *I*, *J*, *K*, and *M* keys as a "cursor diamond." *I* took you up, *M* brought you down, and *J* and *K* were left and right, respectively. They'll still work on your Apple //c. Just hit the *esc* key and try them.

If that's not enough, you can also use *esc* followed by the *A*, *B*, *C*, and *D* keys. This time *esc* is only good for the following keypress. If you press *esc* and the *D* key, the cursor will move up a line. But if you want to do it again, you have to press both *esc* and *D* once more. Likewise for *A*, which moves you right one position, *B* (left one position), and *C* (down).

These are somewhat awkward to use. If you forget to press the *esc* key each time (as you will when you've grown accustomed to the arrow or cursor-diamond *I-J-K-M* key sequences), you'll have a line full of *A*'s or *B*'s or *C*'s or *D*'s that you'll have to go back and erase.

A Little Screen Magic

How about some ways to spice up what appears on the screen? First, use the NEW command to clear the machine's memory, then type in:

```
100 PRINT "WHEN IN ROME..."
110 INVERSE
120 PRINT "...DO AS THE ROMANS DO."
130 NORMAL
```

The words may be obvious. The Apple's reaction may not be. The first line you print appears quite normally on the screen, in a black background. The second, however, is a little different. The text itself is black, this time, and the background of the line it's printed on is a solid block of the color that's normally the foreground. It's called "inverse video," and the command in line 110 did it.

The screen would have stayed in INVERSE if we'd left out line 130 and the NORMAL command. Inverse video is very jazzy, but use it sparingly. It can definitely become tiring on the old eyeballs.

Let's replace lines 110 and 130 with the following:

```
110 SPEED=50
130 SPEED=255
```

Run the program. The first PRINT statement goes right along in a manner to which you've become accustomed. The . . . second . . . line . . . however . . . moves . . . somewhat slower than the first. The SPEED command accepts values between 0 and 255; 255 is the normal or "default" speed.

Ignoring the caps lock Key

Applesoft insists that its commands be entered in uppercase letters. That's the law. But your Apple //c has lowercase capability, and, in fact, some things deserve to be in lowercase (after all, why else would Apple have provided it?). Wouldn't it be nice if you could write a program line like this:

```
10 IF X<>28 THEN PRINT "Jim is only 28 years old."
```

Well, you can. All it would take is a little juggling with the *shift* or *caps lock* keys. Applesoft needs its *commands* (like GOTO and IF and INVERSE) in uppercase, but what's between quotes in a string doesn't qualify as a command.

Better still, the magicians at Apple have put one over on Applesoft. Let's try our old friend Jim again:

```
100 if x<>28 then print "Jim is 28 years old."
```

The literal looks good. It starts the way most English sentences start, with a capital letter, and ends with a period. Those lowercase commands, however, would send chills up the spine of any longtime Apple programmer. Want to see some magic? LIST it:

```
100 IF X<>28 THEN PRINT "Jim is 28 years old."
```

Voilà! No fiddling with the *caps lock* or *shift* keys at all. Applesoft translates all of its own commands, even the variable name, into capitals. In fact, it converts everything *not* in quotes into uppercase. That's quite a feat. You can even use the word "list" in lowercase, if you like. Keep in mind, though, that not every Apple can follow along.

You may see a warning message, "BE SURE THE CAPS LOCK KEY IS DOWN," but it applies only when you respond to questions and other programming commands *when working with DOS commands.* When we get to DOS (beginning in Chapter 10), lots of things will get more complicated.

Getting Out of BASIC

In the previous chapter we showed you how to create a matrix holding your friends' names and vital statistics. Using a PRINT statement inside the program, you could send a list of them to the screen. And by using PR#1 before you ran it, all of the output would be directed to the printer, just the way your program lines were when you used PR#1 and then LIST.

But doing it that way is sloppy. The word RUN would also appear in print at the beginning of the page, and the Applesoft prompt,], would turn up at the end. You certainly can do without them.

What about including the PR#1 in your program? You'd need a companion PR#0 to get back to the screen, but it seems as though it should work. Close, but no cigar. Anytime you send output somewhere other than the screen, your Apple does a small rearrangement of memory. Outside a program, it causes no harm, but inside, it confuses the heck out of the computer. And if you had started the machine with a disk in the drive, you'd discover that using just a PR# command from within a program would disconnect DOS—the highly essential disk operating system!

What you have to do is send the Apple a signal that warns it about what you're going to do, so it can take the proper precautions. This signal is a *control character*—a character whose ASCII code is less than 32. The one you need is the one whose ASCII value is 4.

Let's look at a sample program that illustrates the point. Suppose you had already assigned a matrix for the values and filled it using the READ and DATA statements. When it came time to print the information, you could do the following:

```
500 PRINT CHR$(4);"PR#1"
510 FOR X=0 TO 14
520 FOR Y=0 TO 2
530 PRINT A$(X,Y),
540 NEXT Y
550 PRINT
560 NEXT X
570 PRINT CHR$(4);"PR#0"
```

Here you see the application of the CHR$ function. PRINT CHR$(4) "prints" the character with ASCII value 4 (which just happens to be invisible on the screen) and tells the Apple, "Hold on a minute! What follows requires some special action!" The object of that special action, PR#1, is used as a literal string immediately following the control character, which is why you put the semicolon after CHR$(4). After the printing is finished, line 570 redirects output to the screen. Applesoft uses the same format to send output to any of the slots or the disk drive from within a program.

Fancy Math

BASIC has a reasonably large repertory of mathematical functions. If you plan to use your //c for heavy calculating, the following functions are at your fingertips:

ABS (for ABSolute) gives the absolute value of the number following in parentheses. For instance, PRINT ABS(–3) will put the number 3 on the screen.

ATN (for ArcTaNgent) finds the arctangent of the number in parentheses: that is, the angle (in radians) corresponding to the tangent of the number following the command. Typing PRINT ATN(30) would produce the result 1.53747533.

COS (for COSine) finds the cosine of the number in parentheses (where that number is an angle in radians). Typing PRINT COS(4) would produce the result –.65364362.

EXP calculates the value of "e" (the base of natural logarithms) raised to the power of the number following in parentheses.

INT (for INTeger) returns a numeric value equal to the integer value nearest and below the number following in parentheses. In other words, it lops off all the decimal places of positive numbers or finds the integer just less than a given negative number. PRINT INT(8.245676) would return 8; PRINT INT(5.994321) would give a result of 5.

LOG (for LOGarithm) gives the value of the natural logarithm of the number following in parentheses (which must be a nonzero, positive number). PRINT LOG(12) would result in 2.48490665; PRINT LOG(–12) would get a ?ILLEGAL QUANTITY ERROR message.

RND (for RaNDom) gives a "pseudo" random number between zero and .99999999. It requires a number (or numeric expression) to follow the command to serve as the "seed" from which the random numbers are calculated. For every repetition of the RND operation, a new "random" number is calculated in sequence. If the seed is negative, the RND function is reseeded each time it is called, essentially giving the same number. Zero returns the same number each time. Your guess is as good as mine what result you'd get from typing PRINT RND(8)!

SGN (for SiGN) returns a value based on whether the number following in parentheses is positive, negative, or zero. Positive returns a 1, zero a 0, and negative a –1.

SIN (for SINe) gives the sine (in radians) of the number (expressed in radians) that follows in parentheses. For instance, PRINT SIN(9) would produce .412118485.

SQR (for SQuare Root) gives the square root of the number following. BASIC has problems finding the imaginary SQRs of negative numbers and responds with a ?ILLEGAL QUANTITY ERROR message, should you try. PRINT SQR(65536) results in 256; PRINT SQR(–16) results in a ?ILLEGAL QUANTITY ERROR.

TAN (for TANgent) gives the tangent of the number (expressed in radians) that follows in parentheses. For instance, PRINT TAN(10) would produce .648360828. Some values of TAN can result in a ?DIVISION BY ZERO error message.

BASIC is very versatile. If this list does not include a mathematical function you need in your work, you can create one using the DEF FN statement, which lets you give any function or formula a variable name. To see how it works, try this:

```
10 DEF FN A(X) = X + 10
20 PRINT FN A(2)
30 PRINT FN A(100)
```

Remarks about REM

One BASIC command seems to do almost nothing at all. REM advises BASIC to ignore everything else that follows it on a program line.

The REM command is of immense value in documenting your software. It allows you to add comments to program lines to tell others (and yourself, after your memories of the program become hazy) why you did what you did or what a program line is supposed to do. Documenting your programs properly helps others learn from your experiences and helps you share your programming knowledge with others.

REM statements do take up valuable room in memory, however. When you want to make a program as small as possible, the first thing to be eliminated will most likely be the REMs.

You can insert REMs anywhere in a program or even make an entire program from them. Try this:

```
10 REM THIS LINE WILL NOT PRINT
20 PRINT "THIS WILL": REM "BUT THIS WON'T"
```

8

Graphics Dazzle

The graphics talents of the Apple // family have long been among the most important features setting it apart from the pack. But graphics programming isn't exactly easy. The most dazzling graphics you see on your machine are likely to come from prewritten software, be it a game or a fancy business package. Still, it won't hurt to pick up some of the fundamentals of the graphics capabilities Applesoft offers.

There are three graphics modes on the Apple //c:

Text
Low resolution (lo-res)
High resolution (hi-res)

Text as Graphics

Let's start with the most limited one, the one you might not even think of as a graphics mode: text. True, it's very limited, but within the scope of most programs, it can be very handy. Applesoft does not normally allow text to be mixed with graphics in either the lo-res or hi-res modes; you must have special programs that create text on a graphics screen rather than place it there as a result of normal keyboard entry.

In the text mode, the Apple //c has 960 screen positions to fill, and the screen is divided up as shown.

The figure should look familiar to you, at least in format: it's your old friend the matrix. The Apple text screen is 40 columns across by 24 rows down. The upper left-hand corner, called the *home position* when using text, is matrix element (1,1). The last element, the lower right-hand corner, is (40,24).

Apple Text Mode Screen Map

```
1,1                                            40,1
----------------------------------------------->
|
|
|
|
|
----------------------------------------------->
1,24                                           40,24
```

Now that you know how to describe the spot where you're putting something, the next question is how you put something there. You're looking for a way to glide across the screen both vertically and horizontally with a minimum of effort. Apple has provided the tools for you to do that—they're called HTAB and VTAB. Type in this simple program:

```
10 HOME
20 VTAB 10 :HTAB 15 :PRINT "I'm here..."
30 FOR X=1 TO 400:NEXT X
40 HOME
50 VTAB 20 :HTAB 4 :PRINT "No, I'm over here..."
60 FOR X=1 TO 400:NEXT X
70 HOME
80 VTAB 3 :HTAB 11 :PRINT "Try again--over here!"
90 FOR X=1 TO 400:NEXT X
100 GOTO 10
```

Of course, you should RUN the program. It's nothing to write home about, but it should give you a smile. There is no obvious end to it. Indeed, given the opportunity, it will run on forever. This is one case where *control-C* will come in handy.

By the way, lines 30, 60, and 90 are called *empty loops*: they do absolutely nothing—but they take time to do it. It's a useful technique when you want to slow down a program. Later on, try omitting them in this program and see what happens.

Notice the format of the commands: VTABv and HTABh where *v* represents the vertical component and *h* represents the horizontal component. Each is a separate command (and hence must be separated from other commands by a colon or the end of a program line). If you're using them in pairs, it doesn't matter whether VTAB or HTAB comes first.

Neither needs the other; if you give a VTAB command without a corresponding HTAB, the next character you PRINT will simply turn up in the column immediately to the right of the last one PRINTed. An HTAB without a VTAB will PRINT a character in the very same row as the last one PRINTed—unless, of course, the last character you printed caused the Apple to advance to the next line—a response to an INPUT statement, say, or a PRINT statement not ending in a semicolon.

Lo-res Graphics

Text mode is fine for *very* low level screen manipulation, but things are always brighter when you use a little color. If you're not using a color television or a color monitor, it will still be worthwhile to follow along. You won't see the colors, but you will see shadings and differences on your monochrome monitor.

Let's change modes. Use the *esc* and ↓ keys to bring the cursor down to the bottom screen line. Make sure your cursor's all the way at the bottom of the display.

Now type:

```
GR
```

(for GRaphics) and press the *return* key. You'll see a flash of light and color run across the screen, and then it will clear to black. With the exception of enough space to accommodate four lines of text at the bottom, your display is now dedicated to the Apple //c's lo-res graphics mode. If you don't want to go any further, you can go back to text mode by entering the word:

```
TEXT
```

and pressing *return*. It's the standard bail-out from all Apple graphics modes.

Unlike text, the lo-res graphics screen is divided into 40 columns *and* 40 rows. It makes for a nice, square display area. As with the text screen, you'll need to know the graphics screen's coordinates in order to do anything. It's laid out like this:

With HTAB and VTAB, it didn't matter which came first. Not so here. Still, Apple's X-Y coordinate system is very easy to get the hang of. The X value represents one of the forty columns that run from left to right across your display. They're numbered 0 through 39. Another way to think of it is the horizontal distance from the left side of the screen.

The Y value represents one of the forty rows, numbered 0 through 39, which run from the top to the bottom of the display. You can also think of it as the vertical distance from the top of the screen.

As in our pictorial representation, the upper left-hand corner of the screen would have an X coordinate of 0 and a Y coordinate of 0. When you

Apple Lo-res Screen Map

refer to any spot on the screen, it's important to use the coordinates in the correct order. It's always the X first, followed by the Y. We'll try some practice in a minute.

Color Helps

The most important part of having color graphics capabilities is color. In lo-res mode, the Apple uses the reserved word COLOR to hold the value you select from among the sixteen choices.

Time to pick one. Enter:

```
COLOR=9
```

That, obviously, selects orange. Until you give a different COLOR command, everything you do on the lo-res screen (but not on the four text lines beneath it) will appear in orange. Enter the line at the top of the next page.

Lo-res Graphics Colors

0	Black	6	Medium Blue	11	Pink
1	Magenta	7	Light Blue	12	Light Green
2	Dark Blue	8	Brown	13	Yellow
3	Purple	9	Orange	14	Aqua
4	Dark Green	10	Gray	15	White
5	Gray				

```
PLOT 39,0
```

An orange square will appear in the upper right-hand corner of your display. PLOT lets you light up a particular spot on the screen with the color of your choice. Try:

```
COLOR=2
PLOT 0,0
```

You should see a blue square in the upper left-hand corner of the screen. You might want to take a moment right now to adjust the colors on your TV or monitor so they match the ones you're looking at. Once you've done that, try these commands:

```
COLOR=13
PLOT 0,39
COLOR=1
PLOT 39,39
```

If all went well, you should be looking at a screen with four colored squares in the corners: clockwise from the top left, you should see blue, orange, magenta, and yellow in color. Your first excursion into the world of graphics has proven a profound success.

But four colored squares? They leave much to be desired. With a few well-thought-out FOR . . . NEXT loops, you could PLOT more squares and form a pattern (otherwise, drawing a line 17 squares long would require 17 PLOT commands). But right now, we may as well explore some of the other commands available.

Making Sense of the Mess

Those four lines at the bottom of the screen don't give you much room to work on your programming. Type in the TEXT command, which will switch you back to text mode.

Slight problem. The area that was formerly the lo-res screen is now almost entirely covered with inverse @ symbols!

Nothing's wrong with your computer. The low-resolution graphics mode shares some of the same internal memory space that the text screen uses. What you're seeing on the screen is the residual effect. It requires more information to describe a colored square than to define an ASCII character, but the inverse @ symbols are the only portion of the color information that the text screen can understand. It mistakenly assumes that the information represents an ASCII character which it knows and tries to display.

You need to clear the screen. You could type HOME, which you know erases the display and leaves the cursor in the upper left-hand corner of the screen. How about a shortcut?

Press and release the *esc* key. Cross hairs will appear inside the cursor. Now hold down the *shift* key and press the *2* on the top row of the keyboard. You're actually sending the Apple the shifted value of that key, which is the @ symbol. As it happens, that's just a coincidence.

As if you'd typed HOME, the screen clears and the cursor flashes at you from the top left of the display. The point is that no matter what's on the text screen, the *esc-@* (*esc-shift-2*) sequence will *always* clear the screen.

Adding Lines

Wouldn't it be nice to draw lines? Enter this program:

```
10 HOME: GR
20 FOR X=0 TO 15
30 COLOR=X
40 IF X=0 OR X/4=INT(X/4) THEN VLIN 39,0 AT 0
50 IF X=1 OR (X-1)/4=INT((X-1)/4) THEN HLIN 0,39 AT 0
60 IF X=2 OR (X-2)/4=INT((X-2)/4) THEN VLIN 0,39 AT
   39
70 IF X=3 OR (X-3)/4=INT((X-3)/4) THEN HLIN 39,0 AT
   39
80 NEXT X
90 PRINT CHR$(7)
100 GOTO 20
```

The program should produce a multicolored border around the screen. The GR command in line 10 puts you into graphics mode.

CHR$(7), in line 90, is another control character, *Control-G*. When you PRINT it, it sounds the bell—here, every time the FOR . . . NEXT loop has finished. That gives you audible confirmation that something is going on. To get the program to quit, use *control-C*.

The HLIN and VLIN commands draw the border. HLIN draws a horizontal line, and VLIN draws a vertical one. Like all BASIC commands, they have a certain syntax that allows the Apple to understand them. It's as follows:

```
HLIN <starting point>,<ending point> AT <row number>
```

and

```
VLIN <starting point>,<ending point> AT <column
     number>
```

Suppose you want to draw a vertical yellow line down the center of the screen. That's approximately column 20. To cover all forty possible locations, you'll want the line to extend from row 0 at the top to row 39 at the bottom. Try this:

```
COLOR=13
VLIN 0,39 AT 20
```

You could make a giant cross out of it by complementing that line with a horizontal line, extending from column 0 to column 39, positioned at row 20. You'd do that with:

```
HLIN 0,39 AT 20
```

If you'd like to try some lines of your own, just use the GR command again to clear the screen. Play around as long as you like. When you're done, you'll be ready for the high-resolution mode.

Hi-res Graphics

High-resolution graphics (often abbreviated hi-res) and the Apple //c were meant for each other. Up to this point, you've been dealing with a very limited graphics screen. The maximum number of points available was only 1,600 (40 × 40). That's nothing compared to hi-res, where you can play with 280 dots horizontally and 192 vertically—53,760 in all!

There are two different hi-res displays. HGR allows text in the bottom four lines of what would normally be the text screen. This limits vertical resolution to 160 dots. Graphics commands that exceed this boundary, but are still within the overall limits of the graphics screen, are allowed but not displayed. HGR2 allows graphics only, with a full 192-dot resolution. You'll be using the first type here, but every command you learn will work with either one.

One disadvantage of increasing the resolution of the graphics screen is that you lose some of the colors you had in lo-res mode. According to Apple, you have eight colors.

Apple Hi-res Graphics Screen Map

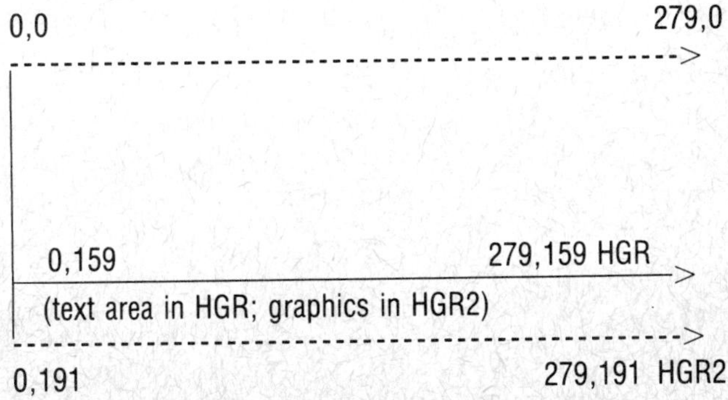

Hi-res Graphics Colors

0	Black1	4	Black2
1	Green	5	Orange
2	Violet	6	Blue
3	White1	7	White2

Now, there are definitely eight items in that list, but somehow they don't seem to add up to eight colors. There are differences between the two whites and the two blacks, but the differences are only in the *way* the Apple displays them rather than in the colors themselves. Be thankful anyhow: on older Apple //'s, those with serial numbers below 6000, colors 4 through 7 were the same as 0 through 3. By the way: if you have a monochrome monitor, some of the following exercises may be invisible.

HPLOTting

Commands in hi-res are similar to those in lo-res, but in most cases you must add an *H* to the front of them. For instance, setting the color for a hi-res screen is done using HCOLOR, rather than COLOR. Type:

```
HGR
```

This gets you into hi-res. Now try something easy:

```
HCOLOR=6
HPLOT 279,0 TO 279,159
```

You'll see a blue line stretching along the right side of your screen. Here you see the fundamental difference between PLOTting and HPLOTting (aside from the addition of the *H*). The syntax for the command is:

HPLOT <X position>, <Y position> TO <X position>, <Y position>

There's a variation as well. If you want to continue a line from the last point you specified, you don't need to specify the start coordinates. As an example try:

```
HPLOT TO 0,159
```

The last line you plotted ended at screen coordinates 279,159—the lower right-hand corner of the screen. Now, with this command, the Apple assumes you want to start at that point and continue to 0,159—the lower left-hand corner of the screen.

The Different Colors of White

Let's complete the border and learn something very interesting at the same time. Switch back to text (with TEXT) and make sure there's nothing in memory by typing the NEW command. Then enter this short program:

```
10 HGR
20 HPLOT 0,0 TO 279,0 TO 279,159 TO 0,159 TO 0,0
```

Line 20 is just an extension of your ability to use HPLOT TO. Before you run the program, set the drawing color to WHITE*1* with:

```
HCOLOR=3
```

Now run the program. You've completed the border around your screen, but do you see anything interesting? You should.

Even though you've selected white as the drawing color, only the top and bottom lines are white. The left side is violet and the right side is light green. But the mystery goes on!

Now set the color to WHITE*2* with:

```
HCOLOR=7
```

Run the program. Again, white prevails on the top and bottom, but this time, the left side is blue and the right side is dark green. But don't stop. Change the color to violet, then blue, and then orange. Strange, isn't it?

When you tried to draw a violet box, only three sides appeared. The right side was missing. The same thing happened when you tried it in blue. And in orange, the left side was missing and the right side was dark green!

Your monitor is all right and so are your eyes. The problem lies within the Apple itself. The way colors are arranged and handled, the color of any one dot is not only dependent on the drawing color you've set, but also on the color of the dot next to the one you're trying to draw *and* on whether that dot is an even- or odd-numbered column.

It's a complicated arrangement. Fortunately, unless you become an experienced programmer, you'll be doing most of your graphics work with programs that keep track of all that for you automatically. Computers are designed to save you time, remember?

Creating Simple Movement

Let's put together a simple program that will teach you a thing or two about the hi-res mode. We'll build it a step at a time. Begin with:

```
1 HOME:HGR
5 FOR C = 1 TO 6
6 IF C = 3 OR C = 4 THEN 100
8 HCOLOR = C
```

Line 1 clears the screen and sets HGR mode. In line 8, the variable C selects the HCOLOR value; line 6 makes sure that value's discarded if it becomes white (3) or black (4).

```
10 FOR Y = 0 TO 159 STEP 2
20 HPLOT 0,Y TO 279,0
```

Line 10 begins a counting loop that selects the Y coordinate of the starting point for drawing. The STEP 2 at the end of that line means that Y increases by 2 each time the program goes through the loop.

The value of Y is used in line 20, which plots a line from the left side of the screen to the upper right-hand corner.

```
21 IF Y < 2 THEN 30
22 HCOLOR = 0
24 HPLOT 0,Y-2 TO 279,0
26 HCOLOR = C
27 IF Y = 158 THEN HCOLOR = 0:HPLOT 0,Y TO 279,0:
   HCOLOR = C
30 NEXT Y
```

This section goes back and erases the last line drawn. Actually, it redraws it with black selected as the color. Of course, if Y is not greater than 2, there's no place to go back to, so line 21 checks for that. Finally, in line 27, if the value of Y has reached the largest number it can achieve, you erase that line as well. If you don't, the NEXT Y statement will put you outside the loop, and the line will remain on the screen.

```
40 FOR X = 0 TO 279 STEP 2
50 HPLOT X,159 TO 279,0
51 IF X < 2 THEN 60
52 HCOLOR= 0
54 HPLOT X-2,159 TO 279,0
56 HCOLOR= C
58 IF X = 278 THEN HCOLOR=0:HPLOT X,159 TO 279,0:
   HCOLOR=C
60 NEXT X
100 NEXT C
110 GOTO 5
```

With the exception of line 100, which changes the color value, and line 110, which starts the whole thing all over again, this section is a repeat of the first—with one important difference. It plots lines from the upper right-hand corner to points along the bottom of the graphics screen. Just as in the first half, the previous line is erased each time.

This program simply draws a continuously moving line that originates in the upper right corner and terminates at points on the left and bottom of the screen. You'll have to use *control-C* to get it to quit.

Switching to HGR2

If you'd like to use the full-page high-resolution display, just change HGR in line 1 to HGR2. Go through the program you've entered, and, everywhere it limits movement to 159, change it to 191. The line will then "scan" the full length and width of the screen.

You'll still need to use *control-C* to stop it, but that won't be a problem. What will surprise you is that with HGR2, even when you've stopped the program, you won't see any text on the screen. The second hi-res display hides it all. But it doesn't affect any of it.

Get back to text mode by typing TEXT and hitting the *return* key. (You'll have to do it without seeing what you're typing.) Leave that program in memory and clear the screen (you can use either HOME or the *esc-@* sequence—it doesn't matter). Your screen is blank. Now type HGR2 and press *return*.

The sprinkle of color you see whenever you call in a graphics screen is actually the screen clearing. The Apple displays whatever's currently on that screen and, as you watch, turns it all to black. Now everything is blank! The screen won't show you what you're doing. Keep your eyes on your fingers and the keyboard, carefully type LIST, and press *return*.

Look at the screen. Apparently nothing happened. But now switch over to the text mode by using the TEXT command. You'll see the entire program—unaffected by the use of HGR2. It was listed, just as you requested, but, with the second graphics display sitting on top of it like a window shade, you couldn't see it. The first graphics display, HGR, has the same effect, but if your listing extends into the four text lines HGR leaves you at the bottom of the screen, you'll see that part of it.

What Remains

There are many additional graphics features available on the Apple //c. You can capture an image you've drawn within what's called a *shape table*. It's a matrix of sorts that holds the values for color and relative internal position of all the dots, and it lets you play with your image—place it anywhere on the screen, or rotate it to a different angle.

It's one of the more sophisticated features of Apple graphics and is neither simple nor difficult. But it is complex and out of the bounds of what you're doing here. Besides, there's plenty of Apple // software out there that can do that kind of job for you with less pain and strain.

There's also a double-hi-res graphics mode that gives you twice as many horizontal dots to play with, but using it involves graphics *pages,* which are more complicated than we have room for here. Although double-hi-res graphics are available on the //c and //e, they're no picnic to use, and programmers are only beginning to take advantage of them.

That's graphics in a nutshell—and it's also the end of the Applesoft section of the book. Now you're ready to tackle your disk drive.

9

The //c's File Cabinets: DOS—Disk Operating System

Information is very important. You spend much of your life gathering, organizing, and using it. In the real world there are a variety of places to keep that information. File cabinets, desk drawers, even shoeboxes have often become repositories for a variety of facts and records.

But what happens when you need to retrieve information quickly? There's often a mad dash to search through all of your various hiding places. You unfold and read scraps of information, and you shuffle papers until you find what you want. As your information pool becomes larger and larger, you might start storing only certain types of data in certain places and even mark your file drawers or shoeboxes accordingly.

In your household file, for example, you might insert tabs to mark off special sections for various bill categories. When it comes time to hunt down a particular bill, you know which shoebox to retrieve and which section in that shoebox contains the information you want.

Whether or not you use such a system yourself, you can easily see the merits of keeping your important paperwork in order. What happens when a computer enters the scene? Can you duplicate with electronics and advanced technology the simple yet semiefficient system you had before? More important, can computers really operate on the same level as you do? The answer is simple—yes.

Why Happiness Is Flat

The floppy disk is the new electronic equivalent to the file drawer. Actually, since the disks we're all accustomed to are scaled-down versions of the larger ones initially introduced, the proper term is *diskette.* But since the 5¼-inch diskette has become the single most popular storage medium, we'll bow to common usage and refer to it as a disk.

You already know that when a floppy disk is manufactured, a coating similar to that on magnetic recording tape is applied to a circular flat sheet of polyester film (now usually Dupont's Mylar). Around that is placed a rectangular, nonremovable jacket. The inside of the jacket is coated with a soft fibrous material that cleans dust particles from the disk's surface as it rotates. The overall stiffness of the covering helps to protect the delicate disk inside from being damaged.

How Apples Stay Compatible

Since their introduction, disks have evolved into a variety of sizes and styles. The first disks were 8 inches in diameter. But as computers became smaller, the technology was refined to allow equivalent storage room in less space, and the 5¼-inch disk was born. Now, with new advances in both media preparation and motor technology, the newest development is a 3½-inch floppy disk in a hard plastic case. This most recent entry is the basis of storage in such sophisticated machines as Apple's Macintosh and the Hewlett-Packard HP-150.

A new type of storage also evolved. Multiple disks using a different technology were stacked together to create a much larger storage device. Since the new configuration used either 5- or 8-inch surfaces that were rigid in composition, they were called *hard disks.* While the capacity of floppy disks was measured in hundreds of thousands of characters per disk, the new hard disks could hold tens of millions of characters in the same size enclosure. Hard disks allow information to be stored and retrieved far faster than floppy disks, and they're correspondingly more expensive. But while new technologies for mass storage are rapidly arriving on the microcomputer scene, floppy disks are so inexpensive and reliable that they will no doubt be the standard microcomputer storage medium in the next few years. Still, the //c's external disk-drive port will accept hard-disk drives today.

While Apple has assured continued compatibility among its // series through most of the Apple //c hardware and firmware, they wisely refrained from providing a cassette port. Instead, the Apple //c comes with one disk drive already built into its cabinet. The drive is a "half-height" unit, meaning that its physical height is about half that of the regular Apple disk drives. However, it can run the same programs as any of the other Apple // series computers.

Why They Call It DOS

The processes of moving data to and from disks is internally very complicated. The computer has to make certain that the information is flowing flawlessly in the proper direction, and must take many factors into account while the data is being shuttled from one location to another. A master operating system is required to oversee the workings of the disk drives. Apple provides you with one. You'll find it neatly stowed inside the packing material.

There's never too much of a good thing. In the brightly colored holder card you'll see a disk. Turn the card over, and you'll see that there are really *two* disks packed there. These contain the disk operating systems provided with the Apple //c.

One is called DOS 3.3 (short for *D*isk *O*perating *S*ystem), and it's part of a common thread that runs through all of the Apple // series computers. This operating system has evolved from version 3.2.1 on the Apple //. As you can see from its label, it's compatible with every Apple // system.

The other disk is labeled ProDOS. This is a new disk operating system Apple Computer originally developed for the Apple /// under the name SOS (*S*ophisticated *O*perating *S*ystem) and then brought over to the // series.

ProDOS is in some ways a significant improvement over DOS, although at this point most software developers have shied away from using it. You need at least 64K of memory to use it, which is something not all of the Apple // series has. ProDOS has been targeted at Apple //e users and is now being pitched to owners of the Apple //c. It has many surprises, and we'll discuss it in detail in Chapter 12. First, though, you'll get a look at old reliable DOS 3.3 and at some of the things that both systems have in common.

Booting and What It Does

You already know that the internal disk drive starts to spin when you turn your machine on. This is because the Apple //c wants to know what you're trying to do and is peeking at the disk to find out.

The first way the disk helps is in "booting"—or starting up—the system. Before disks made it easy, any start-up instruction you wanted to give a computer had to be physically loaded into it, either by typing in instructions or feeding the machine reels of paper tape punched with binary arrangements of holes. This simple act could take many minutes and require many separate, complex steps. Since the computer digested all of this "initialization" information itself to turn itself on, the process was compared to pulling oneself up by one's bootstraps. Over time the term was shortened to "booting."

If you're ready to boot your Apple //c, you'll need to start with a bootable disk. Find the pair of operating system disks. You'll notice that the DOS 3.3 and ProDOS disks do *not* have write protect/enable notches in them. Taking human nature into consideration, Apple has protected you from the opportunity of accidentally erasing anything from either of them. This is a worthwhile precaution indeed, since you can't do much computing if you've erased the instructions that turn your computer on.

There are eight ways to insert the disk into the drive, but only one of them will work. Take the disk labeled DOS 3.3 and hold it label side up with the oblong access oval pointing toward the internal drive. If the machine is on, gently push the disk into the drive and close the door. Reset the machine (hold down the *control* and keys and press the *reset* switch). Then release all of the keys when you hear the bell tone.

If your computer is turned off, insert the disk into the drive and close the door. Turn on all your additional hardware (in the order we discussed in Chapter 4) and then turn the computer on. You'll soon see the Apple //c logo at the top of your screen.

A Personal Caution

Apple has always maintained that no harm will befall a disk if you leave it in the drive when you turn the machine on or off. That's true enough if the disk drive is operating in fine fettle, but it can do very unpleasant things to a disk if it happens to be out of whack. I've lost only one disk this way in four years, but one was enough to make me fussy.

My advice is that you should *not* have disks in your drives when you turn your computer on or off. At worst, you merely get an extra CHECK DISK DRIVE message, and have to go through the reset procedure to reboot the disk. And removing the disk before turn-off won't cost you any time at all. However, if you want to take the slight risks involved, feel free to follow standard behavior and leave your disks in—the odds are actually very much in your favor.

Why Is the Disk Drive Spinning?

In the first few seconds that the disk spins, the read/write head will retrieve the basic boot-up information the computer needs. If everything goes smoothly, you'll see the DOS 3.3 logo on the screen. Soon a second message will inform you that the machine is loading Integer BASIC into the top 16K of RAM (ready for you to use, but not active until you do). Finally, you'll be asked to MAKE SURE THE CAPS LOCK KEY IS DOWN. Obey: DOS absolutely insists that all commands you give it be in uppercase. You'll see the Applesoft ready symbol,], letting you know that the Apple //c is waiting and ready. And you'll also see the cursor.

At this point, DOS is ready to handle all your disk drive activities fairly automatically. It knows you have at least one active drive and assumes it is connected through a controller card in slot 6. The fact that there are no slots in the Apple //c doesn't matter to it. DOS also anticipates the existence of a second drive, but will not act upon its suspicions unless you confirm them. Through all of your dealings with it, you will distinguish your disk drives by referring to either drive 1 or drive 2. If you have only the internal drive, it will always be drive 1.

The Most Important Step—Making a Backup

If you're just starting out, there is one urgent task you *must* attend to. The DOS disk you've just placed in the drive so confidently is the original disk. If anything happens to it, you're pretty much up the creek. An ounce of prevention is always better than an unexpected trip to the computer store, so make an exact copy of it before you do *anything* else.

Reach in the box for a blank disk—now you know why we told you to buy some. If you have an external disk drive for your Apple //c, insert the blank disk in the external drive. If you have only the internal drive, just put the new, blank disk aside for a moment. In either case type the words RUN COPYA and press *return*.

You've seen the command RUN in the Applesoft chapters. Used alone, RUN forces whatever program is currently in memory into immediate execution. But once loaded, DOS intercepts all Applesoft commands, checking for those of its own. When DOS sees the word RUN it looks for another word—the name of a program—to follow it. If it doesn't find a name, it runs what's already in memory. If it does find a name, it copies the program with that name from the disk into memory (wiping out any program already there) and runs it.

The program on the DOS disk called COPYA lets you copy the entire contents of one disk onto another. That's what you're about to do right now.

Keeping Your Disks in Order

All original disks are sacrosanct—you should take every possible precaution to preserve their integrity. The first thing you must always do is copy your original disks (except in cases where nervous software publishers designed the disks in such a way that copies are difficult or impossible to make), put them carefully away, and only use the copies. Good disk-handling practices dictate that you make *two* copies in addition to the original.

Finding the Slots and Drives

In less time than it takes to read this sentence, DOS looks at your disk, finds the program named COPYA, loads it into memory, and starts to run it. At the top of the screen you'll see the words APPLE DISK DUPLICA-

TION PROGRAM. Then you'll discover that the program needs some information from you to work properly.

First, you'll see the words ORIGINAL SLOT:. This is a request for you to identify the slot that controls the disk drive that contains the disk you want to copy. This is less difficult a question to answer than it might sound (especially considering you don't have any slots). The program assumes that you're following the Apple norm of slot 6. You'll notice that it has printed DEFAULT = 6 on the same line as its request. You can either type the number *6* or just press the *return* key to accept the default value (the standard setting that the computer will use unless you tell it otherwise).

Almost immediately you'll see another word—DRIVE:. At this point you have to identify the drive that contains the disk you want to copy *from*. The default answer it gives you this time is 1. Since your DOS disk is in the internal drive, which it thinks of as drive 1, enter the number *1* or just press *return*.

Next you'll see the words DUPLICATE SLOT:. The program wants to check which slot controls the disk drive containing the blank disk you want to copy the other disk *to*. If you have only the internal drive, you're probably still holding that blank disk in your hand, wondering what to do with it. It's not in any drive, and therefore is not associated with any of the slots. (If you do have a second drive attached to the Apple //c, hang in there for a moment. You're in great shape because you've already put your disk in the second drive and you're virtually ready to go.)

Don't worry if you only have one drive—you'll be using it to copy *to* as well as *from*. Slot 6 controls the drive you're going to use for copying both from and to disks, so press *return* to accept the default value of 6 or press the *6* key, whichever you prefer. Again the word DRIVE: appears. This time DOS wants to know which disk drive holds the blank disk you'll be copying *to*. For those of you with an external drive the choice is the default value, 2. If you have only a single drive, press the *1* key.

Do those of you with two drives remember how many disk drives one slot can control? The answer is two. Therefore (as the screen told you) you know that the correct number for *both* the ORIGINAL SLOT *and* DUPLICATE SLOT questions is 6. The DRIVE number under the former is 1. But the DRIVE number under the DUPLICATE SLOT is 2.

Your screen should now look like the following (with minor variations for the last drive number):

Screen Messages for Disk Copying Program

```
            APPLE DISK DUPLICATION PROGRAM

   ORIGINAL SLOT:   6
           DRIVE:   1

  DUPLICATE SLOT:   6
           DRIVE:   1 (or 2)

      — PRESS 'RETURN' KEY TO BEGIN COPY —
```

After you've answered the questions about which disks are in which drives, press *return*.

If you have two drives, everything will begin to happen automatically; the second disk will begin to spin, and the program will immediately begin reading your original DOS disk. If you have only one drive, you'll be told to INSERT ORIGINAL DISK AND PRESS RETURN. Your DOS disk is already in the drive, so press the *return* key. After it has read the disk for a moment you'll be asked to insert the duplicate disk. Now's the time to use the blank disk you've been hanging on to. Pop the DOS disk out of the drive and insert the blank disk.

The next step is a crucial one, and no matter how many drives you have, it's one the machine handles quite efficiently without any help or advice from you. The program is now ready to format your disk, and the word INITIALIZING appears on the screen. Those of you with two drives will move automatically from the initialization stage to the actual copying. If you have just one drive, however, you face some more hard work, but it's all fairly straightforward—just follow the prompt at the bottom of the screen that tells you which disk to insert when.

The Meaning of DOS

Simply stated, the Apple //c DOS is a repository for all the computer's disk-handling instructions. DOS controls how the computer reads and writes information on the disk and keeps track of where on the disk it is. When you boot the DOS disk, DOS is loaded into the machine's RAM memory and becomes a temporary extension of the machine's firmware (programs that are permanently stored on chips inside the cabinet).

As mentioned earlier, the computer needs to have a system for finding data on disks, a blueprint of where on a given disk it can expect to find certain critical *kinds* of information. But first, it has to make sure that there is no existing information on the disk to confuse it. If you were to strip off the outside jacket of a new disk, you'd see a circle of raw recording material that has probably picked up random information from stray magnetic signals during the manufacturing process and during normal handling in transit from the factory to you. Your computer would try to interpret this "random noise" and become bewildered. So before you use any disk, you have to remove all these extraneous signals. The initialization process takes care of this for you.

Building the Face of a Disk

In order to organize your information, DOS must first do some organization of its own. The disk is only raw material when it's fresh from the box. It's much like an open tract of land waiting to be developed. DOS initializes the disk by subdividing this area into smaller segments called tracks. The tracks are then further broken down into sectors. On many computers, this operation is called formatting. Apple refers to the entire process as *initializing* the disk.

DOS 3.2.1 (the earlier disk operating system for the Apple //) and DOS 3.3 (the present system) are compatible only in that they understand the same commands. The way they format a blank disk is different.

As you can see from the illustrations, the tracks consist of thirty-five concentric rings within the plane of the disk. These are electromagnetic boundary lines understood by the disk and controller mechanisms. You can't see them by looking at the disk, but the computer's magnetic disk-drive heads can.

DOS Disk Formats

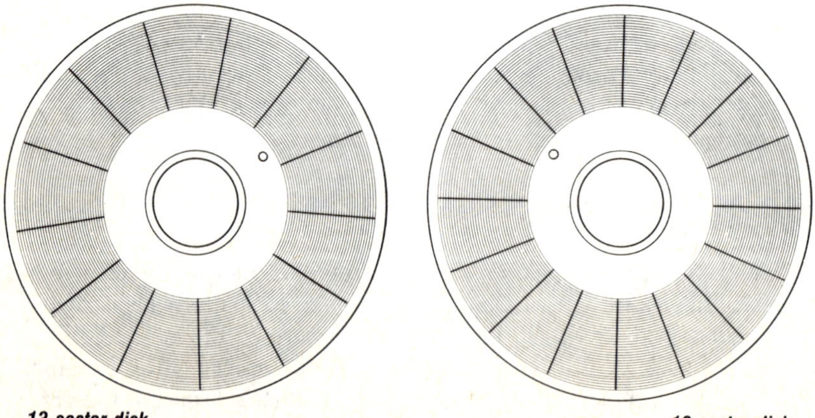

13-sector disk (DOS 3.2.1 Disk)

16-sector disk (Dos 3.3 Disk)

Disk Formats: 13 sectors vs. 16 sectors.

The concentric rings represent the disk tracks. The wedges radiating from the center holes represent the sectors. Regardless of physical size, each sector stores the same amount of information.

The Difference in the DOS Versions

The major difference between DOS 3.2.1 and DOS 3.3 is in the way they initialize a disk. The former subdivided each track into thirteen sectors, while the 3.3 version makes a sixteen-sector track. If we do some simple math as shown, we can see that one system can store considerably more information than the other in the same physical amount of space.

Making Another Copy

When your first copy is finished, you'll be asked if you want to make another. Since you're going to need two copies, the answer is yes. Take your new DOS copy out of the disk drive. In the box of disks you purchased, you'll find pressure-sensitive labels you can write on. On one, print DOS MASTER, on another write DOS WORKING COPY.

DOS 3.2.1 vs. DOS 3.3 Disk Storage

On the Apple // series, each disk sector holds 256 characters. There are 35 tracks and, on DOS 3.2.1, each track was broken down into 13 sectors. That means:

	256	characters per sector
×	13	sectors per track
=	3328	characters per track
×	35	tracks per disk
=	116480	characters per disk

The most you can store on a DOS 3.2.1 disk is 116,480 bytes, or characters, of information. That's about 81 double-spaced pages of typed material (presuming a 54-line page with 75 characters a line).

A similar computation for DOS 3.3 shows the bonus that an extra 3 sectors per track can yield:

	256	characters per sector
×	16	sectors per track
=	4096	characters per track
×	35	tracks per disk
=	143360	characters per disk

If you use the same page size as before, you'll see that the larger storage space afforded by DOS 3.3 will now let you keep 100 pages of material, an increase of about 23%.

Peel off the label marked DOS MASTER and, making sure you don't touch the access ovals on the disk, stick it on the upper left or right corner. Put a gummed write-protect tab over the small notch in the side and place this disk back in the box, in safe storage.

Since you've already told the machine (by pressing "Y" for "yes") that you want it to make another copy, place a blank disk in the external drive (single-drive users: follow the appropriate instructions described earlier) and press the *return* key.

The Possibility of Possibilities

At any time during the copy process the computer may tell you that it has found a problem. (Usually, though, if you follow the instructions carefully, such problems won't crop up.) You may, for example, see a message telling you that the computer can't write to the blank disk, or can't initialize the disk. If you do get an error message, COPYA will stop and ask you if you want to make another copy. This is, essentially, "Do you want to try again?"

If you see this message while you're trying to copy the DOS disk, pull the disk out and check it. Make sure you haven't inadvertently covered the write-protect notch. If you have, just peel off the protective tab. If the write-protect notch is not covered, however, carefully examine the surface of the disk exposed through the oval-shaped slits.

The disk drive mechanism writes from beneath, so the side you want to look at is the one that faces down as it goes into the drive. If the disk surface looks irregular or scratched, there's a good chance that the disk itself is damaged and unusable. It doesn't mean that *you* did anything wrong, it just means that somewhere along the line the polishing equipment was working incorrectly. Try another disk. In fact, even if you can't see any logical reason for it not to work, try another disk. Sometimes, even though there are no visible surface imperfections, the disk is just a lemon. It happens.

Assuming the second copy has been made by now, label that disk as well. It's now your WORKING COPY. Don't place a write-protect tab on this one, or you won't be able to work with it. Now take the original disk you've just made copies of and place it back in its sleeve. Find a safe place for it. Barring a freak disaster that destroys both of the other two copies, you should never have to touch it again.

Place your working copy of the DOS disk into the internal drive (from now on when we say "the DOS disk," you'll know we're talking about the working copy you just made, and not the original). In the next chapters we'll examine exactly what the DOS disk has to offer.

Disk Copies and How to Use Them

Which Disk?	Use It As:	What to Do with It:
Original	Archive Copy	Put this disk away where the light of day will never see it unless a dire emergency occurs.
First Copy	Master Copy	Keep this disk stored nearby, but don't use it in day-to-day operations. In the case of an unusual situation, it can be used to make another copy.
Second Copy	Working Copy	Use this version every day. Don't be careless with it. But if anything does happen to it, you'll still have the master copy to bail you out.

10

DOS Commands: Power at Your Fingertips

With the DOS disk in your drive, type the word CATALOG (and press *return*). You'll see a long directory of the programs on the disk. There are only as many entries showing as will fit on the screen. Press any key and the rest of the list will appear. You'll notice that the list contains much more than just the names of the disk's programs.

Sample DOS Disk Directory

```
DISK VOLUME 254

*A 003 HELLO
*I 003 APPLESOFT
*B 006 LOADER.OBJ0
*B 042 FPBASIC
*B 042 INTBASIC
*A 003 MASTER
*B 009 MASTER CREATE
*B 003 COPY.OBJ0
*A 009 COPYA

(. . . and there's more)
```

Don't worry if your own list differs slightly from what you see here.

Reading the Directory

At this point you will have a very comprehensive display of information on the screen. The top line holds an intriguing name; we'll save it for last. Right now, look at the list itself, particularly the asterisk in the leftmost column. What does this indicate?

Disks used under DOS can be considered roughly equivalent to file cabinets that hold only one topic per drawer. The files on each disk are similar in many ways to normal file-cabinet drawers. Each contains information that can be accessed by opening the drawer. Your files are opened and closed before and after use just like real file drawers.

(The difference between files and programs is that programs usually perform a function while files are simply a collection of information. However, the words are sometimes used interchangeably, and "file" is often a catch-all phrase for any unit of software that shows up as an entry in your directory.)

Like drawers, files can also be locked and unlocked. How? Let's try an experiment. The prompt "]" and the cursor are waiting for you to type in a command. As you can see by looking at the directory, there is a program on your disk called HELLO. Give it a whirl. Enter:

```
UNLOCK HELLO
```

Your drive will immediately start spinning. You can tell when the disk motor is working because the red light on the front of the disk will briefly flash on. Now get another CATALOG of the disk. The asterisk has vanished! Now try:

```
LOCK HELLO
```

And get another CATALOG. The asterisk is back again!

While the file is locked, you can't change it in any way. If the locked item is a program, you would be able to run it. If you changed any of the program lines and then tried to put the file back on the disk, DOS wouldn't let you. If it was an information file, you could read from it but you couldn't write anything in it. Let's see what HELLO has to offer.

A Load on Your Memory

Directly to the right of the asterisk is a letter. You'll notice that each entry in the directory is prefaced by a letter. This letter is an important clue to the nature of the material listed.

The *A* tells you right away that HELLO is a program and that it runs under Applesoft BASIC. At the keyboard, type:

```
LOAD HELLO
```

In a few seconds the Applesoft prompt and cursor will reappear and the screen will look otherwise unaffected. But is it? Remember that the Applesoft LIST command will display the contents of an Applesoft BASIC program. Type in LIST and the program listing will roll down the screen.

Just as does RUN SOMEPROGRAM, LOAD SOMEPROGRAM wipes out any program that happens to be in memory at the time. By the way, if you can't read as fast as the program scrolls, you can momentarily freeze the flow of output from the computer. While the program listing is rushing by, hold down the *control* key and press *S*—then release them both. All activity in the Apple //c snaps to a halt. To continue the action, press any key and it will resume. This can come in very handy very often.

So far, you've seen that a program can be run from the disk (remember that COPYA is also an Applesoft program). Your DOS has been set up to run the HELLO program whenever you boot the disk. HELLO loads a copy of Integer BASIC into the upper 16K of memory, which DOS wants done before anything else. This is accomplished with the help of a special program, which will be covered shortly.

Now that you've loaded HELLO, there is a copy of it stored in memory. Let's try to take the copy in memory and transfer it to the disk. Type:

```
SAVE HELLO
```

After a few seconds your screen should display the message FILE LOCKED. This tells you your effort to copy the file from memory back onto the disk was unsuccessful, because the file on the disk was "locked," or configured expressly to prevent you from meddling with it.

DOS assumes you've changed every program once you've loaded it into memory. If the version of the same file on the disk is locked, you can't put the file back until you unlock it. So now unlock the HELLO file on the disk, using the technique described earlier, then try the SAVE command again. This time you'll find it works without any error messages. If your disk contains a file with the same name as your program, that file must be unlocked before you can copy your program from memory onto the disk. This is to protect you from wiping out an important file on the disk by saving something else with the same name in its place on the disk.

Now you know how to save your Applesoft programs and RUN them without typing them in. Just be sure you've booted your machine with a DOS disk before typing in your program. Then, whenever you like, you can save your program to the disk with the command:

```
SAVE <program-name>
```

and run it with the command

```
RUN <program-name>
```

where <program-name> is the name of your program.

The Name Game

One important thing to remember is that there are a few things you can't do when naming your files. File names can't include delimiters (commas, semicolons, quotes) or an equals sign; they can't be longer than thirty characters (and, as in BASIC, a space counts as a character); and they can't begin with a number.

Now that you know what you can't do, let's see what you can. You've left HELLO unlocked, so let's experiment some more. Try entering this:

```
RENAME HELLO,GOODBYE
```

The disk will spin for a few seconds. Try CATALOG again. HELLO is gone, and in its place is the same program with the new name GOODBYE.

RENAME can be entertaining as well as useful. The syntax for it is:

```
RENAME <original-name>,<new-name>
```

However, since we know that DOS is going to look for HELLO when the disk is booted, and not GOODBYE, put it back the way it was:

```
RENAME GOODBYE,HELLO
```

And since you don't want anyone meddling with it, lock it for safekeeping by entering LOCK HELLO. If you're nervous, you can check that HELLO is there, safely locked, by getting a CATALOG again.

RENAME isn't just for fun and games. Suppose you were working on a program or text file and you already had a copy of it on disk. Since you've improved the file, you want to save the revision. If you just go ahead and save it with the same name, you'll erase the old copy and replace it with the new one. But there are times when you want to keep the old file on the disk for reference. You can save the new version with a new name, or you can rename the old version (providing you haven't locked it against just such a thing) and save the new version with the same name it had previously. Let's do the latter.

First, UNLOCK HELLO (you can't RENAME it if it's locked), then LOAD it. Imagine that you've been tinkering with the program in memory and now want to save it. First, enter: RENAME HELLO,HELLO2. Then type SAVE HELLO, followed by LOCK HELLO (you still want to keep it safe). If you examined the directory at this point, you'd see both programs were on the disk. That's all it takes. It's a very simple operation—absolutely painless.

The Big Wipeout

But what happens if you no longer want HELLO2 on your disk? You get rid of it by deleting it from the CATALOG. And that just happens to be the command you use. Try it:

```
DELETE HELLO2
```

As long as you haven't locked it, it will be gone. BUT BE CAREFUL! Whenever you delete a file, please be sure that's what you really want to do. When it's gone, it's gone for good. You should always have copies of your important files so that if something like this happens, you won't have to start again from scratch.

Down for the Count

Don't worry too much about getting rid of something. It's good to delete files and programs periodically (this is called disk housekeeping). If you never did, your disks would soon be filled to the brim with a mixture of important current files and ancient unused ones, and you couldn't add any more to them.

It's simple to keep track of how much space you've used or how large particular programs or files are. The catalog listing gives you some of this information, in the space between the name and the letter that describes the type of file. It's in the form of a three-digit number that tells you how many sectors the program is using.

Some quick math will tell you that on a disk with 35 tracks and 16 sectors per track, you have a maximum of 560 sectors to work with. HELLO, for instance, uses 3 sectors. If it were the only thing on the disk, you'd have 557 more to work with.

While that tells you something about the current and available disk storage, it would be useful to relate that to the amount of computer memory each program would use when run. That's a little trickier than it sounds. Again, math should tell you that if HELLO occupies 3 sectors and each sector is 256 characters, or bytes, in length, then the program is 768 bytes long. Maybe.

DOS never uses less than one whole sector. If one of your disk entries is 2.5 sectors long, DOS will allot 3 sectors to it when it gives you a CATALOG. In any event, this will tell you only the physical size of the entry. If it's a data file, its actual size is fairly close to what's listed in the directory. But if it's a program, things aren't that easy.

Programs have to account for their physical size, but also for those changeable things called variables. Variables take up memory, but not until you run the program. Also, some programs, like COPYA, use information from a file. If you were to load and list it, you'd see that it borrows from another file called COPY.OBJ0. The part of this COPY.OBJ0 file it uses would have to be counted in with LOAD's overall memory consumption, but there's no easy way to figure this out by looking at the numbers CATALOG produces.

Also, when a file or program exceeds 255 sectors in length, the count starts again at 000. So if you know you have a very large file and CATALOG tells you it's only 003 sectors, odds are good it's actually 258.

Notice that the COPY.OBJ0 program just mentioned is listed in the directory as a *B*-type file, as in *B*inary. These B files may be either files or machine language programs. They're stored in a special *compact* format to take up less space on the disk and load and save quickly. There are quite a few of them in the list, and most are programs. We'll get to these shortly.

There are two other types of files commonly found on Apple DOS disks. The first is a *T*ext file. These are most often the product of word-processing programs, although there are other sources. If you could look directly onto the disk, you would be able to read a text file as it was stored. This is not true with most other files, such as binary files. If you tried to read a binary file directly off the disk, you'd see what looks like gibberish, although the computer can understand it perfectly well. The computer does not try to compress text files into the more efficient binary format.

Integer BASIC and Where to Find It

The last type of file has an alphabetical indicator *I*. Looking down your list, you'll only see one, APPLESOFT. This is an Integer BASIC program, as are all *I*-type files. Try typing:

```
RUN APPLESOFT
```

The screen clears and for a moment looks just as it did when you booted the DOS disk. Only now, at the bottom of the screen, there's a ">" and the cursor. What happened to the Applesoft prompt? What does the greater-than sign mean?

You've met the cursor already. But the ">" is the Integer BASIC prompt. This prompt tells you that the computer is ready to execute Integer BASIC commands. Any programs you write or run now will follow the instructions coming out of the upper 16K of RAM, where Integer BASIC was loaded when you booted the disk.

Actually, the Integer program APPLESOFT is the equivalent of the Applesoft program HELLO. They both use *another* file called LOADER.OBJ0 (or LOADER for short), which is the real workhorse. LOADER checks which version of BASIC is in firmware and loads a different one from the disk into the upper 16K of memory. Notice that there are two binary programs on your disk, one called FPBASIC, the other INTBASIC. If LOADER sees that your firmware contains Applesoft, it loads INTBASIC—

Integer BASIC. If it finds Integer BASIC in your firmware, it loads FPBASIC. The FP stands for *F*loating *P*oint, or decimal BASIC, which means Applesoft. Running the APPLESOFT program didn't give you the message that it was LOADING INTEGER BASIC, because you have Applesoft in firmware, and Integer BASIC was already loaded. On the DOS level, the Apple //, //+, //e, and //c are all essentially compatible, since they all offer both Applesoft and Integer BASIC.

To get out of Integer BASIC, type FP and press the *return* key. To get back into Integer BASIC, type INT and *return*. You don't have to run the APPLESOFT program to get into Integer BASIC. Once you've booted with a DOS disk that has loaded Integer BASIC into memory, all you have to do is type INT. You probably won't use Integer BASIC much, but at least now you know how to access it. Keep in mind, however, that when you switch in and out of Integer BASIC, whatever else you had in memory is forgotten.

Initializing on Your Own

While COPYA can initialize disks for you, there are times when you'll have to initialize disks on your own. In fact, you'll need to know how in order to proceed with the tricks in the next chapter. Remember, a blank disk can only boot the system if it has been initialized.

Get out a blank disk. If you have two drives, put the blank disk in the external disk drive and don't worry about your DOS disk. If you have a single disk drive, take the DOS disk out of the internal drive and replace it with the blank disk. In either case, enter NEW [*return*] to clear everything out of the computer's memory.

If you have two drives, type in:

```
INIT HELLO,S6,D2,V254
```

If you have just one drive, type:

```
INIT HELLO
```

The grinding noise you will hear is perfectly normal. Your drives will soon stop churning, and the Applesoft prompt will return. Are you ready to view your handiwork? Type:

```
CATALOG
```

and in response you'll see:

```
DISK VOLUME 254
 A 002 HELLO
```

Those of you with two drives will see a CATALOG of the disk in your external drive, while those of you with only one will view a CATALOG of the disk in your one and only drive. And *both* catalogs are the same.

INIT is the DOS command to initialize a disk. Used alone, about the only thing you'll get from the command is ?SYNTAX ERROR. INIT must be used in conjunction with a program name. In this case, with a little help, you've chosen HELLO. It will go to the disk drive you have last referenced and format the disk it finds there, placing the program that you named on it. If there is no program in memory at the time, DOS will supply you with a dummy file and give it the name you've selected. That's why your disk shows an Applesoft program called HELLO that is two sectors long. If you try to load it, you'll get nothing.

Notice that users with two drives were told to put a comma after the filename and to add S6,D2,V254. Specifying *S*lot 6, *D*rive 2, *V*olume number 254, you've set all of the parameters needed by INIT. This was necessary to tell the system you wanted it to work with the second drive.

Since you have only one disk controller card, you could have ignored the S6 parameter and used INIT HELLO,D2,V254. Those with one drive did not even include the V254 and their VOLUME NUMBER was still 254. That number is the default supplied by DOS if you don't supply one.

Why should you supply one? If you decide to keep a list of which floppies contain what information, you can use this as a unique disk reference number. It can be anything from 0 to 255. If it doesn't matter to you, you can omit it, but all of your initialized disks will have the same default volume number.

DOS makes sure that users with one or two drives both get the correct drive when using the CATALOG command. Those with one drive automatically directed the Apple //c to the internal drive. Those with two drives routed the last disk command to the second drive by using the D2 parameter.

When you gave it the CATALOG command, DOS went to the appropriate drive and reported the list of programs it found there. Now put the disk you've just initialized back into its sleeve and keep it handy; you'll be needing it shortly. Those of you with one drive should now put the DOS disk back into the internal drive. Those with two drives should enter CATALOG, D1 [*return*]. This will tell DOS that the internal drive is now the *default drive*—the one DOS will look to first.

Watch Out!

Be careful with the INIT command! You can reINITialize an old disk, and sooner or later you'll want to. But be sure to remember this: *initializing any disk wipes out every single bit of data on that disk!* Fair warning.

11

Help and Fun: The DOS Programs

Now that you've initialized a disk, what do you do with it? When you use the INIT command, as mentioned in the last chapter, you create a bootable Apple // disk with a program that will automatically run when the disk is used to start the machine. In the example in the previous chapter, no program was created, so DOS supplied a default file using the name HELLO. INIT then went out to the machine and copied DOS directly from it and onto the disk.

Breaking the Bonds of Slavery

There's one minor problem. A disk created this way was originally called a *slave* disk because it was closely tied to the machine upon which it was created. When DOS was copied, it specified a designated section of memory where it was loaded when the disk booted. This corresponded to the maximum memory available on your particular computer.

All Apple //'s are not created equal. The Apple //e and Apple //c both have 48K of memory, with an additional 16K used to hold Integer BASIC under DOS. (The other 64K, standard in the //c and optional on the //e, isn't available to DOS without a lot of fancy programming.) Many of the older Apples have a scant 32K, and some few might have a dismal 16K (DOS uses 10.5K RAM, so this is actually possible).

A disk initialized on a 48K machine would not boot on a 32K Apple //, since the smaller machine would not have the extra memory it thinks it should. A disk INITialized under 32K would not boot on a 16K system for the same reason.

On the other hand, while an initialized disk from a 32K system would boot on a 48K computer, DOS would think it was in a 32K environment, and would ignore the last 16K of memory. In other words, the memory would be there, but DOS wouldn't know it.

Mastering the Disk

MASTER CREATE to the rescue. It will create a disk that will boot on any Apple // model. Get a CATALOG of the DOS disk. Listed among all of the other programs, you'll see MASTER and MASTER CREATE. They're closely related. Next to the word MASTER is the A indication that tells you the file is an Applesoft program. MASTER CREATE has a B beside it, which lets you know it's a machine language program, stored in binary form. This binary file is run from MASTER, much the same as COPYA uses COPY.OBJ0.

Now try typing RUN MASTER, and follow the few instructions supplied. If you're like most new users, you'll end up totally confused.

In the first place, MASTER performs its functions on the disk in drive D1—your internal drive. But all you're told is to insert the disk into a drive, without being told which. You're also told that you can change the name of the disk's greeting program. In case you haven't made the connection, that's HELLO. Here it's called the greeting program for the obvious reason that it's the first program that's run when you boot the disk. In effect, it's how the Apple says hello to, or greets, you. This is important.

Automatic Execution

If you write your own programs, there will be times when you'll want them to run automatically when the computer is first turned on or whenever the disk is booted. If you've initialized a disk to look for a program named HELLO as its greeting program, you'll be forced to save that program with the name HELLO for it to turn itself on. Let's face it: that's a silly name. It's acceptable to beginners as a clue to what it does, but after you've dripped sweat and worked long hours nursing a program from its infancy to fruition, the last thing you'll want to do is call it HELLO.

You could initialize a disk with the name you've selected, as in:

```
INIT <myprogramname>,Dn
```

where <myprogramname> is the actual name you've selected and the *n* in Dn is the drive number. But if you have many initialized diskettes already (or even if you don't), you'll still need to run MASTER. And you might want to change the name of the program; perhaps you've thought of a better one.

This is your chance. When MASTER CREATE prompts you to enter the name of the greeting program, you can select any name you want for it. (It's not permanent, however; you can change it later by running MASTER again). This name will be imprinted in DOS until you run MASTER CREATE another time. Of course, you don't *have* to change the name—you might like the one you gave it in the first place.

This process creates what is called a "turnkey" system. When you "turn the key" (Apple //c uses on/off switches, not keys, to turn it on, but originally computers did use keys), your program will run automatically.

DOS Independence

Aside from that, MASTER also displays the message:

```
LOADING DOS IMAGE
```

This tells you that MASTER is gathering all of the necessary DOS information and will soon write it on your disk—with one important difference. While INIT uses a fixed image of DOS (tied to the memory size of the computer), MASTER uses a theoretical image of DOS. When this is finally loaded, it will look through memory, find the highest memory "address" (the upper limit of your computer's memory), and settle itself neatly in there. The result is a bootable disk that is entirely independent of the computer memory size.

But while this works very well for DOS, you may not like the fact that it limits you to running just one program automatically. You may want to have the computer run a whole series of your programs one by one. Actually, this is fairly simple, but you can't do it with the programs on the DOS 3.3 disk. You do it with a command that uses a special program you create that is designed expressly to manage a series of programs.

Letting Your Computer EXEC You to Freedom

Apple has thoughtfully provided you with a way of directing virtually all of your computer's affairs. Suppose you had a series of programs. The first collected information from you. The second put that information in one particular order, the third rearranged it into another, the fourth did some calculation based on the results of the second and the third, and so on. This can easily be done by running one program after another, but your physical presence isn't required after the first program. The Apple //c can run all the programs for you and free you from the drudgery of waiting for one program to end so that you can start the next.

The actual commands to run a series of programs under your own supervision would look something like this:

```
RUN <program one>
RUN <program two>
. . .
RUN <the last program>
```

You'd obviously substitute the names of the programs you want to run for what's inside surrounded by angle brackets. However, if you issued these instructions, you'd be forced to sit there and monitor everything until the last program ran.

An EXEC file is a text file that contains the same instructions you'd give it yourself if you were sitting in front of your computer. It uses standard Apple // instructions and is "run" just like a program. But it does the supervision, so you don't have to. Let's try one.

Make sure your Apple //c is on and that you've used a DOS disk to boot it. Then enter the following:

```
10 PRINT CHR$ (4);"OPEN EXECTEST"
20 PRINT CHR$ (4);"WRITE EXECTEST"
30 PRINT "CATALOG"
40 PRINT "LOAD EXECMAKER"
50 PRINT "LIST"
60 PRINT CHR$ (4);"CLOSE EXECTEST"
```

This program will create a simple EXEC file. Save it to disk by typing:

```
SAVE EXECMAKER
```

If you want to save it anywhere other than the disk you're currently using, stick a ",Dn" on the end, where *n* is the drive number of that disk. Now run EXECMAKER. It will create a text file (which will have the designator T). If you could look at the contents of that file, you would see that EXECMAKER stored the following lines in it:

```
CATALOG
LOAD EXECMAKER
LIST
```

If you were to type them in individually, these would be separate DOS commands. In the EXEC file, your Apple also treats them that way. Type NEW, to clear the memory (you don't have to do this, but it proves the instructions that follow are coming from a disk file and are not just something stored in memory), and then EXEC EXECTEST.

The first thing that will happen is that a catalog of the disk will appear on the screen, just as if you entered the DOS command CATALOG. If you're using a full DOS disk, the catalog will stop after it's filled the screen with entries, just as it normally does when you enter the command from the keyboard. Press any key to let it continue. The last two directory entries should show up as:

```
A 002 EXECMAKER
T 002 EXECTEST
```

Your disk will light up a few seconds later (as it loads EXECMAKER). Immediately following that, a listing of your EXECMAKER program will scroll onto the screen as your computer executes the third and final command in the EXEC file.

By running this file, you have passed control of your computer over to the EXEC file you created. This one is just a simple group of commands. They can get far more complex, and even include additional programs. If you like, you can have an EXEC file run from your HELLO program, or you can have it run from inside any program you're using.

Use EXEC on Free Software

Bulletin boards, on-line services, and user groups have literally hundreds of Applesoft programs available for no more than the price of a disk or a phone call. Some of these programs are worth precisely what you pay for them. But some are terrific.

Unfortunately, many people spend hours downloading these programs to their disks and discover that they won't LOAD no matter how hard they try. The reason is that those files are sent as ASCII characters and end up as *text* files. BASIC can't read them (or RUN, LOAD, or LIST them) unless you fool it.

Instead of trying to LOAD the program, EXEC it into memory by typing EXEC <filename>. From then on, you'll be able to LIST it, RUN it, SAVE it, and revise it. In fact, it's probably a good idea to SAVE it first, because then it will be in a form that BASIC can LOAD directly.

A Note on DOS Files

The EXEC process created a text file on your disk. Let's retrace the steps to show precisely how it was done.

Chapter 7 explained that whenever you're *inside* an Applesoft program and want to do something *outside* of Applesoft, you have to preface the request with ASCII character 4. A disk instruction is definitely outside Applesoft, so you must use the ASCII character 4 here. If you look at line 10 of our EXEC program, you'll see you did just that.

That program illustrates all the steps you need to create a file this way. First, before you can do *anything* with a file, you must OPEN it. Line 10 shows the general format, although there are some differences for other types of files. Once you've opened a file, you have to explain to DOS exactly what you want to do. There are only two options, READ or

WRITE, no matter what type of a file it is. That's why you've included line 20. Reading means taking information out of the file. Writing means putting data into the file. DOS file handling doesn't offer you a broad range of choices.

After you've told DOS what you want to do, DOS assumes that all the instructions that follow will be instances of that activity, as is the case in lines 30 through 50. Line 20 tells it you're going to write to the file, and the following three lines do the actual writing. Finally, when you're all done, you have to CLOSE the file. Line 60 makes short work of this.

Actually, you do need a bit more finesse for certain complex DOS operations. But the principle behind all DOS file operations is the same. You open the file, you specify what you want to do, you do it, and you close the file.

FILEM and FID

Another program of towering importance on your DOS disk is actually two programs, FILEM and FID. FILEM is an Applesoft program that runs FID, so we'll deal with FID.

First, a brief note on binary files: At one time, there were no FILEM and no MASTER, just MASTER CREATE and FID. FILEM and MASTER are binary programs and are run by "saying" BRUN <filename>, where <filename> is the name of the binary program. The *B* in front tells the computer that the file you want it to load and run is in binary format. BRUN tells DOS that it's about to execute a binary (machine language) program. Apple probably thought it was too much to introduce users to BRUN immediately, so they created Applesoft lead-in programs to help you out. Note, however, that not every B file is a program. Some are copies of graphics screens; others are data from programs. You'll get a FILE TYPE MISMATCH error message if you try unsuccessfully to BRUN a nonprogram B file.

When you run FILEM it will tell you that it's executing FID, and FID will show up on your screen as a menu with nine options. Most of these choices can be done with Applesoft commands, but the important one, COPY FILES, *cannot*. (If you're copying just programs, you can LOAD them, swap disks, and then SAVE them, but for actual files or binary programs, that's not possible.)

When you select the *copy* option, FID will ask you to tell it which slot and drive you're copying from, as well as which slot and drive you want to copy to. After that you'll be asked which files you want to copy.

This can be a tricky question. If you want to copy a single file, it's simple. One name isn't difficult to remember. But if you're copying six or seven (or even two or three), the names can all run together into one mental blob. FID understands. When it asks you for a filename, you can use an "=" (equals sign). This is a "wild card." It can stand for any filename, or in this case, any and all files on the disk.

You're also asked if you want prompting. If you don't want to copy the whole disk, this is a nice option. First FID will read the entire disk. Then it will ask you if you really do want to copy each file, one by one, before it does so. Answering yes or no will permit or forbid each copying operation.

CONVERT13 and MUFFIN

As mentioned in the earlier DOS chapters, Apple didn't always use 16-sectored disks. In fact, there are still a few of the 13-sectored oldies floating around. If you ever find yourself with one of these anachronisms, you can use it by first running the DOS program CONVERT13.

This is another case of an Applesoft program that leads into a binary program—in this case, MUFFIN. There are only two options available with MUFFIN: convert files or quit. If you choose the first option, the screen will display a list of questions, much as it did with FID. MUFFIN's questions ask for slot and drive numbers and finally filenames.

Here, too, an equals sign will suffice as a wild card, and prompting is an option for those who neither want the entire disk converted nor remember the names of the handful of files which need to be.

The Other DOS Programs and Their Friends

There aren't too many more programs on the disk that you haven't already discovered. Most of the rest are Applesoft programming aids. If you're not writing your own programs, you really won't have much use for them.

DOS 3.3 System Master Disk

Program	Description
HELLO	The Applesoft greeting program. On the System Master, it checks the current contents of ROM and loads the complementary language into high RAM.
APPLESOFT	Performs the same function as HELLO on an Integer BASIC system.
BOOT13	A binary program that lets you run (not just convert) 13-sectored disks created with earlier versions of DOS.

(continued)

Program	Description
CHAIN	A binary program that loads and runs an Applesoft program without erasing the current program in memory or disturbing its variable contents—as long as both programs are in Applesoft.
CONVERT13	An Applesoft program that, in turn, runs MUFFIN.
COPY	The Integer BASIC version of Apple's full disk-copy program.
COPY.OBJ0	A machine language program used by both COPY and COPYA to do the actual copying.
COPYA	The Applesoft version of Apple's full disk-copy program.
FID	A binary program that can be used to copy individual files, renumber, unlock, or verify disk contents.
FILEM	The Applesoft program that runs FID.
FPBASIC	The Applesoft language version that is loaded into high RAM on Integer BASIC versions of the computer.
INTBASIC	The Integer BASIC language version that is loaded into high RAM on Applesoft BASIC versions of the computer.
LOADER.OBJ0	The program that does the actual loading of the alternate language. On the System Master disk it's called by the HELLO program.
MASTER	The Applesoft BASIC program that runs MASTER CREATE.
MASTER CREATE	A binary program that places a relocatable DOS image on your *slave* disk, converting it to a *master* disk. It also allows you to change the name of the DOS greeting program.
MUFFIN	The binary program that converts files on 13-sectored disks onto 16-sectored disks.
RENUMBER	An Applesoft programming tool that can be used to renumber the statements in your Applesoft BASIC program and/or merge two programs.

(continued)

Program	Description
SLOT#	An Applesoft program that will tell you which slot and drive you're currently using (don't laugh, you *could* forget).
START13	The Applesoft program that runs BOOT13.

Another Apple disk, called SAMPLE PROGRAMS, contain programs that illustrate many of the points you've covered here. Remember to make a backup copy of this before you start playing with it, however—*all* original disks are sacred.

DOS 3.3 Sample Programs Disk

Program	Description
HELLO	DOS's greeting program.
ADDRESS	An Applesoft program that demonstrates the use of random access files. It uses BLACK BOOK to hold the data you create.
ANIMALS	An illustrative "game" that lets you build a data file.
APPLE PROMS	The data file used by RANDOM.
APPLESOFT	Integer BASIC version of HELLO.
APPLEVISION	General demonstration program (very cute).
BLACK BOOK	The data file for ADDRESS.
BRICK OUT	The primal Pong game, for the stout of heart with paddles or a liking for the arrow keys.
COLOR TEST	For the color TV that's not quite adjusted correctly.
DELETE.ME.1 DELETE.ME.2 DELETE.ME.3	Three programs which demonstrate how to delete a file—three times, no less.
EXEC DEMO	An Applesoft program demonstrating the creation and use of EXEC and EXEC files.
FPBASIC	The memory version of Applesoft.
GET TEXT	A demonstration program that allows you to read text files.

(continued)

Program	Description
INTBASIC	The memory version of Integer BASIC.
LOADER.OBJ0	The machine language program used by the DOS greeting program to load the alternate language into memory.
LOCK.ME.1 LOCKED.UP.1 LOCKED.UP.2	Demonstration programs that let you practice locking and unlocking files.
MAKE TEXT	A sample program that will let you create sequential text files.
ONERR DEMO	Funny name, but a program that can show you how to check for and deal with error conditions.
PHONE.LIST	A plain old sample Applesoft program.
POKER	Not the game. It's a sample program that translates machine language into text files.
RANDOM	A sample Applesoft program that demonstrates reading and writing random access files.
VERIFY.ME	Learn how to verify a file with this Applesoft program.

12

ProDOS

Once you start adding programs and files to your disks, you'll discover one of the real drawbacks of DOS. You can fill disks with so many programs, data files, text files, and binary files that the contents become totally disorganized. There is no foolproof way to group similar programs together for easy reference, except to create several disks, each dedicated to one kind of file, and then copy the related files and programs from one disk to the others. But this has its problems as well, since there are certain files that would fall into more than one category. Having to switch disks back and forth can be a genuine nuisance.

There is another serious problem with DOS—it was never meant to handle large amounts of information. After all, a DOS 3.3 disk holds a mere 143,000 characters. In the real world, that's not very much. And now that there are far larger capacity disk drives available, 143K is not satisfactory at all. Obviously, the time is right for something new, and that something is ProDOS.

Floppies used with ProDOS 1.0 are physically the very same ones you use with DOS 3.3, but once they're formatted by each system, the similarity ends. To extend our metaphor from previous chapters, ProDOS disks can also be envisioned as a series of file cabinets. But while DOS 3.3 essentially gave you just one file drawer per disk, ProDOS 1.0 moves you closer to the way most people keep information by giving you a vastly more flexible organizational framework.

Perhaps the easiest way to explain the ProDOS enhancements is to have you think about how a file cabinet really works. It has three main components: the cabinet itself, the drawers, and the contents of the drawers (which are usually file folders holding the information).

Imagine that you are a voracious reader who has collected a large library of books over the years and would like to keep track of them. You can start by wheeling in a filing cabinet and marking it LIBRARY, in big letters. Now everyone who saw it would know what it was, not just you. If you were out and wanted someone to look into your library file, it would be easy for him or her to figure out which of your many file cabinets contained your library data.

Assume that your books in this imaginary library fall into three main categories, Science Fiction, Mystery, and Philosophy. So you label the first file drawer "Science Fiction," the second "Mystery," and the third "Philosophy." Straightforward enough.

Now you go to the individual drawers and start filling each one with file folders that correspond to the books in your collection. All you need to put in these folders is the title and a short synopsis of the plot. For the Science Fiction section, you've also decided to subdivide your drawer into front and back halves. The front will contain your Science Fantasy titles, while the back holds all the fiction in your library that is based on real science. Your files are arranged something like this.

Diagram of a Hierarchical File Organization System

```
                                LIBRARY
                            /      |      \
                          /        |        \
     SCIENCE FICTION            MYSTERY        PHILOSOPHY
             |                     |                |
   Fantasy         Science      Title 1          Title 1
      |               |         Title 2          Title 2
   Title 1         Title 1      Title 3          Title 3
   Title 2         Title 2       . . .            . . .
   Title 3         Title 3      Title n          Title n
    . . .           . . .
   Title n         Title n
```

When you finish cataloguing the last book in your collection, you've made a very workable system for finding any book on your shelves. You've also done a good job of building a real-world model of a ProDOS disk.

Volume Names

The first thing you did to your file cabinet was name it, to avoid confusion later. If you have twenty other file cabinets, and you hadn't named them, you'd spend many wasted hours going to the wrong one when you needed information. The best you could get out of DOS 3.3 in this respect was a volume number, not a name. While volume numbers are a good way to keep track of your disks, you'd then need still another file just to keep track of which volume numbers referred to which main disk subjects.

It would be better if you could put an actual name on the disk. This way anyone looking at it would immediately know what the disk was for. With ProDOS you can do just that. Every ProDOS disk has a name that you select. It's called the *volume name*. Here, *volume* is used as another name for disk, as you might call any large amount of data a "volume" of information.

Root Directories and Subdirectories

The next thing you did, after identifying the main physical container, was label each of the drawers. With DOS, if you tried to organize disk files the way you organized a file cabinet, that's about as far as you could go. But this is just a starting point for ProDOS. With it, you can establish a series of primary directories, called *root directories*, each with its own slate of files, much the same way you labeled all of the drawers in your filing cabinet.

This leaves you with only one thing to worry about—your sorting of science fiction material into two subcategories. ProDOS also takes this further organizational refinement into account by offering you subdirectories. These are directories within the root directory that further define the handling of your information, like a section divider in a drawer. You don't have to use subdirectories if you don't want to. But there are circumstances when they come in mighty handy.

So far, ProDOS has done a commendable job of simulating a file cabinet. The disk is the cabinet itself. The name on the front of the cabinet is the disk's volume name. Each drawer can be specified by a root directory, and any divisions within the drawers can be further refined using ProDOS's subdirectory facility.

Why Use Subdirectories?

You don't *have* to use root directories and subdirectories. You can treat a ProDOS disk just as you would a DOS disk with the ordinary primary directory only. This, however, will be a colossal waste if you're using a hard disk, which can hold the equivalent of dozens of boxes of floppies. Since there is a limit to the number of hard-disk directory entries, you'll quickly run out of space in the section set aside for the directory, even though you have lots of open space for files and programs on the rest of the hard disk. Subdirectories are the only way to cram more files on your hard disk. Furthermore, they let you organize all disks—including floppies—in a far more accessible and useful way.

Once you've built your ProDOS directory, though, how do you find information that is buried under several layers of organization? It looked easy in DOS, but all these root and subdirectory parameters make it look complicated. It isn't.

Finding Your Way Through the Disk

Let's take an imaginary journey to the public library to look at a certain reference book. To get to the library, you walk out your front door, make a left onto Jay Street, catch the K bus, get off the bus thirty blocks later at Em Street, walk up the steps, and over to the reference desk.

There, the information librarian tells you where to find the book you're looking for. To reach it, you have to walk down the hall, into the elevator, up three floors, past the "Reference" sign, to the shelf marked "Not to be removed from this room," where all books are arranged alphabetically. The one you're looking for should be in the "P" section.

If you had to tell someone else how to get to that book from your home, you could write down the precise path from your front door to the "P" section in the Reference room. That's the exact same way you tell ProDOS to behave—all you're missing are the the actual commands ProDOS uses.

Walking Down the Old ProDOS Path

If you were using DOS and you wanted a catalog of the disk, you could do it by entering:

```
CATALOG,Sn,Dn
```

CATALOG reads the directory, and Sn and Dn specify the slot and drive number, respectively, where the disk can be found. It's a little cryptic, but it gets the job done.

ProDOS is much more straightforward about it. You have to tell it where things are, but in a different way. As in DOS, if you wanted to see the catalog of the disk you were working on, you'd simply type CATALOG. But what if you wanted to see the contents of your external drive? All you do is tell it what path to take to get to that disk.

For instance, if you did have a disk whose volume name was LIBRARY, you'd enter:

```
CATALOG /LIBRARY
```

The slash (/) is the ProDOS signal that what follows is a *pathname,* and just as the term implies, it is the direction it takes to find the disk specified. Even if it was in the external drive, ProDOS would need no further instructions.

It would look at the disk in the internal drive and see if its name was LIBRARY. If it was, it would catalog it. If it wasn't, it would go to the external drive and check there. Again, if it found the disk it was looking for, you'd soon see the list of its contents on your screen. If neither of them had the correct volume name, you'd see a VOLUME NOT FOUND error message.

CATALOG or CAT?

Under ProDOS the word CATALOG has two forms, the normal full-length CATALOG and the short form, CAT. The former produces an 80-column display that can get very confusing if you're using the Apple //c's 40-column mode. The lines overlap and the information is visually lost in the scramble of screen lines. If you're not using 80 columns, you would be well advised to use the abbreviated CAT version. The only information you lose is about creation and modification dates. If you didn't set the date and time when you first entered ProDOS, it won't matter anyway.

So if you've given ProDOS the pathname to the volume you want, you'll get a basic list of what root directories are there. But what if you want to see more? After all, there is more to a disk than root directories. If adding a slash to the volume name provided a path to the disk, why not try the same for a root directory? There's only one hitch. Assume you want to try looking for SCIENCE.FICTION:

```
CATALOG /SCIENCE.FICTION
```

You'd quickly discover that ProDOS couldn't find what you were looking for. It assumes that the pathname immediately following the command is to a *volume.*

Spaced Out

Unlike DOS, ProDOS doesn't know how to handle spaces. While DOS could deal with a filename like SCIENCE FICTION, ProDOS would become very confused. If you need two words to describe a volume or a directory name, separate the two with a period, as in SCIENCE.FICTION. By the way, SCIENCE.FICTION is as long as a ProDOS name can get. Fifteen characters is the official maximum.

Instead, try using a ProDOS multilevel pathname like this:

```
CATALOG /LIBRARY/SCIENCE.FICTION
```

You first define the volume you want to look at, then specify any root directory on that volume, again preceded by a slash. If there is a subdirectory involved, it would be:

```
CATALOG /LIBRARY/SCIENCE.FICTION/FANTASY
```

That's all there is to it. Armed with these simple tricks, you and ProDOS can now quickly find the proper path to any file on any disk, no matter how complex your organizational structure is.

THE ProDOS Filer

When you booted the DOS 3.3 disk, it left you in Applesoft, ready to program—if that's what you wanted. ProDOS is a bit different. It simply leaves you staring at a menu.

ProDOS Menu

System Utilities Main Menu
Copyright Apple Computer, Inc., 1984

Work on Individual Files

1. <COPY FILES>
2. Delete Files
3. Rename Files
4. Lock/Unlock Files

Work on Entire Disk

5. Duplicate a Disk
6. Format a Disk
7. Identify and Catalog a Disk
8. Advanced Operations
9. Exit System Utilities

Type a number or press ↑ or ↓ to select an option. Then press *return*.
For Help: Press or

Volume Commands

As with DOS, the most important part of using the ProDOS disk is to make sure that you have a backup copy. Your original is sacred. To do this, select option 5, Duplicate a Disk, from the ProDOS menu.

The choices you see are similar to those given you by the DOS COPYA, with the exception that D1 is now the Internal Drive and D2 is the External Drive. If you have an external drive, use it. Otherwise you'll spend much too much time swapping disks in and out of the internal drive.

This segment of the program will ask you to give a volume name to the blank disk. At the same time, it will supply the volume name of the original disk as the default value. This time accept the default, which should be /UTILITIES.

Don't stop once the initial copying operation finishes. Make an additional copy just as you did (or at least were supposed to do) for the DOS master disk. It's better to spend the extra time now than to be sorry later.

Formatting a Disk

ProDOS has its own way of initializing disks. It doesn't have a utility like the INIT command from Applesoft. You cannot initialize a blank disk.

Instead, you use the ProDOS FORMAT option. Remember, there are real differences in the two operating systems and what they each require. DOS was a single-level operating system. INIT allowed you to place a memory-dependent copy of DOS on the disk you initialized. That just isn't done with ProDOS.

When you format a ProDOS disk, you do not place an image of the operating system on it. All you do is prepare it to be used. You can't assume that a ProDOS-formatted disk will boot.

To format several disks, select option 6 on the ProDOS menu. It will ask which drive to use (this depends on your hardware configuration), and then what volume name you want to give it. You can supply one of your own or accept what ProDOS suggests, which will be BLANKxx, where the xx is a two digit number ProDOS supplies. If you do select the default name, you'll also notice that ProDOS increments the numeric suffix (the xx) at each successive format operation. It's trying to be helpful.

What Happened to INIT

To get a directory, use option 7. Tell it in this case that you want to use the built-in drive and send the listing to the display. Aside from the statistics that are available, the list of files and programs on your Utilities disk should be very close to this:

```
USER.PROFILE
*STARTUP
```

```
*SU
*SU1.OBJ
*SU2.OBJ
*SU3.OBJ
*SU4.OBJ
*PRODOS
*BASIC.SYSTEM
```

These are an assortment of text, BASIC, binary, and ProDOS files (a new file type, not seen under DOS). Three of these will demonstrate how ProDOS works.

The first is, naturally enough, ProDOS. This is the operating system file that contains all of the instructions and procedures that constitute ProDOS. For a disk to be bootable, it must have this file on it.

When ProDOS finishes loading, it looks for a file with a .SYSTEM suffix. The one shown here is BASIC.SYSTEM, which indicates that it will enter the BASIC environment. No matter what .SYSTEM file it is (it could also just as easily be PASCAL.SYSTEM), ProDOS will attempt to use it. If there is none, you'll get a nasty message on the screen and the boot process will not continue.

After that, the .SYSTEM file looks for a program named STARTUP. It's equivalent to a DOS greeting program, like HELLO, and is run automatically if it's found. If none is found, the computer reverts to whatever language or program is contained in the .SYSTEM file.

That's why INIT is ineffective. It would have to copy both ProDOS and BASIC.SYSTEM and it can't do that. Right now, though, you're going to make a bootable disk. And what you find out from it may surprise you.

What Happened to Applesoft

Select option 1, *COPY FILES,* from the ProDOS menu. ProDOS will ask for the source disk (in this case the built-in drive), and then the destination disk. Pick whichever suits your hardware (as with COPYA, you'll be asked to remove and insert disks if necessary).

It will then ask you whether you want to copy some or all of the files on your source disk. You've already made enough backup disks, so now you're going to copy just two files into the disk you've just formatted (you *must* have a formatted disk). Tell ProDOS you want to copy only *some* files, by pressing the *return* key and accepting the default. The screen will change as the names of the programs on your disk are examined, and your display will look like this:

```
<USER.PROFILE>
STARTUP
SU
SU1.OBJ
SU2.OBJ
SU3.OBJ
```

```
SU4.OBJ
PRODOS
BASIC.SYSTEM
```

Notice that the first file name is enclosed in greater-than and less-than brackets. ProDOS is always on the lookout for ways to help you. In fact, it will always make a suggestion whenever you have a choice. Here, it asks you to select which files you want, and it suggests that you try the first. You can tell which choice it feels is best by looking at the one it has marked.

Everything you do now will be controlled by the four arrow keys on the lower right corner of the keyboard (you can also use the *tab* key, but let's stick with the arrows until you get proficient).

Using the ↓, move the brackets down the list until they enclose the word ProDOS. Now press the → key. A small checkmark will appear next to it. Do the same to the next file, BASIC.SYSTEM. If you make a mistake and select the wrong file, move back up and use the ← to remove the checkmark. In fact, there is almost always a way to correct erroneous entries. When you're done and ready to do the actual copying, press the *return* key. The actual copying process is far easier with two drives, but will work with one. You'll be prompted about which disks to put where and when.

HELP!

At any point in your travels through any of the ProDOS utilities menus, you can bail out of a wrong or unsure act by pressing the *esc* key. It's a direct path to safety.

When you're done, don't return to the menu; instead, be sure the disk you've just copied files to is in the drive and reset the machine. (If you don't remember how—hold down the and *control* keys and press the *reset* switch at the top of the keyboard.)

The system will load and the screen will clear. You'll see the familiar Applesoft prompt,], and the cursor. But the top of the screen will look like this:

```
PRODOS BASIC 1.0
COPYRIGHT APPLE, 1983
```

What happened to Applesoft? Much of Applesoft is the same as under DOS, but there are important differences. It wouldn't do if everyone referred to both the version of BASIC that under DOS and the one that ran under ProDOS as Applesoft. This ProDOS version is much more businesslike. It even accepts lowercase disk commands from BASIC.

Now that you know how to format a disk and make it bootable, examine some of the other ProDOS features. Replace the Utilities disk in the internal drive and reboot the system. When you see the menu, select option 8, Advanced Operations. There are a few new frontiers to be found there. A new menu will greet you.

ProDOS Advanced Operations Menu

Advanced Operations
ESC: Main Menu

ProDOS Only
1. <SET THE PREFIX>
2. Create a Subdirectory

Additional Operations

3. Change a Disk's Format
4. Verify That a Disk is Readable
5. Configure the Serial Ports

Type a number or press ↑ or ↓ to select an option.
Then press *return*.

For Help: Press or

Prefix

The one new construction you'll find here is the PREFIX. The word has an obvious meaning in English, and Apple has attempted to make ProDOS as obvious as possible. A prefix is a combination of letters or words that go in front of other letters or words.

Every ProDOS disk activity needs to know which disk you want it to use. You must provide this as the first piece of information after any disk-handling command. That's where PREFIX comes in. It's what ProDOS looks at if you don't give it a volume name to work with.

After you select option 1 from the Advanced Operations menu, you'll be asked to choose either the disk in the internal or external drive as the source of the prefix. Alternately, you can specify another volume name, but the disk it represents must be in one of the Apple //c's drives or you'll get an error message.

For now, take ProDOS's suggestion again and choose option 1 (set prefix) by pressing the *return* key. Part of the screen will clear and you'll see a two-choice menu and the message:

```
New Prefix: /UTILITIES/
```

This is the pathname of the volume in the built-in drive. From now until you change it, DOS will look to this pathname automatically without your having to type it in.

But there are more uses to PREFIX than just that. As well as the volume name, it can also hold any directory pathname(s) you need to get to a specific file—thus saving you much typing.

If you choose to set the prefix by slot and drive (option 1), rather than by pathname (option 2), the prefix will only include the volume name. If, however, you select the pathname option, you can include root and subdirectory information as well.

Dealing with Non-ProDOS Disks

DOS 3.3 has a provision for running older-style DOS 3.2 disks, and ProDOS can also handle disks created under older operating systems. Use the Advanced Operations menu to select option 3, Change a Disk's Format. This name is somewhat misleading, since you're not really going to *change* the format of a disk. What this lets you do is convert files from one disk to another. The menu offers three choices:

```
Which conversion do you want to make?

1. <DOS 3.2 -> DOS 3.3>
2.  DOS 3.3 -> ProDOS
3.  ProDOS -> DOS 3.3
```

This is very similar to the DOS 3.3 MUFFIN utility. Here, however, you can upgrade information from the old DOS all the way up to ProDOS (a process that unfortunately requires two steps). Alternatively, you can transfer material from ProDOS back down to DOS 3.3. ProDOS gives you one shining new feature older operating systems lack. When you use ProDOS utilities to transfer material between disks with different formats, you do *not* need a preformatted disk. The transfer utility will format the disk prior to copying the files. That includes both DOS 3.3 and ProDOS formats.

The Serial Ports and ProDOS

Subsequent chapters will show you how to set up the printer and modem ports for non-Apple equipment if you're using Applesoft. ProDOS will do the job for you automatically—but setting up the mechanisms to do it can be very tricky.

From the Advanced Operations menu, select option 5, Configure the Serial Ports. Your screen should look like this.

ProDOS Serial Port Configuration Menu

What do you want to do?

1. <SET PORT 1>
   Apple Imagewriter (166/1124)
2. Set Port 2
   Apple 300 Baud Modem (252/1111)
3. Edit the Device List

The Apple //c has two serial ports, one primarily for the printer, the other for the modem. You can switch these back and forth if you want, and you can select the parameters under which the device connected to either of them operates. The foregoing menu is your pathway to customizing your ports.

Suppose you want to work with a printer other than the Apple Imagewriter. Let's say you already have a serial printer and have no great need of graphics. You want to do word processing and you have a letter-quality printer like the NEC 7715 Spinwriter. To do this, you'll have to reconfigure port 1.

The menu indicates that it is currently set to handle the Apple Imagewriter. Beside the listing for the Imagewriter is a number: 166/1124. Press *return* and you'll see the menu for port 1, listing the Imagewriter, Apple's 300 and 1200 baud modems, and Apple's Color Plotter—all with seven-digit numbers after them. Also, there are three additional listings that say YOUR DEVICE, as well as two more, at the bottom of the list that say *I Know My PIN* and *I Don't Know My PIN*.

There are seven parameters that pertain to all serial devices connected to the Apple //c:

- Modem or Printer
- Data & Stop Bits
- Operating Speed
- Parity
- Screen Echo (On or Off)
- Linefeed after Carriage Return or Not
- Length of Transmitted Line before Carriage Return

There are also seven digits to the right of the devices as shown in the preceding menu. Apple calls these the PIN numbers and uses them to identify the characteristics of the devices. Each digit corresponds to one of the parameters on the list.

Press *esc* to return to the main serial port configuration menu, and choose selection 3, Edit the Device List. ProDOS displays a list of the possibilities and suggests that you might want to edit option 5, one of the YOUR DEVICE options. Press *return* to accept the default.

Enter your device name; NEC 7715, and press *return*. You'll be asked if you know what PIN to use. This time the default is YES, but if you don't yet know how to specify all the parameters, respond with NO.

Your first choice is the mode setting. You have two options:

```
1. Printer Mode
2. Communications Mode
```

Since you're connecting a printer, select 1. As soon as you've indicated your choice, the screen will display another menu, on data bits and stop bits:

```
1. 6 Data Bits/1 Stop Bit
2. 6 Data Bits/2 Stop Bits
3. 7 Data Bits/1 Stop Bit
4. 7 Data Bits/2 Stop Bits
5. 8 Data Bits/1 Stop Bit
6. 8 Data Bits/2 Stop Bits
```

The NEC 7715 can accept a wide range of data bit/stop bit combinations. In this case, select a common setting—8 data bits and 1 stop bit. The following screen asks you to choose the transmission speed:

```
1. 110 Bits per Second
2. 300 Bits per Second
3. 1200 Bits per Second
4. 2400 Bits per Second
5. 4800 Bits per Second
6. 9600 Bits per Second
7. 19200 Bits per Second
```

This is what's normally referred to as the baud rate of your printer. The 7715 can be set to a variety of speeds up to 1,200 bits per second, so pick number 3.

Next, ProDOS needs to know whether or not your data uses a parity error-checking scheme. As discussed briefly in an earlier chapter, every character the computer uses can be expressed in terms of a unique eight-bit ASCII binary number. A binary number is made up of *1*'s and *0*'s only. The parity checker counts the number of 1's in the binary representation of each character's ASCII code, making sure that the total number of *1*'s in the character sent from the computer matches the total of *1*'s received by the external device—in this case the printer. You can check the parity in several ways:

```
1. No Parity
2. Even Parity
3. Odd Parity
4. Mark Parity
5. Space Parity
```

The Spinwriter can handle any of these. In this case, we'll select option 1, No Parity.

You'll then have to decide if you want the information that goes to the printer to be simultaneously copied, or "echoed," to the screen. You have two choices only:

```
1. Do Not Echo Output On Screen
2. Echo Output On Screen
```

Choose option number 1; otherwise, if you happen to be in 40-column mode and the document you are printing is 80 columns wide, the screen display will be unreadable.

The next option asks if you want a linefeed sent after a carriage return. When you hit the *return* key on an electric typewriter, the carriage returns to the leftmost position and the paper feeds up one line (or more if you've set it for that). The *return* key actually causes a carriage return *and* linefeed. To a computer, a linefeed (which rolls the carriage up a line) and a carriage return (which moves the printing mechanism to the leftmost position on the carriage) are two entirely different operations. While there are times when they should work together, there are also times when they shouldn't. You have to tell the computer whether or not to combine the two. Your choice is:

```
1. Do Not Send Line Feed after Carriage Return
2. Insert Line Feed after Carriage Return
```

Both the Apple //c and the NEC 7715 printer can be set either way. Most software that you'll use will send its own linefeeds and expect the printer not to do it. Since you'll need to set the printer that way, set the Apple //c to insert a linefeed, in order to maintain compatibility with the bulk of the software you'll use. This is option 2.

The menu will then ask whether you want to insert a carriage return periodically throughout your data:

```
1. Do Not Insert CR
2. Insert CR after 40 Characters
3. Insert CR after 72 Characters
```

```
4. Insert CR after 80 Characters
5. Insert CR after 132 Characters
```

When the print head on some printers reaches its rightmost position, it returns automatically to its leftmost position. On other printers it doesn't. You should take no chances. The NEC 7715 has a 15-inch carriage, which translates into approximately 132 characters of print per line; select option 5 to tell the Apple //c this. Doing so, you've made the last of the choices needed. Your screen clears and now displays the statistics you've selected:

```
Printer Mode
8 Data Bits/1 Stop Bit
1200 Bits per Second
No Parity
Do Not Echo Output on Screen
Insert Line Feed After CR
Insert CR After 132 Characters

The PIN is 153/1125

Is this information Correct?
 <YES> no
```

The PIN is a shorthand way of recording the numbers of the choices you just selected, in the order in which you chose them. ProDOS will ask if you want to save the configuration to disk, and if you think you'll ever own a NEC 7715, you should. Otherwise tell it no.

You can now look at the PIN displayed beside the Imagewriter and figure out what all of the settings for it are. Remember, its PIN is 166/1124.

- 1-Printer Mode
- 6-8 Data Bits/2 Stop Bits
- 6-9600 Bits per Second
- 1-No Parity
- 1-Do Not Echo Output to Screen
- 2-Insert LF after CR
- 4-Insert CR after 80 Characters

Modem PINs would start with a 2 and end with a 1, Do Not Send CR. The manuals of most printers and modems will give you a precise range of parameters these serial devices were designed to use. You can then check the options and determine their PIN. And, you can make either of the two serial ports support a printer or a modem—or both of them if you have the software to handle it.

If you ever find yourself stuck with a recalcitrant printer or modem and have to use a DOS program that can't set the device, you can use the ProDOS utilities to configure everything properly. Once you set up the port, the only way to change its configuration is to reset it or shut off the Apple //c.

13

Printing It Out

There are three distinct types of printers, based on the internal mechanism that in each case puts the image on the page. Impact printers are by far the most common. These can produce either fully formed characters (like a conventional typewriter), or letters and numbers made up of little dots (like those on your monitor's screen). Thermal printers are generally inexpensive. They work by cooking tiny areas of specially coated heat-sensitive paper, but do not yield the most professional-looking results (though Apple's announced new Scribe is a thermal printer with the promise of putting its images on regular paper—and in color to boot). The newest kinds of printers use lasers to etch a blackened image onto the paper, or nozzles that squirt fine jets of ink on the paper's surface.

Dot Matrix

Dot-matrix printers range in price from anywhere around $300 to ten times that amount. The higher the price, the faster the printing speed and the higher the print quality. Inexpensive dot-matrix printers bang out as few as 50 or so characters per second, while expensive ones can rattle off as many as 450 per second.

Your computer starts the printing process by sending your printer a unique ASCII code for each character you want to print. Printers are notorious for requiring their own nonstandard special codes to do things like print in italics, but virtually all of them rely on ASCII codes for input.

As their name implies, dot-matrix printers form characters out of a square block of wires arranged in a matrix, or grid. When the printer receives an ASCII code, it looks in an internal table stored on a chip, and "maps," or translates, the code into the correct combination of wires that will print the character. The process is very much like selectively lighting up bulbs on a scoreboard. Your monitor uses a similar technique to create characters out of dots on your screen—look closely and you'll see the matrix that makes up each letter and number.

These wires are then banged up against the ribbon by a delicate electromagnet, transferring a printed impression onto the page. As you might imagine, there are a wide variety of characters that can be formed by the combination of dots in the grid. Most dot-matrix printers can also print graphics, by using individual wires to print individual dots to form the kind of grainy pictures you see in newspapers.

The More the Merrier

The more wires there are in the matrix, the better the image. This is why magazine photos look better than newspaper photos; there are more dots to the inch in glossy magazines than on newsprint. Wire-firing mechanisms can be expensive, and low-cost printers usually print characters that look coarse and very unlike typewriter-quality text. The gaps between the dots are very pronounced.

However, most of the newer dot-matrix printers on the market allow you to select a pseudo-letter-quality mode in which the wires pass over the same line more than once and fill in the gaps. Some of the very costly printers can produce dot-matrix output that is so sharp and crisp that it really does rival typewriter type. The disadvantage to passing over the same line more than once to boost the quality is that the speed is reduced dramatically. To compensate for this, most dot-matrix printers offer at least two modes—one for "letter quality" that produces attractive characters relatively slowly, and one for "draft" quality that produces coarser, single-pass letters very quickly.

Quite a few companies market dot-matrix printers. Perhaps the best known are Epson, Okidata, and C. Itoh. Models of the C. Itoh printer are marketed by NEC as its NEC 8023 printer, and by Apple as the Apple DMP and Imagewriter. Epson has been adopted by IBM as the standard printer for the IBM PC. And Okidata has an enormous following of satisfied users as well.

A company called Centronics was at one time a leader in dot-matrix technology. The common parallel connection many printers use is unofficially called the "Centronics parallel interface" because this company popularized it. Unfortunately, their printers are no longer as popular in the mass consumer marketplace. The printer output of the Apple //c is serial rather than parallel (although it is possible to use parallel printers). A parallel printer handles eight bits of data at one gulp. A serial printer handles information *serially*, in a long string, one bit at a time rather than eight.

Hooking Up a Parallel Printer

While the Apple printer output is strictly serial, companies such as Quadram market external devices that can reconfigure the serial output of a printer to a parallel signal. Some printers, especially the more expensive ones, contain modular printed circuit boards that can be easily converted to turn the output from parallel to serial. Contact your dealer, or the printer manufacturer, for more help in this area.

There are several key things you should look for in a dot-matrix printer. Upper- and lowercase characters are a must! Even in today's age of technological miracles, there are still very low-priced dot-matrix printers on the market that do not allow the "tails" (descenders) on letters like *g*, *j*, and *y* to extend below the bottom of the line of print. This was barely acceptable in the very early days of printer technology and is to be avoided at all costs now, as it looks absolutely awful.

Good dot-matrix printers should also provide you with a variety of type fonts and styles. You should be able to emphasize characters, by printing them in **boldface**, or *italics,* or by elongating or compressing them. Some even give you whole different families of typefaces, or allow you to create your own customized typefaces and send, or *download,* them from a disk file to your printer. Such tricks can come in very handy if you want to print out your own letterhead or fit a wide spreadsheet onto a narrow page, or give your letters and reports a distinctive, artistic appearance.

If you want to reproduce the handsome graphic displays Apple computers are known for, you'll need a dot-matrix printer with graphics capabilities. Some even use special ribbons and firmware to generate color images. However, if you use your computer exclusively for word processing or spreadsheet manipulation, this feature is not important.

The other feature you'll probably want to consider is physical size. Some dot-matrix printers will accommodate a sheet of paper a maximum of 8½ inches wide. With standard character sizes and print spacing, this will give you an 80-column output, which is sufficient for virtually all ordinary applications. There are times, though, when this won't be enough. While it's possible to use a compressed print mode to cram additional characters onto an 8½-inch page, compressed characters are small and packed very closely together, so you sacrifice some readability.

Other printers, or wide-bodied versions of the smaller ones, can handle a sheet of paper up to 14 inches wide. In normal print mode this will give you a 132-column output. If compressed print is available, you can almost double that number of characters. On the other hand, larger printers take

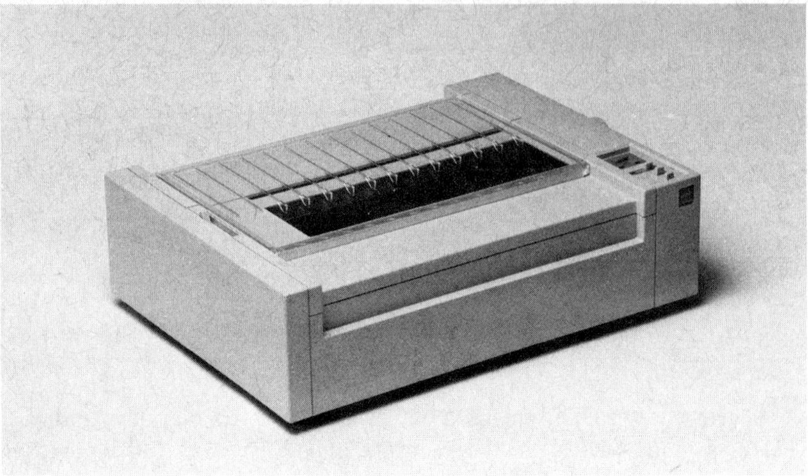

The Apple Imagewriter printer.

up proportionately more room on your desk, so if you're already cramped for space, one more extra-wide cabinet may make your system almost unusable.

Apple's Imagewriter has the edge over most of the small-carriage competition. Since you cannot plug printer cards (or any other kinds of expansion cards) into the Apple //c, it is up to programmers who create software to make sure their packages will work within the limitations of the Apple //c printer output. Since the Imagewriter is an Apple product, it is totally compatible with all of the software Apple will produce—graphics included. How third-party software authors handle the printer may not be as wonderful.

If graphics are not important to you, and you're working with text and/or numbers only, then most of the serial-interface dot-matrix printers currently on the market will suffice. Remember, as a rule, the more you pay,

DIN vs. D-Plug

One of the trickiest pieces of Apple //c hardware is the nonstandard cable that connects your computer to a printer. While most printer cables have what is called a "D-connector" (since it is shaped like the letter *D*) at the computer end, the Apple //c has a five-pin DIN connector in order to save room at the back of the machine. If you are trying to connect your existing printer to your computer, you may have to purchase a cable adapter, or have your computer store make a special cable for you.

the faster and more businesslike the printed output will be. But unless you're prepared to spend well over $1,000, the characters any dot-matrix printer will produce will not look as sharp as those done on a typewriter or true letter-quality printer. And no matter what printer you eventually choose, make absolutely sure that it supports *serial* output, and that you can find a cable for it.

High-Quality Output

Letter-quality printers produce character output that can rival (or even surpass) the best typewriters. On the other hand, if you need to reproduce graphics, letter-quality printers will not do as good a job as dot-matrix printers. However, if you are using a computer to type reams of business correspondence, customized form letters, high-level memos and reports, or even typeset material for a book or periodical, a letter-quality printer is a must. The principal suppliers are NEC, Diablo (Xerox), Qume (makers of the Apple Daisy Wheel Printer), and C. Itoh.

To yield such high quality, letter-quality printers (which are sometimes referred to as "fully formed character printers" since they print whole letters one at a time rather than just patterns of dots that resemble letters) use special printing elements. These type elements are called either *daisy wheels*—because the characters are arranged on stalks emanating from a central hub like petals on a flower—or *thimbles*—which are just like daisy wheels, except that the petals are bent upward so that the unit becomes thimble shaped.

While these print elements are made either of metal or reinforced plastic, they do wear out after extensive use. Such deterioration isn't exactly unexpected, considering these printers can hammer out book-length manuscripts. Fortunately, the elements are simple to change and relatively inexpensive. Typical elements cost from $8 to $20, with specialized ones going for as much as $40 or $50.

Because the print elements are so easy to change, it's a snap (literally) to switch typefaces. Most printer manufacturers offer several dozen different typefaces, both for standard and proportionally spaced output. To switch typefaces, all you have to do is snap the old one out and drop the new one in. The entire process takes five or ten seconds. And since each of the typefaces is as sharp and clear as the finest typewriter output, having a letter-quality printer and a drawer full of print elements is almost like having a typesetting shop at your fingertips.

Since there are no sharp wires impacting against the ribbon, letter-quality printers can also use carbon, or "film," ribbons which produce the sharpest, clearest, crispest output possible. The output of the best letter-quality printers is unmatchable. However, the fastest letter-quality printers run slower than all but the slowest dot-matrix printers. Speeds range from a pathetic 12 characters per second for the bargain-basement models, to a rapid 55 characters per second for the top-of-the-line machines. The range of prices is about the same as that for dot-matrix printers, though fewer truly cheap letter-quality models are available.

When you select a letter-quality printer, it's important to consider the type of work for which you will be using it. As with the dot-matrix machines, some of the lower-cost models will handle a standard 8½-inch-wide sheet of paper only. If you have to produce miles of printouts every day, don't even consider a low-priced model. The slow speed will become a real bottleneck. Also, the heavy output load will destroy cheap plastic models that aren't made for working nonstop. Very expensive 55-characters-per-second printers such as the Diablos and the Spinwriters are built like battleships to take the punishment of printing all day long without complaint.

Common Features

Both dot-matrix and letter-quality printers share certain common paper-manipulation, or "forms-handling," features. While inserting individual sheets of paper into the printer is fine for small printing jobs, it's not practical to sit next to the printer stuffing single sheets into the platen for longer runs.

To make such applications easier, many printers can use continuous forms. These are sheets of paper joined together in one continuous zigzag a thousand or so sheets long. At a predetermined interval, usually 11 or 14 inches, there is a perforation running across the width of the page to allow you to separate individual standard-sized sheets.

An extra ¼ inch of perforated paper is added to each edge, along the entire length, with small holes spaced about ½ inch apart. These holes are grabbed by spikes on a device called a tractor, which pulls the paper through the printer very precisely. Once you're finished printing, you tear the strips off the pages and are left with more or less ordinary 8½-by-11- or 11-by-14-inch sheets.

Unfortunately, the edges usually look ragged where the perforations were. If this ragged edge bothers you, you can buy "microperf" paper, which has finer and tinier perforations, or "tipped-on bond" paper, which lightly glues a sheet of normal stationery to a carrier sheet with tractor holes in the sides. In either case, when you are done printing and tear the microperf paper along its tiny perforations, or peel the tipped-on bond from its carrier sheets, the output is free from that ragged-edged "computer" look. If you're typing customized form letters, or anything else with a personal touch, ugly serrated perforations can create entirely the wrong effect. You can also have your business stationery or forms specially printed on microperf or tipped-on forms.

A dot-matrix printer with spikes on the platen to pull the paper through is said to have "pin-feed" capabilities. In most cases, this means that a primitive tractor is built into the printer. The majority of dot-matrix printers are built with such pin-feed mechanisms. Fancier printers often use a removable tractor mechanism that allows you to use single sheets as well as tractor-feed forms. A good dot-matrix printer should be able to handle both single sheets and continuous forms.

Letter-quality printers, on the other hand, must have a provision for accommodating single sheets, since they're used extensively for typing on custom-printed stationery and business letterheads. Tractors are usually offered as accessories, and clip on top of the printer almost as an afterthought. A simple letter-quality printer tractor can often cost hundreds of dollars.

Businesses with heavy demands for customized letters would probably want to investigate cut-sheet feeders, special mechanized hoppers that can insert various-sized stationery (and even envelopes) into the printer without any fuss. Trying to do this yourself manually can be an exercise in futility, as you have to keep precise pace with the speedy printer and feed the paper in exactly the right spot at exactly the right time. Cut-sheet feeders can do this all automatically, without missing a beat. However, they tend to be expensive, and reliability can be a problem.

The real advantage of forms handling is that you can theoretically use your word processor to create a large batch of correspondence, and then print it all out at once without having to baby-sit your printer. Unfortunately, it doesn't always work that smoothly. If your equipment is sturdy and well maintained and you check to make sure the ribbon is not almost gone and there is enough blank paper ready to roll into the printer, you may be able to set the system up, turn it all on, walk away, and come back to see a tall stack of finished work. But if something goes awry, the entire batch can be ruined. It's not difficult, for instance, to miss a closing underline symbol and return to see the entire job underlined rather than just the word you wanted to emphasize. If the form's length on one page somehow comes out wrong, every page that follows may start in the middle and continue printing over the perforation. But when the system is functioning properly, it's a real workhorse and can save you untold hours of routine labor.

When Silence Is Golden—Thermal and Ink-Jet Printers

While impact printers all have one characteristic in common—their strident noise—thermal printers are exceptionally quiet. The mechanism that drives them is similar to that of a dot-matrix printer. Thermal-printer characters are made up of rows and columns of little dots. But these printers don't have to bang wires up noisily against a ribbon. Instead, characters are "printed" on paper that is coated with a heat-sensitive film by momentarily heating patterns of wires in the thermal print head. As the heat is transferred, the special paper reacts by changing color. Different characters and symbols can be created depending on which of the tiny heating elements in the print head are activated.

There are major drawbacks to thermal printers. You have to use spe-

The Apple Scribe printer.

cially treated paper. It has a slick feel to it that most people seem to hate. It has a chemical-covered surface that can rub off and even smell awful. Since it usually comes in rolls, it tends to curl up. It often has a gray or off-color background rather than the pristine white most folks favor. The print quality just isn't very good and will fade with time.

Announced but unavailable at press time, the Apple Scribe printer will use thermal-printing technology to print on plain paper in black or in colors. According to reports, the print head actually melts paraffin-based ink to deposit it on paper. Though unproven thus far, this new technology may well turn out to be a breakthrough in low-cost printing.

Ink-jet printers are equally quiet. However, right now the ink-jet technology is not well suited to text work, unless you really want to invest a bundle for a top-of-the-line model. For graphics work they are exceptional, and with few moving parts, they should last quite a long time with limited maintenance. Manufacturers are also beginning to introduce color ink-jet printers. As the technology improves and the price comes down, these may surge in popularity. But the problem of clogging has not been entirely solved. If you go for long periods of time without using an ink-jet printer, the ink in the nozzle can dry and harden. As with everything else, you can and should take maintenance steps to prevent this.

Unfortunately, most ink-jet printers currently require the addition of an internal printer card, an impossibility for the current Apple //c. Whether or not they can be used with the Apple //c will depend, mainly, on how programmers handle the graphic output and whether or not the special interpreting instructions found in the printer cards can be surmounted.

Laser Printers

These are by some accounts the best of both worlds, since they can produce crisp letter-quality printouts at dizzying speeds and absolutely gorgeous graphics. A laser output scans across a metallic drum, and then a process similar to Xeroxing does the rest. Lasers can be controlled extraordinarily precisely, and, since their output is so strong, with incredible speed. The software that drives the control mechanism can contain literally hundreds of typefaces and variations on each of them, for maximum flexibility. And they are whisper silent.

Laser printers are also extremely expensive. They start at around $5,000 and climb very rapidly thereafter. Yet, several companies like Canon have introduced speedy, powerful, relatively inexpensive laser printers at recent trade shows, and it is possible that there may be a laser printer in your future. Not the immediate future, though.

Technical Details

Most, if not all, of the programs you'll be using on the Apple //c will control the printer output for you. You really won't need to know anything about how these applications handle your printer. If you want to use it on your own, however, there are quite a few things you should understand.

Since the Apple //c printer output is serial rather than parallel, the computer thinks of the printer as a sort of communications device. Before even one bit of data is sent, you have to insure that certain communications "parameters" are properly set. This is because communications from one device to another can be sent at a wide variety of speeds and in a wide range of configurations.

The first of these settings is the *baud* rate, or speed of the data transmission. The *word length*—whether your characters are being sent to the printer as combinations of seven bits or eight bits—is also critical. The eighth bit isn't generally used except for graphics. You also have to specify the number of stop bits, which tell the printer when it's reached the end of each character. If your printer and computer are connected, but even one of these settings doesn't match, you'll end up with totally garbled output, or none at all.

Printers usually come from the factory with preset "default" settings for these parameters but allow you to change them to match precisely with your computer's output. Of course, it's easiest to hook things together properly when your computer lets you change the options as well. The Apple //c is one computer that does.

For printing, the Apple //c uses serial port 1. When you turn the machine on, the values for baud, word length, parity, and stop bits (as well as a few other things that you'll see in a moment) are preset.

Apple //c Printer Serial Default Parameters

Baud:	9600
Word length:	8 Bits
Parity:	None
Stop Bits:	2
Width:	80 column
Echo:	Off
LF/CR:	Yes
Command Character:	*control-I*

Parity refers to a system that checks the accuracy of the characters sent and received. Remember that all the computer sends to the printer is a long stream of *0*'s and *1*'s. If a computer checks parity, it counts the number of *1*'s in each word, and adds a *1* or a *0* at the end of the word to indicate whether that number was odd or even. If the device at the other end of the connection makes the same calculation and thinks the number of *1*'s is even when the computer says the number is odd (or vice versa), it knows there was an error in transmission. However, since the default is for no *parity check*, this isn't critical here.

A word here essentially means a character. *Width* indicates the width of the line the printer can handle. With the original Apples, this was 40 columns because the screen display was that wide. Now, as the world advances, this has changed.

Echo determines whether the printer output will be simultaneously sent to the screen. This setting is the way it was for the 40-column Apples.

Some printers can supply their own *linefeed* (a command that advances the paper up one line) when they receive a carriage return from the computer or program. Others can't. Using the *LF/CR* parameter, you can have the linefeed supplied by the Apple //c if your printer cannot.

These, by the way, are the same settings used by the Apple Imagewriter, so you don't have to change anything to make the computer work with it. But what happens if you have another printer, and its settings are different? Simple—you change them.

The *command character* is the key to initiating any of the changes. Though it may sound complicated, it's easy. First use:

```
PR#1
```

(All of this and everything that follows assumes that you placed the *caps lock* key on.) This opens port 1, the port you want to work with. Next press *control-I*. (First press and hold the *control* key, and then press the *I* key.) Release them—and don't press anything else yet.

Command Parameters

You now have your choice of what you want to change, and it will depend on what combination of numbers and/or letters you enter next. They're all listed in the following table, but before you look you should understand the setup. You'll see some symbols that look like letters, but aren't. These symbols will be either *n, nn,* or *nnn.* Where these occur, they actually stand for numbers. The quantity of *n*'s will be a limitation to the number of digits in the number it represents. For instance, *nn* can be a two-digit number, while *n* would have only one digit, and *nnn* could have a maximum of three digits.

You may also see uppercase letters, either alone or in combination with the *nnn*'s. The legend *nnB* would mean you'd enter a two-digit number followed immediately by the uppercase letter *B*. Likewise *nD* would require a single digit entry followed immediately by the letter *D* (again, in uppercase).

Remember—don't forget the *control-I*!

Apple //c Printer Serial Parameters

control-I and	Maximum numeric values	Alteration to the printer port
nnnN or nnn	1-255	Set new line width. If used with the trailing N, output is *not* echoed to the screen. If the N is omitted and a carriage return is used to end the command sequence, the echo status remains the same.
nnB		Set baud rate according to following table:

nn	Baud Rate	nn	Baud Rate
1	50	5	150
2	75	6	300
3	110	7	600
4	135	8	1200

(continued)

control-I and	Maximum numeric values	Alteration to the printer port

nn	Baud Rate	nn	Baud Rate
9	1800	13	7200
10	2400	14	9600
11	3600	15	19200
12	4800		

nD		Set the word length and stop bits according to the following:

n	Word Length	Stop Bits
0	8	1
1	7	1
2	6	1
3	5	1
4	8	2
5	7	2
6	6	2
7	5	2

I		Echo printer output to screen.
K		Disable automatic linefeed after carriage return.
L		Generate linefeed after carriage return.
nP		Set parity according to the following:

n	Parity	n	Parity
0	None	4	None
1	Odd	5	Mark (or parity 1)
2	None	6	None
3	Even	7	Space (or parity 0)

R		Reset printer port to default values and exit.

(continued)

control-I and	Maximum numeric values	Alteration to the printer port
S		Send a 233-millisecond BREAK character (used by some printers to synchronize with the serial port).
Z		Ignore (ZAP) further commands until a *control-reset* or PR#1 has been performed.

As an example, if you wanted to set up the printer port for 1200 baud output, with a seven-bit word length, two stop bits, and no parity, you'd use the following command sequence (we're using ^I to represent the two-key combination of *control* and *I*; when you enter the command, remember to use the actual two-key combination):

```
PR#1
^I8B^I5D^I0P
PR#0
```

You can exit the printer port at that point, as was done here with PR#0, or you can send information to be printed to it. If you exit, you do *not* reset the parameters you've changed. They remain as they were (whether you've actually changed them or just used the default values) until they are changed or the machine is reset. Remember that from Applesoft (that is, from within a program), you *must* prefix the PR# command with CHR$(4).

In the example, ^I8B selected the eighth value from the baud rate table, which is 1200 baud. ^I5D selected a seven-bit word with two stop bits (the values opposite 5 in the word length–stop bit table) and ^I0P chose none, or no parity, from the parity table (an *n* value of 0, 2, 4, or 6 could have been used—they all select no parity).

These commands could have been on separate lines, if that makes you more comfortable, or, as shown here, all on the same line. In either case, the selection of each parameter must be preceded by a ^I.

The choice of ^I as a symbol to represent the two-key combination *control-I* was not made arbitrarily. It's a common computer convention to represent a control character with a caret (^) followed by the letter you want to use. It's shorthand, and saves some space.

14

Hooking Up with the World: Modems

Many experienced computer users' modems and microcomputers have almost become substitutes for normal telephones. You can use your computer to communicate with other users, order merchandise, leave messages for friends who are asleep or away on business, send documents across the country, have your hardware problems solved for free by experts, fill up disk after disk with free software, or even phone in your work rather than commute each day on the freeway or subway.

That's really not as farfetched as it sounds. There are many resources available to computer owners who can invest in a few hundred dollars' worth of equipment. In this chapter we'll examine several services that some computer users say they can't live without.

Bulletin Boards for Machines

Several years ago, a clever computer user who felt it was wasteful to have his system sit idle while he slept and worked wrote a software package that let others call his computer and leave messages on it when he wasn't using it. The computer essentially became a bulletin board. In recent years these computer bulletin boards (CBBS) have proliferated, and there are thousands of them spread all over the nation. They've recently begun to specialize—there are computer bulletin boards for beginners, hackers, doctors, single people, and more special-interest groups—plus dozens for each specific machine on the market.

Several very large companies entered the field, and for a fee, now offer many of the services users can get at no charge from the many national amateur bulletin boards. These giant companies, led by The Source and CompuServe, also offer news, games, stock prices, certain kinds of airline reservations, and a handful of other services they think people can't live without, all for a stiff hourly fee. The one real advantage to these big national networks is that users with wildly different systems can communicate with each other. Someone with an Apple //c can find himself or herself chatting with a computer whiz typing away on a giant mainframe computer halfway across the country.

Even more potentially exciting are the many databases springing up. These can give you the resources of a vast electronic library at your fingertips. You can avoid the lines at the local library and look up facts on everything from obscure legal cases to tropical diseases to who starred in old movies.

At some point in the not too distant future, services such as these may even replace libraries (or at least the libraries will be available to your computer). If you'd like a more comprehensive look at what's out there, you might want to try *Getting On-line: A Guide to Accessing Computer Information Services* by M. David Stone (Prentice-Hall, 1984). It's packed with information on which systems are available and the features each one offers, and is certainly a cheaper alternative than trying each one.

But you can't do any of that unless you have the correct equipment. Right now you're halfway home: you have the Apple //c. The only other thing you need is a modem and cable for it.

What's Out There

Modems, like printers, come in a variety of types. Some work without phone lines and are used to connect one computer directly to another over short distances of 100 feet or so. The ones you'll probably be interested in, however, do use the phone lines to communicate with other computers. There are two basic types: acoustic and direct connect.

You don't have to know too much about how modems work to use them. All they really do is translate (or modulate) the *digital* (*1*'s and *0*'s) signal coming out of your computer into an *analog* signal that can travel freely over phone lines, and then reverse the process at the other end of the connection, demodulating the analog signal back into a digital stream of binary bits the other computer can understand.

Two manufacturers, Hayes and Novation, currently lead the modem field. But Apple and others are aggressively marketing their own modems. The first two companies make plug-in card versions for the Apple // series, but since you don't have any usable slots, these won't do much for an Apple //c.

Hayes and Novation, as well as many other modem manufacturers, sell "outboard" modems, external devices that connect through the Apple //c's serial port 2. You can use both acoustic and direct-connect outboard modems.

Acoustic Modems

An acoustic modem is usually a flat rectangle with a rubber cup at either end. The handset of the phone fits into this "cradle" and the rubber cups form an acoustic seal. Outgoing signals from the modem enter the mouthpiece of the phone. Incoming tones exit the earpiece and enter the modem. It plugs into a serial port.

One problem with these is that phones do not always fit into the acoustic cups. When telephones were all one style, this was not a problem. But it's impossible to use some of the new, odd-shaped telephones with the acoustic couplings provided. Besides, the rubber cups do not always do a very good job of sealing out extraneous noise. If odd sounds leak through the seal, the signals being sent down the line can easily become garbled, especially in a noisy environment.

Direct-Connect Modems

The preferred configuration is clearly the direct-connect modem. These plug into your computer's serial port and connect directly into the phone system via a modular plug, just as modern phones do. This type of modem is far more popular than the acoustic type, and has the lion's share of the market. Once you make all the initial hookups, you can forget that all the equipment is there. Modern direct-connect modems are "smart," which means they're programmed to do all the work for you. They can dial, redial, switch parameters, even answer the phone for you, all automatically.

The only major drawback with direct-connect modems is that you have to find a modular jack in order to use them. That's easy enough at home, but in an office with multiline phones, special adapters may be needed. Moreover, in a hotel or motel on the road, the phone jack may be behind the wall to discourage souvenir hunters. If you expect to use the computer in many different places, an acoustic modem may be better for your system.

Keeping Things Straight

Like all serial devices, modems need to have their communications parameters set properly. (It is especially critical when two computers are talking to each other via modem that every communications parameter at both ends be precisely matched.) Conventional phone lines were designed for normal voice transmission and not high-speed data, and therefore modem data rates are slower than those of serial printers. Modems generally operate at either 300 or 1200 baud. The speed at which they communicate depends on the speed setting at the other end of the connection. If the computer you are talking to operates at 300 baud, then yours must also. Some modems, like the Hayes Smartmodem 1200, can work at either speed.

In the beginning, modems could originate or answer transmissions, but only the most expensive could do both. Which one you had depended on whether you were originating the call to transfer information or were receiving it. Now, such problems of distinguishing between answering and originating are all handled automatically by the modem. In fact, current modems contain nearly as much intelligence as many small computers once did.

Features

What should you look for in a modem? Obviously, the best ones are direct-connect models. It is best if the modem can automatically dial and *answer* the phone for you. It's also handy if it can operate at either 300 or 1200 baud—and it should know enough to switch between speeds automatically, depending on the speed coming from the computer at the other end of the line.

If it sounds as though your choices are limited, you're wrong. Hayes markets the Smartmodem 300, which does a great deal, but at 300 baud only. The Smartmodem 1200 is a sound choice if you want dual speeds (you may not now, but you will eventually; 300 baud is molasses-slow and likely to go the way of the dodo sooner or later); it's probably the most popular modem in use today. Apple's two modem offerings also give you everything you'll need for effortless communication. Other modems that have some or all of these features are sold by Novation, US Robotics, Universal Data Systems, Racal-Vadic, and even NEC.

The Apple modem.

300 and 1200/300 baud models are available.

Modems can cost anywhere from $200 for the 300-baud variety to over $800 for the higher-level kind. Buying from a reputable company is always a good idea, and the ones just mentioned (plus others not mentioned) certainly fit the bill. Some manufacturers are rumored to be exceptionally friendly; Hayes is famous for bending over backward to help users. Novation and others are starting to offer a few slightly more sophisticated features, more "smarts" for their smart modems.

There's one ultra-important modem accessory you should know about if you have a direct-connect modem. Since the modem plugs into the jack where your phone goes, you may get awfully tired of playing plug-and-unplug every time you want to use the phone instead of your computer. Besides, if you forget to plug the phone back in, human voices are going to have a very hard time trying to reach out and touch you.

The solution to this problem is a simple device called a modular telephone jack Y-adapter. It plugs right into the jack and turns one jack into two. You can then connect both telephone and modem and never have to look at the jack again. You can find a Y-adapter at almost any Radio Shack store.

If you have "call-waiting," watch out. The signal that lets you know you have a second incoming call will often disconnect modem communications. If you do a lot of work with the modem, you may want to get rid of "call-waiting" on the line you use for telecommunications.

Once you've selected the modem, you have to hook it up to your Apple //c and find good software to make running it easy. The many communications programs available will handle all of the details for you, and we'll cover some a bit later. As with printers, you can configure them to do just about anything yourself. The Apple //c is capable, without program assistance, of becoming a dumb terminal—a keyboard-and-screen combination that can communicate with other computers in the simplest ways. All you have to know is how to adjust it.

Rushing into the Breach

In some cases, all you have to do to use a modem is to connect it to the Apple //c, turn everything on, and start doing whatever it was you wanted to do. When you turn on the Apple //c, the modem port is ready to use a whole set of default values for the parameters it needs to begin operating. The default values are as listed.

Each device, whether it's a modem or another microcomputer, will come with its own set of specifications for the various communications parameters it uses. For your purposes, the Apple //c specifications are all you should really be concerned with.

The Apple //c modem port is not much different from the printer port; they are both designed for serial communications with an external device. In fact, the printer and modem ports can be switched if you want to do so.

Apple //c Modem Serial Default Parameters

Baud:	300
Word Length:	8 Bits
Parity:	None
Stop Bits:	1
Echo:	Off
CR:	No
LF/CR:	No
Command Character:	*control-A*

But if you've left the ports the way Apple configured them, you access the modem port with the IN#2 (not PR#2—IN# is used for two-way communications) command.

Most receiving devices do not require the sending device (in this case, your computer) to generate a carriage return or linefeed. As the text they're receiving reaches the leftmost position on the screen, they supply their own.

You'll also notice that the control character used by port 2 is ^A (*control-A*). This differs from the control character used by the printer port. The entire slate of modem commands is listed here. As before, remember that all of the commands are first preceded by IN#2 to open the port and that immediately before each command you must use ^A.

Apple //c Modem Serial Parameters

***control-A* and**	**Maximum numeric values**	**Alteration to the modem port**
nnnN or nnn	1-255	Set new line width. If used with the trailing N, output is *not* echoed to the screen. If the N is omitted and a carriage return is used to end the command sequence, the echo status remains the same.

(continued)

control-A and	Maximum numeric values	Alteration to the modem port
nnB		Set baud rate according to following table:

nn	Baud Rate	nn	Baud Rate
1	50	9	1800
2	75	10	2400
3	110	11	3600
4	135	12	4800
5	150	13	7200
6	300	14	9600
7	600	15	19200
8	1200		

nD		Set the word length and stop bits according to the following:

n	Word Length	Stop Bits
0	8	1
1	7	1
2	6	1
3	5	1
4	8	2
5	7	2
6	6	2
7	5	2

I		Echo output to screen.
K		Disable automatic linefeed after carriage return.
L		Generate linefeed after carriage return.
nP		Set parity according to the following:

n	Parity	n	Parity
0	None	4	None
1	Odd	5	Mark (or parity 1)
2	None	6	None
3	Even	7	Space (or parity 0)

Q		Quit terminal mode.

(continued)

control-A and	Maximum numeric values	Alteration to the modem port
R		Reset modem port to default values and exit.
S		Send a 233-millisecond BREAK character (used by some modems in special situations).
T		Enter terminal mode.
Z		Ignore (ZAP) further commands until a *control-reset* or PR#1 has been performed.

The command sequences to set the various parameters follow the same formats you used in setting up the printer port, except that in this case they are preceded by ^A. When the Apple //c receives a ^A, you'll see a question mark on the screen, indicating that the computer is waiting for the command sequence it expects to follow.

When you first activate the modem port, nothing that you type and nothing that it receives is sent to the screen. Initially, echo is set to off. If you follow the IN#2 command with PR#1, all of the input, and everything you type, will wind up on the printer.

At some of the higher transmission speeds, sending characters out to the printer *and* trying to print them on the screen at the same time just won't work; everything will begin to go crazy. It's good practice, therefore, to leave the echo off if using 1200 baud and routing the output to a printer.

The Duplex Question and Echo

There are two additional modes to discuss, half- and full-duplex modes. As they refer to the Apple //c, they're very important.

When you "talk" with another computer, it may or may not send back a copy of the characters you send to it. Usually, if you're talking to another personal computer, it won't. If, on the other hand, you're communicating with a large computer service, it will. With echo off and the other side in half-duplex operation, you won't see anything on the screen.

When one of the computers does send back the characters it receives, it is in the full-duplex mode. When it doesn't, it's using half duplex. Only one end of the conversation should be in full duplex; otherwise, the first time a character is sent it will be transmitted back and forth endlessly.

If you are in full duplex, don't use echo. If you do, you'll see everything twice, once when you type it and once when the other side sends it back to you. Conversely, if you're in half-duplex mode, do use it. Most personal computer conversations occur with both sides in half duplex.

If you enter terminal mode and follow the ^AT sequence with PR#2, you can try the various combinations of full-duplex transmission. Remember that *control-reset* will bail you out of any difficulty.

While this may seem complicated, remember that the combination of powerful software and smart modems will do most of the hard work for you automatically. The trick is setting up everything properly the first time—and being able to handle strange situations when someone is trying to send you data using parameters you're not familiar with.

In chapter 18 you'll meet two of the many terminal packages that take full control of the serial port. They give you all of the amenities you need, usually complete with a full menu that allows you to select what parameters you want to use. Which is the way it should be.

15

The Care and Feeding of the Apple //c

Since the Apple //c is a portable computer, it is specially constructed to withstand a bit more wear and tear than computers that were designed to perch forever on the top of a desk. Features such as the volume control are carefully recessed into the side. The keytops are flush with the top surface of the chassis to avoid any chance of shearing off in transit. The handle and case are constructed of sturdy high-impact plastic, and all the parts are precisely fitted together into a solid, compact unit.

The internal circuitry is also lean and tough. Apple has gone to great pains to cram as much as possible onto as few chips as possible. The only really delicate device, the disk drive, is protectively placed in the thickest part of the unit and is such an intrinsic part of the chassis that all you can really see is the slot for the disk and the drive door.

While Apple does recommend that you place the machine inside a carrying case for very long trips, it clearly designed the //c to be moved from room to room, home to office. It's a sophisticated and expensive piece of electronic equipment, and you should treat it with the care you'd lavish on any precision appliance. This means placing it in an attaché case or suitable padded covering when fighting the commuter crowds, and avoiding thundershowers. But you don't have to baby it. It has a bit of extra padding where it counts and was meant to take a certain amount of everyday abuse.

The Apple //c does not require much maintenance, and in fact, there's not much you can do other than keep it clean and out of heavy traffic. But if you want to keep it in tiptop shape, you can observe certain guidelines and practices to increase its life span, which will keep it happy and working and looking like new for a very long time.

There's little doubt that giving a computer the specialized care it requires, and even going beyond what is merely necessary, will prolong the life of your sophisticated and expensive electronic investment. The key words in the common jargon of computerdom are "preventive maintenance."

The minimum you can do is the absolute minimum, nothing. Factory recommendations are minimal because the microelectronics of the Apple //c (or any computer, for that matter) require no mechanical care or maintenance. There are virtually no moving parts to wear out.

Rather than slowly grinding down, modern solid-state electronics fail catastrophically. One moment they work, and the next moment nothing is left except your frustration. No matter what you do, there is a chance your Apple //c—or any computer—might suffer a catastrophic failure.

Fortunately, for the space program and any other critical application that relies on microelectronics, such catastrophic failures are rare. After marginal components have been weeded out of any modern electronic device, you shouldn't expect a disaster more often than once in tens of thousands of hours of operation or years of normal use.

Burning It In

The first preventive thing to do is to try to prevent your Apple from failing *after* its warranty runs out. Rather than trying to extend its life by keeping your use of it to the minimum, push your Apple //c to its limits.

The "weeding out" of marginal components in any solid-state device occurs during the first few hours of operation. If your Apple //c works after you first turn it on and perks happily along for the first few days, barring an outside cataclysm, your computer should cogitate for years without you lifting a finger except to massage the keyboard.

The logical thing to do when you become the owner of a brand-new Apple //c is to pull the fledgling computer from its box, turn it on, and leave it on for the next day or two. You can use the added "burn-in" time for familiarization, learning the new language the Apple speaks, playing your favorite game, or just allowing the fledgling computer to perk along on its own.

Once the computer has proven itself, you can take added precautions that go beyond the factory's recommendations, to assure yourself that your Apple //c will remain in perfect shape.

A Happy Home

The mandatory care the Apple //c requires is, in fact, nothing. But the Apple //c is not entirely trouble-free. Although it requires no maintenance, it also requires that you do not abuse it. That means that you must give it a happy home in the type of atmosphere it likes, and take care of its particular needs.

In fact, the Apple //c does have some moving parts and delicate electrical contacts—in its keyboard. The keyboard's big enemies are mostly airborne—dust and extreme humidity—but the keys (and the contacts below) can also be tainted and trapped by more worldly problems, from grease to peanut butter and runaway coffee spills.

The Apple //c's computer circuitry is likely to suffer ill effects from its environment, too. The climate can be either too hot or too cold or too dry for it, or the machine can suffer when odd things happen to the power lines in your town.

The best advice in trying to give the Apple //c a happy home is to be reasonable. You wouldn't put your clock radio in a sandbox or swimming pool. Don't use your computer there, either.

Maybe your thoughts aren't that absurd, but you might be considering a computer room in your dank basement or in your hot attic. Even though the computer doesn't complain about its surroundings, it still is a bit particular about them. Its internal circuitry is designed to work within a wide temperature range. Apple specifies that it was designed to work in an environment somewhere between 50° and 104° F (10° to 40° C), where the relative humidity is anywhere from 20% to 90%. This means you can use it practically anywhere.

Rather than treating the Apple //c as a mindless machine, pretend that it is a sensitive and good friend. Computers are generally happy to operate under any conditions of both temperature and humidity that humans would be happy with. That does not mean that a computer needs the same perfect temperature that you might demand for absolute comfort. Rather, the best preventive measure is to avoid putting your computer in a hostile environment.

You should give your Apple //c the same consideration that you would give to an expensive machine or to valuable papers and documents. Just as a sugar-laden cup of coffee would be disastrous if spilled on the deed to your home or poured into your stereo receiver, the Apple //c would likely succumb to such a drenching.

In other words, the table on which you set up your computer should be reserved for the computer alone. Keep your breakfast of overbrimming Coca-Cola and chocolate-covered doughnuts away unless the equipment is covered by flood insurance.

All liquids should be kept away from the Apple //c because its keyboard is relatively unsophisticated and has contacts that can be easily gummed up by sugar pollution. These contacts can be ruined in other ways. In highly humid environments, for instance, contact corrosion will be accelerated.

Power-Line Problems

Although the electric line that your Apple //c plugs into is its life blood, it's also your computer's worst enemy. Not that electricity is bad for the computer. In theory, a solid-state computer won't electrically wear out no matter how long you leave it plugged in. But the current supplied by your favorite electric utility is far from the purity that would grant endless life.

Supplied free of charge (and free from recourse) along with the nominal 110–120 volt, 60 hertz (cycles per second) alternating current delivered to your fuse box is a collection of spikes, surges, pulses, glitches, noise, and absences of very brief and prolonged durations. Your computer expects a certain norm, and any deviation is potentially life-threatening to your computer or its data.

Glitches and spikes are real trouble for most computers. Both terms describe essentially the same phenomenon: a temporary pulse of abnormally high voltage on the power line. "Temporary" can mean anywhere from a few millionths of a second to nearly a second long. Abnormally high voltage can range from just a couple of volts above what you are supposed to get to 10,000 volts and higher. Because of the brief durations of spikes and power-line glitches, they are invisible. They won't cause the slightest flicker to your lights, and only specialized equipment can determine whether or not they are present on your power line.

Spikes and glitches can be caused by anything from lightning striking near a power line to brief pulses of power added to the electric line when large motors (in all kinds of appliances from refrigerators to air conditioners and industrial equipment) switch on and off. One large spike can be enough to damage the microcircuits in your Apple //c permanently.

Some studies have shown that the effects of spikes can be cumulative, like getting small doses of poison over weeks and months. Each spike can slightly damage the tiny internal structure of the Apple //c's microcircuits. When enough damage has been done, maybe over a year or more, the computer may mysteriously stop working, or just work erratically, refusing to execute simple functions or giving strange answers to obvious questions.

The best way to protect your Apple //c from power-line spikes and glitches is with a surge suppressor. Many brands and styles of suppressors are available from a large number of manufacturers.

Although operating principles vary, the most common of these devices use a novel electronic device called a "varistor" that effectively swallows up most spikes and glitches and prevents them from getting to your computer. One suppressor can be used to protect your Apple //c and all its peripherals.

Closely related to spikes and glitches are true "surges" and overvoltages, which are power-line voltages higher and longer lasting than normal—with less change in voltage: a dozen or two volts rather than hundreds and thousands. Surges are long enough that you might be able to see the lights in your home flicker or become momentarily brighter.

The low voltage rise of surges means that most inexpensive spike or "surge" protectors actually do little good in eliminating them. Only the best and most expensive "ferroresonant" types of surge suppressors or voltage regulators offer genuine protection.

Fortunately, in most cases such protection is genuine overkill. Practical experience indicates that the Apple //c is probably impervious to many minor surges, and complete protection is likely to cost more than the computer itself.

Power problems in the other direction, low voltage or none at all, are unlikely to harm your Apple //c itself, but likely to wreak havoc with the data and programs in the computer's RAM memory. When voltage dips low enough for a long enough time (and "long enough" is not long at all), the power-line condition is equivalent to turning the computer completely off. That means everything in its RAM memory is wiped out, and when power again reaches the more normal level the turn-on cycle will begin afresh.

The worst damage will be suffered by your patience as you must reload whatever was in RAM, wasting seconds (if you had been using a program safely stored on disk) to hours (if you were developing a lengthy program that you had laborously entered keystroke by keystroke and not bothered to SAVE).

The anguish caused by voltage drops can be prevented by using a voltage regulator, which automatically adjusts the power supplied to your computer to the optimum level. Your computer's memory can be kept fresh through complete power outages by using an uninterruptible power supply (UPS), a device which has a built-in set of batteries and the necessary electronic circuitry to convert their output to normal line current so that its output is constant no matter what happens to the electric supply from your power company.

Even the least expensive regulators and uninterruptible supplies are likely to cost at least half as much as the Apple //c itself. Your frustration and the prevention thereof must be worth a great deal if you are to justify the protection such devices afford. The best solution is to SAVE your work early and often, and keep backup copies of everything you do.

Static Protection

The other electrical enemy of any computer is static electricity—the blue sparks you feel at your fingertips after shuffling across the carpet and touching a doorknob on a dry winter's day. Static electricity is genuine electricity, as the tingle at your fingertips tells you. The voltage generated by a short walk can be tens of thousands of volts. This can be especially troublesome with a computer that you carry around, and shuffle over rugs with.

There is little current behind this voltage, so static shocks are mostly only annoying and rarely fatal—except to computer circuitry. To delicate microcircuits, a static spark can be more deadly than a spike on the power line. The tiny sparks of static can be enough to blast a silicon microchip to data heaven and run the repair bill into hundreds of dollars.

The only protection from static is prevention. If you don't make sparks, they won't hurt anything. Dozens of products are available to help keep static under control—special carpets, chairs, mats, and sprays. There's little doubt that they work. However, although some form of static control may be necessary in the business computer room where one byte of data may mean a million dollars, expensive static protection may be unnecessary in your home.

The Apple //c itself does a good job of warding off static sparks. Sparks usually jump from finger to metal—that is, from your body (which can store a great deal of static electricity) to a conductor (which can drain that electricity off quite quickly). Touching the Apple //c's insulating plastic case doesn't drain off the static charge fast enough to generate a damaging electrical spark.

The best static preventive is inexpensive and good for you. It's worth doing even if you don't care about your computer's health. Static electricity can only build up in your body (or anywhere) when the relative humidity is low enough that the moisture in the air does not slowly drain off the static charge as fast as it is created. Raising the relative humidity of your home to 30% or higher through the use of a humidifier will effectively prevent static shocks to you and your computer. In fact, according to some people, a higher wintertime humidity will help prevent colds and make you feel more comfortable at lower temperatures.

Disk Care

As with the Apple //c itself, the worst enemies of its magnetic storage media are invisible. Certainly disks are vulnerable to the same enemies that plague your important documents and even your furniture—the spilled coffee, the dropped cigarettes, the teething pooch. But compared to the records kept in their paper counterparts, magnetic media require extra thought and care in both use and storage.

The disks used by the Apple //c need the same special treatment that all computer floppy disks demand. You've probably seen many of the warnings a dozen places already. Keep diskettes away from magnets such as those created by hi-fi speakers, power transformers, electric motors, and the bell in your telephone. The errant magnetic fields from such devices can alter or erase irreplaceable stored data.

Take care always to keep diskettes inside their protective sleeves when they're not in the disk drives. That way dust, airborne contaminants, grease, and grime won't pollute the sensitive magnetic surfaces.

When handling a floppy disk, guard particularly against touching its magnetic surface where it shows through the slots in its black plastic case. Tiny drops of oil in a fingerprint can be enough to mess up a disk and gum up the works of a disk drive.

Cigarettes pose a particular danger as they can have lethal effects on computers. Errant ashes have a devious way of collecting on high-precision parts, which include disk drives and even the diskettes themselves. A speck of ash or even a single particle of tar from a cloud of cigarette smoke can be enough to foul some disk units. In an amazingly short time, the airborne tar from cigarette smoke can slowly coat the mechanical parts and bring your Apple //c to a halt. Suggestion: don't smoke near your new computer.

Disk Drives

Although there is no standard recommended care for disk drives beyond proper protection, their trouble-free operation can be safeguarded by regular care and preventive maintenance.

Don't go bananas with the drive doors. Don't snap them up or punch them down. You wouldn't slam your car door shut day in and day out without expecting it to break: disk drives are a lot more fragile.

Disk drives work exactly like other magnetic recording machines and use "heads" to actually record and play back (write and read, in computerese) their signals to and from the disks. Just as with stereo tape recorders, disk-drive heads can get dirty, causing damage to the signals they read and write.

With full-height drives, a cotton swab and some alcohol were useful for cleaning. You could insert them into the drive and get at the head. It's not recommended with the Apple //c; the drive opening is too small.

Several companies manufacture head-cleaning kits. The easiest to use are the ones that come with diskettes that contain absorbent fabric material instead of a recording medium. You simply apply a cleaning solution to the disk, insert the disk, and give the drive a command that sends the head looking for data. As the moistened fabric spins, it cleans the head.

It's every bit as simple as it sounds, as long as you remember two cautionary points. First, your Apple //c uses single-sided disk drives. When the collet comes down to hold the disk in place on the hub, a load button pushes down on the slot in the disk and presses lightly against it to make sure the surface is held flat against the head. Remember: the Apple read/write head uses the *underside* of the disk. When using disk-type cleaning kits, *do not* apply solution to the top of the fabric disk. That can pollute the load button and cause its premature failure.

Don't go ape over cleaning the drive. Most of the drive-cleaning kits are slightly abrasive. Each time you use it, you scrape away a little of the head. If you find yourself plagued by the need to clean your heads every two weeks, your own head may be what needs examining. Even under severe conditions, one cleaning a month would probably be more than enough. If you're starting to run into disk problems, of course, it's worth cleaning the heads to see if that clears up the problem. Otherwise cleaning the heads three or four times a year should be plenty.

Good Housekeeping

A clean computer is a happy computer. Dirt is the mortal enemy of any computer system. It cakes on print mechanisms and causes them to slow down and bind up, and slowly grinds away like sandpaper at delicate disk-drive parts.

If your printer and disk drive are so layered with dust that you need to hire an archeologist just to find them, you'll likely soon be searching out the warranty cards and inspecting the phone book for repair shops.

The best way to keep dust from becoming a problem is by developing a regular clean-up program for your Apple //c. As often as necessary (judged by running your finger over the equipment to see how much dust it collects), simply vacuum the danger away. Use the finest nozzle available to suck dirt from its surface, from between the keyboard keys, and from within the printer.

The dust that inevitably collects on your monitor or television screen can be removed with a soft cloth and ordinary window cleaner. Use paper towels and elbow grease as if the screen were just an ordinary piece of glass. Of course, if you feel wealthy and want to lavish extra care on your Apple //c, you can buy special "CRT" cleaners, but in the end the results will be about the same.

The same window cleaner is perfect for removing smudges and grime from the Apple //c computer/keyboard, disk drive, and printer cases. Take care, however, if you plan on using any spray-type window cleaners. Don't allow any overspray to find its way into *any* openings into the computer (including the disk-drive slot) or between the keys of your keyboard. Rather than spraying to remove smudges from the case or keys, dampen a soft cloth with window cleaner and gently wipe everything off.

For tougher dirt on the outer surfaces of your Apple //c, disk drive, printer, or monitor, almost any household cleaner may be used. The tough plastic cases are immune to most everyday cleaning solvents. Again, apply the cleaner to the cloth.

Be wary of using any strong solvents that frost, glaze, or melt plastics (like acetone or nail-polish remover) to remove really stubborn smudges. They can ruin the textured finishes of the outer plastic shell of the computer and peripherals and might even melt holes in them. If in doubt, dampen a cotton swab with the anticipated cleaning fluid and try the results on the back or bottom of the cabinets.

Your Apple //c is better off when it is protected from the dirt and dust around it. Not only will protecting a //c from grime keep it looking like new, but it will also help prevent potential mechanical problems.

The best protection against dust is a dust cover. Because other members of the Apple // family have proven to be so very popular, several types of dust covers are available commercially, both from dealers and by mail order. While you're at it, consider a dust cover for your printer, too.

As the Apple manuals point out, if you treat your //c with care and avoid physical abuse, you should have no problems whatsoever. However, it is possible to overheat your computer, especially since there are so many parts crammed into such a small space. The telltale sign is erratic performance—the memory devices inside are especially susceptible to heat buildup.

We've said it before, but we'll say it again: the Apple //c was designed so that when the handle is locked in its down position, air will flow through openings in the case and cool the electronics inside. Be very careful not to block any of the vents. This means you should never wedge the computer into a tight space where air can't circulate properly in and around the chassis. And although the case is solid, don't ever pile anything on top of your computer, even if you're tight for space.

Apple also cautions against letting your disks become too warm, and says it is possible that an overheated internal drive could warp—or even *melt*—the hapless disk inside. The same precautions apply here. Make sure there is ample ventilation, and don't use your computer in excessively hot or humid conditions for prolonged periods of time.

If you keep the machine cool and clean, you should enjoy near flawless performance for years to come. Apple has engineered a lot of computer into a small space, and its designers have used the company's years of experience to craft a durable, virtually maintenance-free, precision machine. With a little common sense and a dust cover, you and your Apple //c should do quite well together.

16

Troubleshooting: What to Do If the Apple Turns Rotten

Sometimes things just don't go right. No matter what key you press you get a ?SYNTAX ERROR, or your monitor picture shrinks to a tiny dot in the center of the screen, or you key in LOAD and discover the ten-thousand line program you finished at 3:00 A.M. yesterday morning is nowhere to be found.

Your first urge may be to get a hammer and gently coax your Apple //c back in line with your wishes. Often, however, a cooler head can prevail. Most of the problems that your //c suffers will be caused by minor slips of your fingers or forgotten routines, like following the correct turn-on sequence. Just retrace your steps, and you will probably find that a minor foul-up on your part led to a supposed major failure on the part of your computer.

If not, your second urge might be to cart your //c out to the repair shop for an intensive therapy session with a technician. Since you can tote the Apple //c around by its handle, that solution is even more attractive than it might be with a desktop model. But before you rush to your dealer with your //c in one hand and fistfuls of cash in the other, you might want to check some of the solutions in this chapter.

Is It Hardware or Software?

Sometimes your mistakes or omissions can be subtle, illogical, unreasonable, and obscure. Your first job is always to determine where the problem lies. Is it in the hardware or in the software? If you wrote the program that crashes your system, you're likely to be able to fix it. If you inserted a connector only halfway, it won't take a technician to push it in that extra quarter inch. But you have to know what's wrong in order to do something about it. Obviously, then, the first thing to do whenever you run into a problem with your computer is to determine whether it's a "hard" or "soft" error.

Whenever something seems to have gone wrong with your program, think about what you might have done wrong and try to retrace your steps. In many software programs, the *esc* key or some other key will get you out of trouble. But if nothing else seems to work, your first step should always be to try a *control-reset* interrupt. Often, you'll be back in control with no further ado. If that happens, you've probably run into a software problem. Breathe a sigh of relief; if the problem's in a program you've written, prepare to spend a while trying to find it.

Sometimes a program takes control and even ignores an interrupt. Next step: try a full three-key *reset*. It'll wipe out everything in your computer's memory, including all your data, but sometimes it's the only way out. If the computer starts up properly, you'll be back in business. Again, if the problem's in one of your own programs, LIST it and avoid RUNning it until you dope out the difficulty.

If all else fails, the radical test is to switch off your //c, wait about five seconds, and then turn it back on. You should see the Apple logo greeting and the usual start-up messages. If you don't, you may well have a hardware problem.

Just to be sure, try starting the computer with a different disk in the drive. Try using a different piece of software from the one that's giving you trouble. Disks go bad now and then, and occasionally software vendors accidentally ship test versions never intended to get into your machine. With early versions of some programs, it's possible to venture into dark, mysterious areas the designers never expected you to visit. It's possible that a chunk of bad data is what's giving your machine indigestion. If one program works and another doesn't, your computer is probably alive and well, and your software is ailing.

Hardware Problems

Computer equipment rarely breaks down. Most of the time, hardware "problems" turn out to be the result of something that anyone can fix: a switch in the wrong position, a cable that's worked loose. The only hard part is knowing exactly where to look for the problem.

To help you on your way to computer troubleshooting proficiency, the next few paragraphs will give you a quick run-through of some of the most common hardware-related problems you're likely to encounter.

Serious difficulties, though, are best solved by qualified people. If the most intense experience you've ever had with electronics is changing the

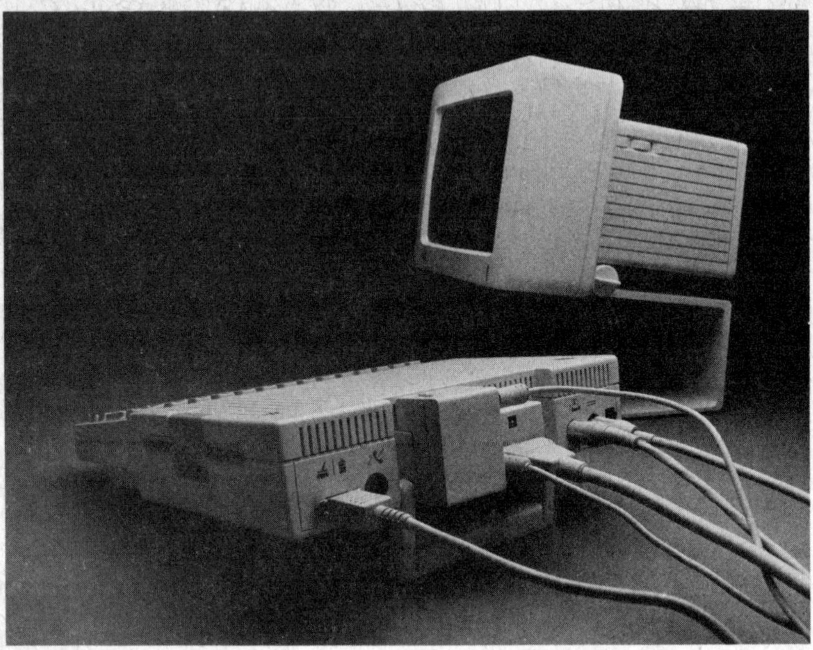

An almost well-connected Apple //c, or why things can go wrong.

The retaining screws of the joystick/mouse connector at left are not securely fastened to the computer; someday soon, the connector may fall out. There is no disk in the drive. The monitor at the rear is not turned on; even if it were, it's apparently not cabled to the computer and therefore unlikely to display anything. And the Apple //c's on/off switch is in the off position.

batteries in your Sony Walkman, trying to repair a computer is probably not the best place to get your education. And keep in mind that the Apple //c, unlike its predecessors, does not have a pop-top that offers easy access to its innards. Before you get deeply involved, check on the congeniality of your local service facility and the integrity of your warranty should you decide to remove the six screws on the bottom and open it up. In the time-worn phrase, there are no user serviceable parts inside the box.

BIG Problems

If the green power *light isn't on . . .*

- Is the computer turned on? If not, turn it on!
- Are the cables from the power supply to the wall *and* to the machine securely connected? If not, be sure to turn the machine *off* and make the connection at the computer side before plugging the cord into the outlet.

- Does the outlet have power? A circuit breaker or fuse may have blown, or a switch to the outlet or power strip may be turned off. Unplug the power supply and try a lamp or some other appliance in the suspect socket.
- Something is genuinely wrong. It's time for a trip to your service center.

If the green **power** *light is flashing . . .*

- Something's wrong with your power supply. Turn the machine off *immediately* and cart it and the power supply off to your local service center.

Display Problems

If you're using a **monitor** *and the screen doesn't light up, remains gray, or produces nothing but static . . .*

- Is the monitor turned on? If not, turn it on.
- Is the monitor plugged in? If not, plug it in.
- Is the outlet live? Check it and correct the problem.
- Is the computer on? If not, turn it on.
- Are the monitor's brightness and/or contrast controls turned up high enough? If not, locate them and turn them up.
- Are you using the proper connector from the Apple //c to the monitor? A composite monitor requires an RCA cable (but *not* hooked up to an RF converter); an RGB monitor requires a special adapter (check chapter 3 for more details).
- Are all monitor cables securely fastened at both ends? If you're using a composite monitor, jiggle the cable at both ends. If the picture flickers and you can glimpse part of an image, the cable may be defective. Replace it. If you're using an RGB monitor, *turn off the computer and the monitor* before making sure the cable is plugged in properly at both ends. If you don't, you may damage both computer and display device.
- Are the cables or adapters defective? Trouble can develop beneath the insulation. Try another if you have one.
- Is the computer's video output defective? Hook up the computer to your TV set and see if that works. If not, chances are the video circuitry of the //c is out of whack and a trip to the service center is in order.
- Is the monitor defective? Try it with another computer or have a technician check it.

If you're using a TV set and the screen doesn't light up, remains gray, or is filled with static . . .

- Is the TV turned on? If not, turn it on.
- Is the TV plugged in? If not, plug it in.
- Is the outlet live? Check it and correct the problem.
- Is the computer on? If not, turn it on.
- Are the TV brightness and/or contrast controls turned up high enough? If not, adjust them.
- Are you using the proper connector from the Apple //c to the TV set? You must use the RF adapter unless your set has a direct video connector (check chapter 3 for more details).
- Are all TV cables securely fastened at both ends? If not, *turn off the computer and the TV set* before plugging them in securely. If you don't, you may damage both computer and TV.
- Is the TV channel you're using the same one you've selected on the RF adapter? If not, change one or the other.
- Is the switch box to the antenna terminals set for *computer* rather than for *TV*? If not, set it to *computer.*
- Is the fine tuning adjusted? A simple twist of the knob may bring the picture into view and clear up any smearing or fuzziness as a dividend.
- Are the cables or adapters defective? Trouble can develop beneath the insulation. Try another if you have one.
- Is the computer's video output defective? Hook up the computer to a monitor and see if that works. If not, the video circuitry is probably on the blink. Take the machine to a service center.
- Is the TV defective? Try it with another computer or antenna or take it in to be checked.

If you're using a TV set, and it's displaying a TV show instead of the //c's output . . .

- Is the switch box connected to the TV set to *computer*? If not, set the switch to *computer.*
- Does the channel selected on your RF converter match the one you're using on the TV? If not, change one or the other.

If you're using a TV set and text characters seem fuzzy . . .

- Is the computer in 80-column mode? If so, change it to 40 columns by using the *esc-4* or *esc-control-Q* sequences.
- In 40-column mode, "color fringing" is normal with color TV sets. If adjusting the fine tuning doesn't eliminate most of it, turn off the color.

Keyboard Problems

If none of the keys respond . . .

- The software you're running may be designed that way. For example, in Applesoft, you may have entered hi-res mode 2, which will not echo your keystrokes to the screen. In that case, type TEXT (then *return*) blind and your work will appear on the screen. In other cases, check the manual that comes with the software.
- You've started without a disk in the drive. If you want to continue, perform a *control-reset* interrupt.
- You've sent keyboard output to a port (modem or printer are likely candidates) without calling for it to be echoed to the screen. Check chapters 12 and 13 for information on the echo feature.
- You've sent a command to the printer when the printer was off, off-line, or out of paper or ribbon. Get the printer up and running and see what happens. With some programs, you'll be able to recover; with others, you may have to perform an interrupt or full three-key reset.
- You've got software problems. If an interrupt doesn't resolve them, perform a three-key reset.
- The keyboard is out of whack. Take your machine in for repair.

If the keys don't produce the letters indicated on them . . .

- The *keyboard* switch is in the wrong position. Press it so that it pops up (off) and returns your keyboard to normal (see chapter 4).

If the ↑ and ↓ keys don't respond . . .

- If you're using Applesoft BASIC, hit the *esc* key to bring them to life for editing purposes.
- If you're using a different program (particularly one designed for older model Apple // machines), the keys may not be able to work. Check the software manual for details.

If the only letters you can type are capitals . . .

- You've engaged the *caps lock*. Press it once and all should be well.

If the symbols in the top row of the keyboard don't appear when you hit them and the caps lock key is on . . .

- That's normal behavior. The *caps lock* key affects only the letter keys, not the ones with numbers or punctuation.

If the delete key doesn't delete anything . . .

- You're probably working in Applesoft, where hitting the *delete* key simply puts a cursorlike box on the screen. Other programs may use the *delete* key as a destructive backspace or disable it entirely.

If a program you've bought won't stop running when you hit control-C . . .

- The program was probably designed that way. The developers don't want you LISTing it or copying it.

If the //c's control and esc keys don't work the way you're used to . . .

- You're probably running a program designed that way. Only at the most fundamental level do the //c's keys work in a consistent way. Programmers may adapt and modify what they do to suit the needs of a particular program.

Disk Problems

If you try to boot a disk and you get a CHECK DISK DRIVE message . . .

- Does the red *in-use* light come on? If not, try again. If it still fails, a trip to the service center is in order.
- Is there a "bootable" disk in the drive? If not, put one in.
- Is the disk properly seated and the drive door closed? If not, make sure they are.
- Is the disk inserted the right way? If not, correct it.
- Are you sure the disk is "bootable"—i.e., one that includes DOS or ProDOS? If not, get one.
- Is the disk damaged? If you think so, try another.

If you try to work with a disk and get an error message after the machine has been booted . . .

- Does the red *in-use* light come on? If not, try again. If it still fails, a trip to the service center is in order.
- Is there a disk in the drive? If not, put one in.
- Is the disk properly seated and the drive door closed? If not, make sure they are.
- Is the disk inserted the right way? If not, correct it.
- Is the disk initialized or formatted? If not, try another disk.
- Is the disk damaged? If so, try another.
- Have you tried to access any of the slots from within an Applesoft program without using the *control-D*—CHR$(4)—prefix? If so, DOS has been disconnected, and disk access will be impossible. Insert a bootable disk and reboot.

Printer Problems

If nothing comes out of the printer . . .

- Is the printer on? If not, turn it on.
- Is the printer off-line (or "deselected")? Many printers have to be turned off-line when you perform a manual line or form feed. It's easy to forget to hit the on-line switch to rouse them back to life again.
- Is the printer out of paper or out of ribbon?
- Is the cable properly connected at both ends? Is the cable connected to the printer port? (It will fit into the modem port, too.) Be sure to turn off both computer and printer before reconnecting them to each other.
- Are you using the proper cable? The printer cable and the modem cable look remarkably similar. The printer cable is not standard, and one internal wire in the wrong place can keep the machine from running.
- If the printer is capable of both serial and parallel communications, is it set to work in serial mode? Are all switches inside and outside the printer set correctly?
- Are the printer parameters set correctly, and is the software sending information to the proper port? With serial devices, parameters must match for proper information transfer to take place (see chapter 13 for details).
- Has an undesired software command sent the printer into some unusual mode (i.e., graphics, special character set, or "wait")? Turn

the printer off for a few seconds and turn it back on again to relieve it of the misinformation.
- Is the printer defective? If the printer offers a "self-test," try running it. If the printer fails, take it to the service center. If it passes, the problem is almost certainly in the cable or the way the communications port and/or parameters have been selected.

If the printer prints "garbage" or the wrong characters . . .

- Are you using the proper cable? The printer cable and the modem cable look remarkably similar. The printer cable is not standard, and one internal wire in the wrong place can keep the machine from running.
- If the printer is capable of both serial and parallel communications, is it set to work in serial mode? Are all switches inside and outside the printer set correctly?
- Are the printer parameters set correctly, and is the software sending information to the proper port? With serial devices, parameters must match for proper information transfer to take place.
- Has an undesired software command sent the printer into some unusual mode (i.e., graphics or special character set)? Turn the printer off for a few seconds and turn it back on again to relieve it of the misinformation.
- Is the printer defective? If the printer offers a "self-test," try running it. If the printer fails, take it to the repairman. If it passes, the problem is almost certainly in the cable or the way the communications port and/or parameters have been selected.

If the printer tears sprocket holes in tractor-feed paper . . .

- Paper may be inserted improperly. Be sure holes are aligned with matching pins on both sides of the printer, and paper is straight as it feeds in.
- Tractors may be adjusted improperly. Be sure sprockets don't put undue tension on holes.
- Paper path may be obstructed. Make sure nothing blocks the paper as it feeds into the printer.

If the print is too light . . .

- Increase the print head force, if possible.
- Replace the ribbon.

If the print is too dark or smudgy . . .

- Decrease the print head force, if possible.

If the printer prints only the top or bottom half of each character . . .

- Check the ribbon. It's probably riding too high or too low.

If the printer chews holes in the ribbon . . .

- The ribbon is probably threaded incorrectly. Rethread it and try again. If the ribbon is badly damaged, discard it and start over with a new one.

Modem Problems

If your modem fails to communicate, or strange characters appear on your screen . . .

- Is the modem turned on? If not, turn it on.
- Is the modem properly connected to the //c, phone line, and wall outlet? If not, turn off the computer before proceeding. Then reconnect the cables properly and turn the power back on.
- Are you using the right modem-to-computer cable? Such cables are *not* standardized. A single internal wire going to the wrong pin can turn the modem deaf to your machine. And be sure you're not using a printer cable; it looks very like the proper cable for the modem.
- Is the proper port open and are the communications parameters properly set? All parameters (baud rate, word length, stop bits, parity, and duplex) must match those of the machine on the other end of the line, or garbled transmission will result (see chapter 14 for details).
- Have you given your "smart" modem the wrong commands? "Smart" modems speak a cryptic language of their own. (For example, some very popular models require that you address them in ALL CAPITAL LETTERS.) If you send them incorrect commands, they may not do what you intend. Turning the modem off for a few seconds and then on again will wipe the incorrect commands from its memory.
- Is the modem or modem port defective? Communications equipment is extraordinarily reliable, and the most common hardware difficulty by far is improper cabling; your communications problem is almost cer-

tainly the result of one of the situations just mentioned. But like anything else, communications hardware can go bad. If all else fails, try your machine with a different modem; try the modem with a different machine.

Audio Problems

If you can't get any sound out of the //c . . .

- Is the volume control turned off or down? If so, turn it on or up.
- Is a cable plugged into the jack? If so, remove it to route sound through the //c's built-in speaker.
- Are you using an external amplifier? If so, is it plugged in, turned on, and set to the proper sound source? Is the cable properly connected?

Software Troubleshooting

Applesoft, DOS, and ProDOS are actually out there willing to help you get out of some major jams. They don't just desert you and make you wonder what happened. They actually give you error messages to help you figure out what's gone wrong.

The error messages on the screen are meant to help you find mistakes and potential problems. Learning what they mean and the possible problems they point to can make you and your computer get along better together.

The following lists of Applesoft, DOS, and ProDOS messages will help you make even more sense out of the machine's cryptic remarks.

The Three Flavors of Errors

There are three formats for error messages. We'll use the ever-popular SYNTAX ERROR as an example:

```
   SYNTAX ERROR   DOS and ProDOS
  ?SYNTAX ERROR   Applesoft BASIC
***SYNTAX ERROR   Integer BASIC
```

In immediate mode, you simply see the message:

```
   SYNTAX ERROR
```

(continued)

In deferred mode (from within an Applesoft program), it will look like this:

```
SYNTAX ERROR IN <linenumber>
```

where <linenumber> is the line number in which the error occurred.

Applesoft BASIC Error Messages

BAD SUBSCRIPT

You've tried to do something to an array or matrix element beyond the range you had previously DIMensioned.

CAN'T CONTINUE

You stopped a program by using *control-C* and attempted to continue its operation with a CONT command. Ordinarily, CONT will work, but depending on what type of an operation it was in the middle of, the computer may well respond that it cannot. This will also appear if you've stopped the program with *control-reset*.

DIVISION BY ZERO

You've tried to divide a number by zero. It can happen either directly (14/0) or when doing arithmetic operations with a variable that has assumed a zero value.

ILLEGAL DIRECT

Some commands, like INPUT, GET, and DATA, can only be used inside of programs and not in immediate mode. This error message appears if you've violated that rule.

ILLEGAL QUANTITY

Some of Applesoft's commands and functions have limitations on the numbers that can be used with them. If you've used an illegal one, you'll get this message.

NEXT WITHOUT FOR

Somewhere along the way, you started a FOR . . . NEXT loop but forgot to include the FOR statement.

OUT OF DATA

If you ask the program to READ from a list of DATA items and there aren't as many items as there are instructions to READ, you will run OUT OF DATA.

OUT OF MEMORY

There are a few reasons for this message. Among them is the obvious: a program is simply too large to fit into memory. You'll also see it if you *nest* more than ten FOR . . . NEXT loops or twenty-four GOSUBs or thirty-six levels of parentheses (not too likely).

OVERFLOW

The result of a calculation was too large to be handled by the variable type you selected to contain it. If you're using an integer variable, switch to a real variable. If you're already using a real variable, we hope the number that caused the error represents your bank balance.

REDIM'D ARRAY

You are trying to redefine (with a DIM statement) a matrix or array that you've already DIMensioned somewhere prior. You've probably sent a GOTO back one line too far.

RETURN WITHOUT GOSUB

While executing its line numbers in an orderly fashion, the program has come upon a RETURN statement. Unfortunately, it has not yet encountered a GOSUB statement to which it should RETURN.

STRING TOO LONG

You've tried to assign more than 255 characters to a string variable.

SYNTAX ERROR

You've made one of a wide variety of mistakes, including spelling and punctuation (missing parentheses and quotes are prime suspects), in the construction of a BASIC statement.

TYPE MISMATCH

You tried to assign the wrong type of information to a variable. Perhaps you're trying to make a numeric variable contain a string, or vice versa.

UNDEF'D FUNCTION

You tried to reference a user defined-function but you haven't used DEF FN to define the function.

UNDEF'D STATEMENT

When you try to send the flow of a program to a line number that doesn't exist, either with a GOSUB or GOTO, you'll get this message. The "statement" it wants to see is the missing line.

DOS Error Messages

DISK FULL
Either all of the directory space has been used up (you've got all the files the disk can handle) or all of the space on the disk is filled.

END OF DATA
When reading from an informational file, you've tried to read more than the file contains.

FILE LOCKED
If you try to rename, delete, write, or save to a file that is locked, DOS will let you know.

FILE NOT FOUND
This one's obvious. DOS can't find the file you've asked it to do something to.

FILE TYPE MISMATCH
Don't try to RUN a binary program or BRUN an Applesoft program unless you want to see this error message.

I/O ERROR
This covers a wide variety of disk errors, including leaving the drive door open, using an unformatted disk or a disk with a bad area on it, or not having any disk at all in the drive.

LANGUAGE NOT AVAILABLE
You've called for FP or INT but no alternate language was available. Check to make sure the DOS greeting program on the boot disk does actually load the language into the high area of RAM.

NO BUFFERS AVAILABLE
Either you've exceeded the maximum number of open files DOS allows or you've used the MAXFILES command to alter that number to the same effect.

NOT DIRECT COMMAND
Same as ILLEGAL DIRECT in Applesoft.

PROGRAM TOO LARGE
You don't have enough memory to load or run the program you've requested.

RANGE ERROR

Check the slot, drive, and volume numbers in the command you used. With the exception of the volume number, none can be 0. On the high end, the maximum slot number is 7, while the maximum drive is 2. If you try to create a random or sequential file with more than 32767 records you will also get this error.

SYNTAX ERROR

Same as in Applesoft.

VOLUME MISMATCH

You've tried to do something to a disk and specified a volume number that did not coincide with the disk's actual volume number.

WRITE PROTECTED

Either there is a write-protect tab on the disk notch, or the disk is not seated in the drive correctly, or there is no write-enable notch at all on the disk. Check that first. If you still get this error message, you may have a hardware problem.

ProDOS Error Messages

CAN'T DELETE DIRECTORY FILE

The name of a file you tried to transfer to a ProDOS disk was the same as the name of a directory that already exists on the disk.

CAN'T TRANSFER DIRECTORY FILE

Don't try to copy a group of files by attempting to copy the directory name. If you do, you'll get this error message. Instead, create a directory on the disk you're copying to and then copy the individual files to that directory.

DIRECTORY ALREADY EXISTS

If you try to create a subdirectory that already exists on a disk, you'll be so informed. Also, if you try to copy files to a directory rather than to files within a directory (for instance: copying OLDDIRECTORY/FILENAME to NEWDIRECTORY/), you'll get the same message.

DIRECTORY EXPECTED

If you try to get a directory of a disk or set the disk's prefix and you inadvertently use a filename instead of a directory name, you'll see this.

DIRECTORY NOT EMPTY

You cannot delete a directory until all of the files it contains have first been deleted.

DIRECTORY NOT FOUND
You've tried to do something (anything) and specified the action at a directory that ProDOS could not find.

DISK DRIVE TOO FAST or DISK DRIVE TOO SLOW
ProDOS has built-in checks to make sure all Apple disk drives stay within a certain speed range. If the speed rises too high or dips too low, you'll be so informed. You've got a hardware problem. It's just possible that the problem is caused by a disk that doesn't turn freely in its jacket. But if different disks produce the same result, it's time to visit Mr. or Ms. Repairman.

DISK WRITE PROTECTED
Same as WRITE PROTECT in DOS.

DUPLICATE FILENAME
The new name you're trying to give your file already exists on the disk or the file you're transferring from one disk already exists on the destination disk.

DUPLICATE VOLUME
Two drives contain disks with the same volume names.

ERROR CODE = XX
An error has occurred, but ProDOS can't determine what it was or it has no specific message. Take the machine in to be checked.

FILE EXPECTED
You've used a volume or subdirectory name when you should have used a filename.

FILE LOCKED
You've tried to alter, save, rename, or write a file that you've locked (it shows in the directory preceded by an asterisk).

FILE NOT FOUND
What you've told ProDOS to do involves a file it can't find on the volume you've specified.

FILES DO NOT MATCH
This message shows up when you use the ProDOS COMPARE utility if the two files compared do not match.

FILE TOO LARGE
You're trying to copy a file to a disk that has insufficient room to hold it.

I/O ERROR

Same as I/O ERROR in DOS.

ILLEGAL CHARACTER

If you try to use a number as the first character in a volume name or a comma in the pathname, ProDOS will give you this message.

ILLEGAL WILDCARD

You used a wild card, either a ? or an =, in a place where ProDOS does not understand it.

INSUFFICIENT MEMORY TO RUN PROGRAM

This usually appears during start-up and means you don't have 64K available. If you are using your Apple //c, a trip to the repair depot may be in order.

INVALID DATE

You tried to tell ProDOS that it was either not one of the twelve months it knows or the wrong day in the month (outside the range of 01–31, depending on the month), or you've used a year range outside of 00–99.

INVALID DRIVE

If you're asked to specify a drive number and you use a letter or a number that's not 1 or 2, you'll be told you're in error.

INVALID PATHNAME

Either you forgot to set the prefix for a disk you want to use or else you've included an illegal character in the pathname.

INVALID SLOT

Entering a letter or a number outside of the allowable range for slot numbers will produce this error.

NAME TOO LONG

You've used a DOS 3.3 filename longer than 30 characters or a ProDOS filename longer than 15 characters.

NO DATA IN FILE

You tried to transfer a file that had no data in it.

NO DEVICE CONNECTED

ProDOS is not receiving the correct signal back from a device (like a printer or disk drive) that you told it was connected. If you've made sure the device is actually connected, have the device and its cable checked. If you've specified the wrong slot number, you'll get the same message.

NO DIRECTORY

If you ask ProDOS to look at a disk that is unformatted, or formatted by DOS 3.3 or Pascal, you'll get this message.

NO PRINTER CONNECTED

Your output device is set to printer port 1 but there is no printer physically connected to it.

NO ROOM ON VOLUME

All the physical space on the disk is used up.

NOT A DOS 3.3 VOLUME

The disk in the slot and drive you specified is *not* a DOS 3.3 disk. This usually happens during the conversion from DOS 3.3 to ProDOS.

NOT A PRODOS DIRECTORY

When you tried to set the prefix, the directory label used was not the name of a ProDOS directory.

NOT A PRODOS INTERPRETER

The .SYSTEM file on your disk, although named correctly, is not the right type of file.

NOT A PRODOS VOLUME

The volume you've directed action to is not a ProDOS formatted disk.

NOT THE SAME DEVICE TYPE

You tried to copy one volume to or compare one volume with another that was not the same type (as you might if you tried to copy a floppy disk volume to a hard disk).

NOT THE SAME DIRECTORY

When you tried to rename a file, you did not use the same directory label.

PATHNAMES INDICATE SAME FILE

The source and destination pathnames are identical. You cannot copy a file onto itself.

PATHNAME TOO LONG

ProDOS pathnames cannot be longer than 64 characters when you set the prefix, or longer than 128 characters when you specify a file.

PATH NOT FOUND

You've specified a pathname that ProDOS cannot find. (You may have told it the correct volume, but not the correct directory.)

PREFIX NOT SET

You tried to perform some action on a disk without first setting the prefix and without specifying the volume name.

SAME FIXED DISK

You tried to copy or compare a hard-disk volume to itself.

VOLUME DIRECTORY FULL

All of the directory space has been used. There's room for a maximum of 55 entries.

VOLUME FULL

Same as NO ROOM ON VOLUME.

VOLUME NOT FOUND

The program cannot find the volume you specified.

WILDCARD MUST BE IN FINAL NAME

You've used a wild card (either a ? or an =) and it was not in the last label of the pathname.

WILDCARD NOT ALLOWED

You used a wild card in a place that ProDOS does not feel was appropriate.

WILDCARD NOT PROCESSED

Using the wild card you specified, the pathname or filename became too large to handle.

WILDCARD USE INCONSISTENT

In copying or renaming files, you used a pathname that included a wild card, but on the other side of the instruction the wild card was not the same or did not appear in the same place.

17

Languages and Applications: Making It All Work for You

No matter how powerful or new or fast your computer is, it's utterly useless until you load a program into it. Computers are essentially stupid. They can execute hundreds of thousands of commands in a second, but they aren't capable of writing even the most primitive instruction themselves.

How Applications Are Born

Computers *do* understand a language. In fact they're flawless speakers of it. This language is buried in the central-processing chip and is made up of a set of instructions, just as the language we speak is made up of nouns, verbs, adjectives, and so on. Programmers can get computers to do astonishing things by writing long lists of precise instructions for the computer to follow slavishly.

Unfortunately, the language the computer speaks is all but incomprehensible to the average human. There are people who can actually sit down and study the pattern of *1*'s and *0*'s that is Shakespearean prose to an Apple //c, and converse with it. Since this arcane language goes straight to the gut level of the machine, it is called a *low-level* language. Programming in it is very fast, and very powerful, since there are few wasted steps and fewer restrictions. If you are conversant in this "machine language," you can get the computer to do practically *anything*.

Most programmers, however, prefer to issue their commands in a language closer to English. The closer it is, the *higher-level* the language. Assembly language is fairly low level, trading what look like choppy English syllables for the endless binary stream. Languages such as BASIC and Pascal are fairly high level, which means they're easy to work with. But what programmers gain in ease of expression, they forfeit in flexibility and speed.

If you had the time and the inclination, you could take a crash course in programming and whip together sets of instructions (called programs) that would put the computer through its paces. In fact, if you were really a whiz at it, you could fashion computer tools that reflected your own particular view of work and play. If deep down you felt that a word processor should check on the spelling of every word as you entered it, and you knew the programming ropes, you could bang together a program to do it for you. Since there are none on the market that do this, you could have the word processor of your dreams—and perhaps even make a bundle selling it to others.

Unfortunately, it's not at all easy to create programs that are a fraction as powerful and fast as commercial software. Remember, manufacturers of the software that fills computer-store shelves and elbows its way onto the best-seller lists hire teams of brilliant engineers who spend countless hours writing, revising, tightening, and polishing their work. If the program is a real winner, you can bet at least part of it is written in assembly language.

If you bought your Apple //c to learn about programming and computers in general, plunge right in. Start with the easier languages, like BASIC and Logo, and work your way down to the lowest level you can stand. You'll learn a whole lot about structure, computers, thinking, and other pompous-sounding but fascinating things.

Programming Languages

If you're like most people, you'll probably end up doing most of your work with commercial software packages. But thousands of users have mastered programming languages and skills well enough to develop their own software. This probably wouldn't make much sense in an area where there is a huge, clearly defined market filled to the brim with elegant packages. Don't try writing a spreadsheet, for instance; it is highly unlikely that you can do better than the magicians whose wares are available at reasonable prices everywhere. But if you want to tinker with a special program for your orthodontics practice or your horticultural research, take the plunge and learn. It can't hurt, and you'll almost certainly have an interesting and rewarding experience.

You've met Applesoft BASIC already. It's a very simple and easily learned language. But there are two other programming languages, Pascal and Logo, that beginners can master without much difficulty.

Logo and BASIC share one sterling feature—they're *interpreted,* which means they can run in the form in which you write them. You can type in a line and run it right away to see if it does what you want. If not, you can change it slightly, then try running it again. Pascal is a *compiled* language, which means you first write the program, then process it through a special translator called a compiler that changes the instructions you've written into a form the computer can more readily understand. You can't just write a line and try it on the spot as you can with BASIC or Logo. On the other hand, programs written in Pascal run much more quickly, since the compiler does the work of translating them from a high-level language into a much lower and more efficient one *before* you run the program itself.

Pascal

Pascal is a high-level programming language named for French mathematician Blaise Pascal, who built a revolutionary calculating machine in 1642. Using no line numbers, this language is quite different from BASIC. Its chief asset is that it forces programmers to write highly structured programs, which many computer experts prefer.

A typical Pascal program might begin with a section of definitions of all the variables you'll be using in the program. It would proceed to specific sections that perform functions such as getting information from the person running the program, storing that information to disk, and printing it on the screen. Then the main body of the program would begin, directing itself back to the individual procedures that can do the bulk of the work.

Pascal is *modular.* The function of the main section of the program is to direct activity to the correct modules, or *procedures* as they're called in the Pascal system, based on the commands and directions you use. The procedures perform their function and then return the flow of control to the main program. This process operates very much as subroutines do in BASIC.

The Pascal Three-Step

But Pascal is unlike BASIC in that Pascal requires three steps in writing a program, each of which uses one of three separate parts of the language. Programs are written using the Pascal *editor,* which is similar to the screen-entry part of a word processor. With it you can move text around, scroll to the bottom or top of your program, and insert or delete words, characters, and lines. You use the editor to write what is called the *source code.* It's from the source code that the real Pascal program is created.

When you're done with the editor, you switch to using the *compiler.* It takes the source code of the program you've just written and turns it into a form the Pascal executing system can understand. Up to this point, your program resembles a conventional document. The compiler reads what you've written and writes another program in machine code that actually tells the Pascal system what you want done.

When you want to run the program, the Pascal *run-time* package is called in. This takes the program written by the compiler and makes it perform all of the things you originally wanted to do quickly and efficiently.

On the plus side, Pascal tends to differ less from machine to machine than BASIC, so the source code you write can be adapted and compiled to run on other computers. For that and other reasons, many experts expected Pascal to become the new salvation of all programmers. Unfortunately, because of the complexity of the structures needed, it was sometimes easier to write the same program in BASIC. However, Pascal is an excellent teaching language (and the only one the Educational Testing Service uses for its Advanced Placement tests), since it does force you to write programs that preserve the source code in a very structured, readable state.

If other people will be working with you to write programs, the organized structure of Pascal may make it very attractive. After two or three months (sometimes days), it can be difficult to follow the flow of logic in a BASIC program. There is nothing to force you to write a BASIC program in any logical fashion. Pascal's modular procedures can give you (and others) a much better handle on what you've written after the fact.

However, there's nothing to prevent you from writing BASIC programs that are every bit as structured and elegant as those in Pascal. And the better BASIC programmers all do; their program listings are works of art. The real problem with BASIC is that it lets you get sloppy—but nothing says you have to. In fact, you should write any program in any language modularly, since you'll find you're using parts of the same programs over and over again. You can create your own library of these modules and use them as the basis of many programs, saving yourself days of repetitious work.

By the way, Apple does have a commitment to Pascal. The operating systems used on the Apple /// and on Apple's Lisa computer were both written in Pascal. The Pascal they've released for the Apple //c is version 1.2—accept no substitutes.

Logo

An interactive, higher-level language used primarily in education, Logo arrived on the microcomputer scene only a few years ago. It was inspired by a rather strange mechanical device, a mechanical "turtle" that could draw lines and figures on a sheet of paper.

Logo was specifically designed to be a useful teaching tool, and it's become extremely popular in educational circles. The little triangular turtle-surrogate marching around the screen fascinates young people and makes learning fun. Logo's vaunted graphics capabilities and their ease of use help too.

When the turtle is on the screen, you move it by issuing a series of commands. Users generally begin with long-form commands, then graduate to shorthand. For instance, you could draw a box by issuing either the instructions on the left or the abbreviations on the right of the following listing:

```
CLEARSCREEN     | CS
RIGHT 90        | RT 90
FORWARD 40      | FD 40
RIGHT 90        | RT 90
FORWARD 40      | FD 40
RIGHT 90        | RT 90
FORWARD 40      | FD 40
RIGHT 90        | RT 90
FORWARD 40      | FD 40
```

Each of these commands is called a Logo *primitive,* because it specifies the lowest level of activity the language can handle. None of them can be broken down into anything simpler. The first command removes any of the screen's contents and places the turtle in the middle of the screen, facing upward. In the Logo system, that's called the HOME position and it has screen coordinates 0,0. The direction the turtle is facing is also called 0. As you saw in the Applesoft graphics chapter, it's easier to refer to movement when you have a system of coordinates.

The first command turns the turtle 90 degrees to the right. The second command moves it 40 dot positions forward (in the direction it's facing). By doing that four times, you draw four lines, each at a 90-degree angle to the previous one, and create the box. But that's such a repetitive function, no language worth its salt would force you to put up with it.

There's an easier way:

```
REPEAT 4 [RT 90 FD 40]
```

You've told it that you want to repeat something, and how many times—and, in brackets, you've said what you want repeated.

You can also train Logo to learn an even shorter command to perform the same action. The turtle is a very good student. Logo's cursor is the question mark [?]. Whenever you see it, you know that Logo's waiting for you to give it a command. Let's teach it how to draw a square.

```
?TO SQUARE
>REPEAT 4 [RT 90 FD 40]
>END
SQUARE DEFINED
?
```

Once you've said TO SQUARE, the Logo cursor changes into the > symbol. This tells you that Logo is in its learning mode. It understands that what you are about to tell it will all be assigned to the word SQUARE. Next you gave it the command you wanted it to learn and followed that with the word END. Logo understands this means the lesson's over, reports "SQUARE DEFINED," and takes you back to the command prompt.

Technically, what you've done is to use Logo primitives to define a Logo procedure. Now, any time you type the word SQUARE, the turtle will turn around and begin its march. You've taught it how. Notice that you didn't include the clear screen command. That's just in case you want to make SQUARE part of a larger procedure.

The whole language can be built image by image and action by action in this way. You can actually create quite sophisticated, complicated graphics with seemingly simple commands.

Other Languages

Your Apple //c will also run Apple's version of FORTRAN (short for FORmula TRANslation) and a language called SuperPILOT (or just PILOT). FORTRAN is a very old language which has, of late, become a bit less popular. It is used most frequently by scientists and mathematicians, for it excels in number-handling situations. Unfortunately, it doesn't handle non-numeric "character strings" well at all. Another drawback of FORTRAN is that because of its origins back in the days when the only means of entering information into a computer was via punch card, it is still dependent on the 80-column punch-card format.

PILOT is a very good language aimed at the educational market. It has excellent graphics creation and handling facilities and excels at creating tutorial material. Unfortunately, it began to blossom at about the same time Logo was introduced. And Logo had a better selling point.

PILOT never really had a chance to achieve popularity because the novelty of a screen "turtle" was just too strong. At the time of Logo's release, there was much controversy over who actually had the rights to distribute it, and the resultant publicity and press coverage overwhelmed what little notoriety PILOT had.

For serious programmers, Apple also offers 6502 assembly language. There are many people who prefer what they call the pure essence of computer programming. Using assembly code speeds up program execution considerably and allows full control over every function of the computer. The potential speed improvement in program execution can be enormous since the program code can be extremely lean, containing only what it absolutely needs.

The drawback with assembly language is that *every* step must be programmed individually and that can take much longer to do than writing in a high-level language with built-in functions to take care of screen handling and keyboard input. Writing in assembler means programming in cryptic terms that are hard to learn. A simple BASIC statement line PRINT "Hello" might take ten or fifteen assembly-language programming lines, since you must load each value into a special holding area and then send each character out to the printer. Nevertheless, there are those who claim it is the *only* way to program.

Those are the main alternatives (though there are others, such as Forth) if you'd like to write your own programs in addition to or instead of using ones that are already available. Just keep in mind that while no prepackaged program may do 100% of what you want it to, you would have to invest a substantial amount of time to write your own. Often, the compromises needed to make your task fit an available prefab program are small enough to make that choice the right one.

Prepackaged Applications Software

If you're like most users who buy a machine for a specific application, you'll be much better off investing your time and money in the best commercial software package you can find. But which ones are the best? What are the features to look for? What is an Apple //c really capable of with sizzling software spinning away inside it?

There are five general groups of software, classified by application:

Popular Types of Applications Software

Word Processing	These programs turn your computer into the space-age equivalent of a typewriter. Simple word-processing programs might only be suitable for short memos or letters to friends, while more sophisticated programs will be able to handle the complex formatting requirements of playwrights and screenplay writers and offer a broad spectrum of other advanced features.
Databases	These programs provide a systematic approach to the storage, updating, and retrieval of information. Database applications can be very simple or so complex that entire programs can be written using them.

(continued)

Spreadsheets	These programs have revolutionized number crunching, allowing you to arrange large quantities of numeric information in rows and columns and to define complex formulas and interrelationships among the various entries.
Communications	These programs let you turn a modem-equipped machine into a communications terminal. With their help, you can hook up your machine to other personal computers as well as to giant mainframes that give you access to databases, electronic mail systems, and much more.
Graphics	These programs cover a lot of ground, from entertaining you with aliens and mazes, to helping you create your own business charts and graphs. Some can turn your computer into an electronic palette, or even help you design a house or a computer chip.

In the past, software manufacturers focused their efforts on single topics. One vendor would become known for its powerful spreadsheets; another would dominate the market with a breathtakingly sophisticated word processor. VisiCorp and Sorcim grabbed the lion's share of the number-crunching market. MicroPro's *WordStar* is the all-time best-selling word processor, and for good reason. In fact, it has probably been responsible for selling hundreds of thousands of Apple CP/M cards. Companies like Ashton-Tate became the unquestioned leaders in microcomputer databases.

The software business became so profitable so fast that thousands of challengers sprang up practically overnight, all clamoring for a piece of the action. Since the leaders all had a head start, many were able to outdistance the competition. Some, however, have shown themselves to be strictly one-trick ponies, and have not kept pace.

The new wrinkle in the industry is integrated software. You didn't have to be a genius to realize what a nuisance it was to have to learn commands and idiosyncrasies of several separate programs, and have to swap disks in and out of your drives dozens of times, just to write a memo that contained the results of a statistical analysis with a few meager charts. Sometimes just getting the data files from one program to another took hours of frustrating agony. A company called Lotus didn't even exist a few years ago; now, however, its *1-2-3* integrated package has lopped off a huge section of the market all to itself, and has spawned an entire new industry—Apple's new *AppleWorks* is exhibit A.

Integrated software elements are often available as independent "modules" that can run as stand-alone applications. That way you can avoid being saddled with purchasing more than you need at any time. But they can also be purchased in complex packages that give you all the various functions at once. These combination packages usually offer great savings over buying the modules separately.

Your needs should determine whether you need a complex integrated package or just one or two single-purpose applications packages. When making a choice, try *not* to let advertising unduly influence you. The best way to decide on a program is to use it. Many computer stores have demo copies and machines available for customers, and many software publishers will send you a demonstration disk at a nominal cost.

Your First Software—and It's Free!

Good software can come from giant companies such as Lotus or MicroPro, or smaller ones that focus on less businesslike applications. Some of the best investments you can make are for top-quality programs that make it easy to play music or to create your own pinball machine.

But Apple has given you an introduction to software for your //c, and it comes packed in the box with your machine, 100% free of charge, on five floppy disks. We'll give you a brief rundown of what's on each of them.

Apple Presents . . . An Introduction

A few years back, Apple standardized its tutorial approach to the Apple // series. The lessons on this disk revolve around using the keyboard, and all in all it's a good way to start.

As the lessons progress, they introduce you to a variety of cursor characters with an explanation of what each one does. The goal is to standardize your programming practices. But some of the disk's suggestions are not entirely accurate.

For instance, it advises you that a blinking underline cursor will respond to the *delete* key as a correction tool, and makes a point of saying that you can press *return* anywhere in a word you've just corrected and the computer will accept it. What it doesn't say is that this is only true under the control of a program that allows you to do it. But you're unlikely ever to see this cursor when you're writing your own programs in Applesoft.

The third cursor you're introduced to is the solid box that you've seen when you activated the Apple's 80-column electronics. Here it's claimed that using the ← causes the characters the cursor backs over to disappear. Again, this is true only if the program you're running at the time permits it. When you're writing your own programs, you'll discover that isn't the case at all.

While the disk does cover the fundamentals, there is a very good chance that this introduction will be misleading to the novice. By all means try the demo, but don't consider it a full-fledged introduction to the machine. It's better as an overall introduction to the world of Apple.

Getting Down to BASIC

This disk gives you a very low-level introduction to BASIC programming. Its chief strength is that it gets your hands on the keyboard and forces you to use the machine.

One of the disk's "chapters" deals with saving the programs you've written, and also offers a look at the CATALOG command. The lesson uses the shortened form, CAT, which may lead users to believe that it will work in all cases, but (as you've already read) it won't—unless you're using ProDOS.

The example given for SAVE is also a bit misleading. In mentioning the external disk drive for the Apple //c, it suggests that saved programs are bound for the external disk drive unless there isn't one. This just isn't the case. Such a blunder can probably be excused under the pretext of simplicity, but there is a real chance for confusion if you haven't read any of the manuals or other reference sources.

The Apple at Work

This is a little bit of Apple advertising. While introducing you to the concepts behind such computer activities as word processing, spreadsheets, and database management, it also previews *AppleWorks*, the company's own integrated software package.

This disk is available in either 40- or 80-column versions to accommodate the particular display you're using. If you can view 80 columns, you may want to look at the word processing in 40-column mode anyway. Likewise, for those of you who are stuck in 40-column mode, take a look at the 80-column output. It will give the best example of what's on the other side of the fence.

The Inside Story

If Mike Hammer ever designed a computer and tried to explain its operation to anyone, he would have done it this way, or so Apple wants you to believe. The background is the office of a grizzled gumshoe. In walks a dame with a problem: her data has vanished after a power failure. She wants our hero to recover the missing data, something he can't do, and proceeds to explain why with a rundown on the workings of the Apple //c.

The internal diagram of the machine is not accurate in relation to the actual placement of components, but the graphics are excellent and the explanations superb. This is definitely one mystery you can go through on a dark and stormy night without fear of goblins invading your dreams.

The Apple at Play

This is the one disk I wouldn't want to be without. It's a collection of games, one of which, *Space Quarks,* was a best-seller from a company called Broderbund back in 1981. *Space Quarks* is an arcade-type game that can occupy your time quite pleasurably for a few hours.

Another, *Lemonade Stand,* is an Apple classic that's been supplied with their computers since time immemorial. It's a version of the old computer standby, *Hammurabi*—a supply vs. demand type game—with limited graphics. A good business sense can give a player the winner's edge. Here are a couple of clues (don't look past the colon if you want to go it alone): Don't make very much lemonade if it looks like rain, and it pays to advertise.

For the gambler in you, there's *Apple 21,* a blackjack simulation from ARTSCI, circa 1980. It was one of the first quality graphics programs done for the Apple. There is also a mortgage and loan simulation that CPAs might enjoy, but it's not really a game.

Even through the internal speaker, the music demonstration is impressive. It plays a beautiful arrangement of a sonata, done in several musical voices. An external amplifier and speaker make this one even better.

Finally, there's a *Quick Quiz,* which isn't exactly a quiz, but a review of everything you should have learned after viewing and using all of the other Apple disks. It's very simple and logical and will give you a rough idea of what you've absorbed.

Overall, these disks get about a B+ for effort and performance. While they're definitely not the greatest programs you can buy, they were designed simply to augment, not supplant, the Apple //c manuals. You should have some fun using them, and, if they bore you after a while, you can always bail out by pressing the esc key.

18

The Big Four: Word Processing, Databases, Spreadsheets, and Communications

In chapter 17 we introduced applications software. Now it's time for a closer look at what you can make your //c do for you.

What's a Word Processor?

Typewriters were technological marvels in their day, allowing anyone with nimble fingers to put words on paper at far greater speeds than with a pen or pencil. And once engineers harnessed electric motors to the keyboard, typewriters became fixtures on virtually every desk in America.

But typewriters had several important drawbacks. Until IBM pioneered a typewriter that could correct mistakes, most typewritten pages were littered with strikeovers, typos, and clumsy erasures. And worse, writers who wanted to revise their work faced the prospect of retyping the entire document just to fix a few words and phrases on each page.

Word processors have changed all that. They've made it possible for every writer to write the way he or she thinks. Very few of us can write off the tops of our heads in perfectly structured, impeccably groomed, freely flowing paragraphs. But with a word processor, it's easy to get your ideas onto the "page" and refine both the content and style before you print out a single word. And you can concentrate on *writing* without having to worry whether you're close to the margin or in danger of typing on the bottom line of the page.

In addition, word processors offer many tricks unheard of a decade or so ago. If you aren't the world's greatest speller, you can run a program that will detect your errors and even suggest changes. If you're often stymied because you can't find the precise word to convey your thoughts, you can consult an electronic thesaurus and choose from a slate of synonyms. And if your business requires repetitive typing that calls for a degree of customization—contracts, customer-service letters, sales proposals, and the like—your word processor can do the lion's share of the work.

Some of the really fancy tricks leave typewriters far behind. If you've just typed a 500-page book about John Jones and you decide to change the hero's name to Randolph Ruskin, the word processor can search for every occurrence of the former name, change it to the new one, and then reformat the manuscript to account for the longer name.

What does a word processor really do? Simply put, it handles words. It's very much like a food processor. It slices, dices, and mulches words. And, just as there's no great mystery behind a blender, there's very little to confound you once you understand what makes a word processor tick.

Every word-processing package available for your Apple //c does the same basic things, but some do them better than others. Just as with any appliance, some are faster, more powerful, easier to use, cheaper, or more reliable.

Playing with Words

In America the standard sheet of typing paper is 8½ inches wide by 11 inches long. Odd-sized sheets can run down to 8 by 10 or up to 8½ by 14 "legal" size sheets of paper with an occasional 11-by-14-inch page thrown in to make typists' lives difficult. In order to be effective, your typewriter should be able to handle whatever size sheets you normally deal with. It should also be able to work with the occasional outsized or undersized page.

A typewriter also must have provisions for multiple line spacing. Typically this is limited to single, double, or triple spacing. Margins need to be set at any desired distance from the left and right edges of the paper, and tab stops placed wherever you want them.

More often than not, aside from putting inked letters on a page, this is the limit of exotic features found on most typewriters. It is the bare minimum you'll find on even the crudest word processor.

What happens when you make a mistake on a typewriter? With most, you must deal with sticky little paintbrushes and drippy opaquing fluid, or shove little flaking sheets of strikeover paper onto the platen. This is definitely something you would want your computer to find a way to avoid.

Some typewriters keep a page or two in memory. These may let you make corrections by showing you a line or two at a time on a small display panel. Half of the heartache with this system is just finding the place in the text that you want to change, and then scrolling it up or down a line at a time to make additional changes.

With other typewriters, each page is remembered and can be retyped at the touch of a button. If you find an error, the typing can be halted, the correction made, and the typing restarted at some point further down the line.

Unfortunately, that's usually the same way editing is done. In all cases, you work primarily on the printed page, doing whatever editing is necessary right on the paper. Then you go back and make the changes in either of the two ways already described. It beats a pencil and pen, but not by much.

The Benefits of Computerization

Nothing really changes when you use a computerized word processor; it just gets infinitely easier. All of the functions your old typewriter boasted are still there—and you have many powerful new ones that will make writing as close to effortless as it can be.

Normally on your typewriter you must either manually return the carriage to the left side or else hit a carriage return button when you come to the end of each line of text. Not only is that needless labor, but it can interrupt your thoughts at untimely places. Ideas don't necessarily stop at the end of a line.

On a computer, you keep typing. The word-processing program handles such things as margins automatically. Your only concern is for the end of paragraphs; only there do you need to hit the carriage return.

Simple editing and error correction can be handled in a variety of ways. If, while you're typing, you notice you've entered something incorrectly, you'll usually have several options. You can backspace to the error and type over it, or you can delete the incorrect word or words and insert new ones. Inserting also works very well when you've forgotten something and don't notice till a few words or lines later.

On a typewriter, if you make a change that adds a word to a line or a line to a page, you must manually adjust the rest of the document to accommodate that change. Word-processing software readjusts the rest of the text in the paragraph and can reformat the entire document at the touch of a key.

Best of all, you can cut and paste your writing virtually automatically. If you find that a paragraph or a page really belongs somewhere else in the document, there isn't much a typewriter can do for you. You can go back and redo the entire piece or you can get out a pair of scissors, cut the sections out, and tape or paste them in where they belong (rearranging the document as you do). Then you either have to find a copy machine that won't show the seams, or retype the whole thing. If the changes are not in contiguous paragraph-size blocks (they rarely are), you end up retyping. Or you avoid making the change, and let your prose suffer.

On your computer, you use one or two keystrokes to mark the beginning of what you want to transfer and another few to mark the end. Then you tell the computer where you want it transferred. With a touch of another key or two, the entire section is transferred and your document is reformatted to accommodate the changes.

If you've ever typed a resume, you're more than ready for some of the advantages a computerized word processor can offer. After looking at the typing job you've done, perhaps you decide it looks too cramped or too spacious. Maybe the indenting is all wrong for the look you want.

You could retype the thing a half-dozen times and still not get it the way you want it to look. With a word processor you can reset the margins and the indents and, with a few simple keystrokes, re-form the entire document. And better still, you can customize your resume to highlight certain areas and play down others for each job opening you're trying to fill. And you can deliver a gorgeous, error-free, crisply typed copy each time.

Not once, so far, have you heard the word *paper* mentioned. You don't need it, at least not all the time. With a typewriter, every time you want to do something you can't start working until you put the paper in and spend a minute aligning the edges.

When you use your computer, you can concentrate on what you're typing, not how you're typing it. You needn't worry how the margins line up—or even if you have any margins. You can do all of the editing and error correcting and formatting when you're finished polishing the ideas and the language.

The only drawback is that you can go overboard once you do start printing. It is so easy to change the margin settings, the indents, the printed line count, the line spacing (single, double, or triple), and the justification (whether both edges of the printed material are aligned or just the left or right side is) that often you'll want to do several copies just to compare the differences.

And with a speedy letter-quality printer, you'll enjoy the ability to print as many *original* copies as you want—without the necessity of retyping every one of them the conventional way.

Word Processors vs. Text Handlers

Word-processing software comes in a variety of styles and complexities. On a stylistic level, the basic difference is in the way they work and what extra features they offer. There are really two kinds of programs that people lump together as word processors—true full-featured word processors and less powerful text handlers.

In some senses that's an artificial difference. Text is what you're processing in both cases. And processing involves handling. In terms of computerized programs, though, these distinctions are descriptions of their relative levels of sophistication.

A true word processor is actually two programs, an editor and a formatter. An editor controls the entry and editing of the text you're typing. A formatter controls the way the final edited text is printed out. Editors do the bulk of the work, but can't even print out a comma themselves. Still, they're useful for certain applications like writing programs, where it's far more important to juggle the commands properly than to print out the program once you're done.

A text formatter uses special sequences of characters in the body of the text that tell your printer how you want the material to look on the page. These format instructions are interpreted when the printing is actually done.

With a good word-processing package, you won't really be able to tell where the editor stops and the formatter begins, since the two processes are intermingled and much of the work is done for you automatically once you make a handful of initial settings. As the level of sophistication drops, the transition between the editor and the formatter becomes more obvious. When it's *very* obvious, you're in the realm of the text handler instead of the word processor.

Any typewriter can put words on a page. So can any text handler. But what happens when you want to add a little panache to your printing? Good computer printers can perform quite a few tricks. Most dot-matrix and letter-quality printers are capable of boldface printing (on some dot-matrix printers this is called emphasized printing), maintaining a wide range of line heights and widths, and even exotic things like superscripting (435^2) and subscripting (NO_2).

Most of the letter-quality printers and some of the dot-matrix printers can also print proportionally spaced text. On a conventional typewriter, a *w* is just as wide as an *i.* If a word like "woman" is directly above a word like "title" both will take up the same amount of space. But if these words were typeset in a book or magazine or newspaper, "woman" would be far wider than "title." Proportionally spaced text has a much cleaner, more professional look than monospace text where every letter has the same width.

Many programs let you align both edges of your text so that neither margin looks ragged. From a distance, fully justified printing looks like an even-sided rectangle. This is done through "microjustification," a process that adds tiny spaces to push the words over until the margins are even. Text handlers without this capability will simply insert whole spaces between words until the lines even out. That can leave wide and unsightly gaps on a line.

Essentially, a word processor should be able to produce a document as professional looking as your printer can make it. If that's your goal, you won't be able to do it without a sophisticated piece of software.

Of the many word-processing programs available for your Apple //c, four stand out, each for a different combination of reasons. Which one is right for you depends on how much power you need and how much you want to spend. We'll try to give you some of the "feel" of them and make you aware of their strengths and weaknesses.

pfs:Write

pfs:Write is part of a family of products available from Software Publishing Corporation. The company combines them into an integrated package which will be discussed later. The word-processing module that is part of this integrated program works fine all by itself, and it is fairly simple to operate.

Write takes advantage of the Apple //c's 80-column display. Although it doesn't ever let you have an 80-column document because of restrictions on the minimum left and right margins, most typed material is not truly 80 characters wide.

When you load the disk, you're greeted by the main menu:

```
        pfs:WRITE          MAIN MENU

   1. TYPE/EDIT         4. GET/SAVE/REMOVE
   2. DEFINE PAGE       5. CLEAR
   3. PRINT

       SELECTION NUMBER:
```

Write is a menu-oriented program, which means that you don't have to memorize a complex command structure. Instead, the program offers you a "menu" of choices. Once you select which function you want, you use the *control-C* key sequence to tell *Write* to start the function. Any and every command you give it terminates with *control-C*.

TYPE/EDIT is the text-entry mode. DEFINE PAGE lets you set up the top, bottom, left, and right margins as well as the headings and footings of your choice. (Headings and footings, also called headers and footers, allow you to label each page at the top and bottom with a title or your name or a page number.) PRINT handles the options for line spacing, start and stop page numbers, single or continuous forms paper, or envelope format. GET/SAVE/REMOVE handles moving documents to and from your disk, while CLEAR erases the contents of the memory.

If you find yourself in any of these menus by accident, or if you decide, once in the option, that you don't want to continue with it, the esc key can be used to return to the main menu. At any menu or option level, you can use the and *H* keys to bring up a help screen with an explanation of the operation you are trying to perform. If you're in the TYPE/EDIT mode, ♂ -*H* will show you all of the editing and cursor control key functions.

When you're working in the TYPE/EDIT mode, you're using the Apple //c's memory to hold your document, which limits the amount you can type. The practical limit appears to be 540 screen lines of text, or the equivalent of ten single-spaced pages, although this is not necessarily the actual printed page count. Single or double spacing can be set through the PRINT option of the main menu, so ten single-spaced Apple //c pages can easily translate into twenty double-spaced printed pages.

This limitation creates some confusion over document length and actual page position. Once you have stored the initial pages of a document and begin a new section, you may well continue the page numbering from the point at which the old document left off. Unfortunately, the displayed page number at the bottom of the TYPE/EDIT screen is absolute to the document in memory, not relative to your settings.

If you're editing a document and you decide that the changes you've made are not what you really want, your original is not disturbed. A document that is saved remains untouched on the disk even if you load it into memory. The copy on the disk is safe unless you save your working copy with the same filename on top of it.

Split documents which are too large to be contained in one working file may be printed continuously by embedding a *J <filename>* in the working text. When the document is printed, the <filename> you've specified is read from disk and printed at the position you've inserted the command. This is very helpful if your typing chores include repetitive phrases in otherwise different documents. You can create a library of these phrases and JOIN them with any text to which they apply.

Write also supports boldface, underlining, and page breaks. This last option allows you to start a new page at any point in your document so that you won't break up a chart or diagram. And you can embed any special characters your printer needs (usually for dot-matrix printers that require these characters for special print modes) in the text.

Cut-and-paste operations are somewhat limited. The maximum number of lines that can be moved is ten. This is a serious limitation if you need to shuffle long paragraphs back and forth. There are also restrictions on rearranging the margins of the document if the text you've entered already uses most of the available memory.

Write supports the processing of form letters with information taken from *pfs:File,* and the inclusion of graphs (if your printer supports graphics) from *pfs:Graph.* Global find and search/replace are also among its repertoire. The *Write* disk is protected against copying, although a backup disk is also supplied.

Apple Writer //

Apple offers its own word processor, and the program is impressive. When you boot the disk, you're greeted by:

```
                  Apple Writer //
            Copyright 1981-82 Paul Lutus
        Copyright 1981-82 Apple Computer Inc

(For HELP while editing,
press ⌘ and "?")
Press RETURN:
```

There is no other indication about what to do next. The presumption, apparently, is that you've read the manual. Pressing the *return* key, as requested, puts you into the editing screen in 80-column mode. The only thing you see is one line at the top of the screen.

This is a "status line" that shows you the current capacity of memory (46,845 characters), the length of your document, the position of the cursor relative to the first character (presumably in the upper left-hand corner), the position of the cursor relative to the left margin, and, if you've chosen one, the name of the document you're typing.

The top line also serves as a tab indicator you can see by pressing the *esc* key. A second press of the key removes the status/tab line, giving you a full-screen display; a third returns the status line for viewing. As you may surmise from the status display, *Apple Writer //* does not keep a page count. But that summarizes 98% of its faults.

If you need help, pressing the ⌘ and *?* keys provides you with a menu of anything (and *almost* everything) it can do:

```
     HELP SCREEN MENU

A. Command Summary
B. Cursor Movement
C. Upper/Lower Case Change
D. Delete Retrieve Text
E. Tabs
F. Glossary
G. Saving Files
H. Loading Files
I. Find/Replace Text
J. Embedded Print Commands

   Press RETURN to Exit
   Enter Your Selection (A - J) :
```

Choosing any of these options brings up an additional screen that outlines what commands are available under any of the categories. Although the manual takes you step by step through the program, with such on-screen help, you really don't need it.

The special features *Apple Writer //* supports are underlining, boldface, and two types of page breaks. The first type is an *absolute* break that will give you a new page wherever you select it. The other is *conditional*; you include a number with the page-break instruction. When printing, if all of the text beginning at the point at which the conditional break was placed and up to the next carriage return will not fit in the number of lines specified, the page will break and the text will resume on the new page.

The cut-and-paste facilities here, too, are limited to a maximum of 1,024 characters. But you have to be careful about marking text for moves—once loaded into its holding buffer, text remains there until it is overwritten, and can become mixed in with the actual material transferred.

Headers and footers are also allowed, but problems occur when the first page of the document does not have a header. Unless you embed a blank header as the last parameter in your document, the header or footer will be included on all pages if you print the document a second time.

All print parameters (margins, spacing, lines per page, output slot number) can be placed in special commands in the body of the text and can be changed from line to line as the need arises.

Apple Writer // also supports global find and replace, as well as embedded control characters which can, among other things, change the type style on dot-matrix printers. These control characters can also be saved to disk and used as needed.

The program boasts several major features that many similar programs lack. With *Apple Writer //* you can create genuine footnotes (as opposed to repetitive footings) to document or explain statements in the text. And it includes another program called WPL (Word Processing Language) through which you can create EXEC-type programs that will run *Apple Writer //* as if you were there even though you're not.

The disk is protected against copying, although a backup is supplied. Once in *Apple Writer //*, you must exit via its own exit routine. To keep you from accidentally erasing text, the usual three-key reset function is disabled when the program is loaded and, short of turning off the computer, there is no other way to leave.

One final note: be *sure* you get the version that specifically states it will run on the //c.

Bank Street Writer

This program from Broderbund was originally designed for kids, but its power is deceptive. On the surface it looks too simple to be of much use, but once you try it you'll probably be surprised by its efficiency. There is no opening menu because there is no need for one. *BSW* uses a prompt line at the top of a double-high-resolution screen to keep you aware of what you need to do.

Without doubt, and with the full admission of its creators, this is a text handler. There are no fancy features other than a few utilities. You reach all the options by pressing the *esc* key. The available items are displayed at the top of the screen and selected by pressing the *tab* key until the desired option is highlighted. You select the feature by pressing *return*, or go back to typing by pressing the *esc* key again.

Deleted characters (and you can delete a range of text as well as single letters) can be restored if you change your mind. Up to fifteen lines of text can be moved around in a cut-and-paste operation.

The program supports full global search and replace functions as well as several disk access routines reached from its TRANSFER MENU. The program questions any action that will remove text that has not been saved, and asks you to verify your choice. All work is done in memory.

The forte of this program is the utilities program lying invisible on the disk. If you press the *esc* key while *BSW* itself is loading, the load is aborted and the utilities are run in its place.

Nearly everything in this program file is changeable. You select options ranging from the drive for the data disk to the use of the Apple //c mouse with the program. It will work in either 40- or 80-column mode, at your option, but even if set for 80-column, it will obey the placement of the Apple //c's *80/40* switch when it loads.

You can assign special character sequences to one-letter commands from within the utility program. These can be placed in your text and used to control the various output features of your printer. Surprisingly enough, considering the simplicity of the program, you can even adjust the serial port parameters from this utilities section—a feature not seen in any other text handler or word processor.

It's not for very long documents, but for letters or quick notes to the utility company, *BSW* is ideally customized for the Apple //c. There is a complete hands-on demonstration program included on the reverse side of the disk, and that may be copied. *BSW* itself, however, is copy protected.

Word Juggler

This program from Quark has migrated over from the Apple /// and runs under ProDOS. This opening menu is formidable:

```
                    Word Juggler

Options
1. NEW - Erases all text and goes to text entry mode
2. CATALOG - Lists all files in a directory
3. LOAD - Loads a document from disk and goes to
   text entry mode
4. STORE - Stores document on disk
5. PURGE - Removes a file from disk
6. FORMAT - Allows a disk to be formatted
7. DEFINE PREFIX - Defines the Prefix to be used for
   disk access
```

```
8. EDIT CONFIGURATION - Allows printer and default
   parameter selection
9. QUIT - Exits the Word Juggler program

Which option ([press RETURN] for text entry mode)?
```

This is a fairly complex program, and those who are new to word processing may avoid it for that reason. However, it has earned a well-deserved reputation as the best word-processing program available on the Apple ///, although it has its share of problems.

To implement all of the possible functions available, the top row of the keyboard serves multiple functions. When preceded by the *esc* key, the numeric and shifted values are ignored and interpreted as text-formatting commands that control justification, line spacing, and physical page characteristics. In addition, several other special commands are available from the keyboard by using a *control* and letter-key combination. A help function is available, but it lists only the cursor control key and *tab* key functions. The setup is confusing enough that most users need the keyboard overlay, a reference card that fits above the keys.

You enter text on an 80-column display with a status line at the bottom. Indicators show the current line and column number (absolute to the current document in memory) plus the amount of free lines available for your typing. Initially you can enter 780 lines of text, and although the page-handling and document-formatting commands must be on a line all to themselves, they do not subtract from the amount of open typing space. Before your document exceeds the allowable space, it must be saved to disk; at printing time, files may be linked together for continuous printing.

Word Juggler supports global find and replace as well as block storage to and retrieval from your disk, and block copy within a document (a block is simply a contiguous chunk of text). All commands that deal with text blocks are self-prompting and explain how the block is to be marked. The program carries you through the operation step by step.

Several of the more popular printers (Epson, Anadex, NEC, Diablo) are supported, and if your printer is not in the list, you can add it. Since that involves writing a machine language source file and is not something a novice (or many professionals) will have the faintest notion of how to do, it's a good idea to see if your printer is supported before buying the program.

Word Juggler appears to be aimed at the word craftsperson and is probably not a program you'd want to dive into unless you had some free time to learn how to use it properly. During the first few days of use the manual is indispensable.

Word Juggler is the only program of the group that comes with its own spelling checker, a wondrous piece of software that checks the spelling of each word in your document against a list of words it knows. It marks words it doesn't recognize and allows you to correct or ignore what it thinks are mistakes. You can also add new words to an auxiliary dictionary and build your own dictionary for specialized reports.

Spelling checkers do not check context: a sentence such as "The judgment is fare" will pass harmlessly through the checker because it is spelled correctly, even though the usage is incorrect. But typing mistakes and spelling blunders will be found and noted. If you're not the world's greatest speller, *Word Juggler*'s electronic dictionary may become your favorite program of all.

What's a Database?

Everyone uses databases all day long. Whenever you check the stock market prices, or look up a word in a dictionary, or consult a recipe in a cookbook, or see how your favorite team stacks up in the league standings, you're using a database.

As an experiment, reach into your pocket or over on the table and get your database book. You may call it your phone book or your address book, but you'll see what it really is in a moment. Look over some of the entries:

Fred Fern
82 Yeaster Ave
Brookline, MA 30032
(900) 555-5665
January 12

Jim Likfre
10101 Binary Lane
Malta, CO 20043
(900) 555-3422
July 18

Gladys Schutz
341 Miller Pond
Munchkin, RI 87333
(777) 828-9999
January 23

Tom Tom
22 Piperson Rd
Pumpkin, OH 45544
(256) 993-3455
March 14

Up until this moment, you've probably just thought of your list of names and numbers as a convenient grouping of your friends, something you used to keep in touch on birthdays and special occasions. But like all information, it can be used to extract other data you might need.

Suppose you wanted a list of everyone whose birthday was in the month of January? You'd search through your information and come up with the names Fred Fern and Gladys Schutz. How about everyone in the 900 area code? Again you search through the information and come up with Fred Fern and Jim Likfre.

As you can see, the raw data in your address book is the basis for many other related groups of information. And that's how a database works. You pour in all of the information you have on a given topic, whether it's friends or enemies or a list of the valuable coins in your collection, and use that base to extract any related information that you need.

The only difference between the database book you carry around with you and the database you would run on your computer is that the computer can do all of the same things you'd do much faster. If there were hundreds of names in your directory, and you were looking for similarities in area code or birthdays, it could take hours to examine every listing. Your Apple //c could sprint through the whole list in a minute or less. If you wanted to copy the names from your book to another list, you could spend many laborious hours typing or writing. Your computer could print out the new information in a fraction of the time.

The world of databases is a world of structures. And every structure has a clearly defined name and purpose.

Naming Your Facts: Database Terminology

Field	One unit of entered information. It could be someone's name, address, or any other piece of data.
Fieldname	A description of what you expect the contents of the field to be. In a simple address file it might be the word NAME.
Form or Screen	The name given to the collection of fieldnames as they are arranged. It is analogous to a paper form that has its own fieldnames and places to put information.
Record	A collection of related individual facts (fields). All the fieldnames you create gather information about one particular subject in a group of related elements. In your address list, one record would be all the information about one person.
File	The total collection of all the records in your database.

You use fieldnames to get field information, which makes up a record, which exists in a group called the database file. There are some very powerful database managers that can turn your Apple //c into the quickest file cabinet you'll ever use.

pfs:File
pfs: Report

The simplest database you can keep is on index cards. Each file is a "primary" database, since there is no real format to the information you can store or the way in which you can access it. The *File* and *Report* series function very much like an electronic index-card file.

The opening menu reads:

```
      pfs:FILE FUNCTION MENU

 1 DESIGN FILE          4 SEARCH/UPDATE
 2 ADD                  5 PRINT
 3 COPY                 6 REMOVE

      Your Selection:
      Filename:
```

File starts with the equivalent of a blank index card. Before you enter any information, you have to create some type of *input screen.* All this program requires is that you select the DESIGN FILE option and give what you're about to do a filename.

If you're familiar with BASIC, after entering the option number (in this case, 1 for DESIGN FILE), your first impulse will be to press the *return* key. You can, but it won't do anything but place the cursor somewhere on the left of the screen. *File* (like the entire pfs series on the Apple //) uses the *tab* key to advance from one option to another. Press *tab,* then enter the filename and a disk-drive designation if you don't want to use the built-in drive. Then use *control-C* to tell the program it should act on the information you've given it. *control-C* is always used as the signal for the program to start processing your information.

It will ask if you want to create a new file or change an existing one. Select 1, CREATE FILE. The next step is very important. The message on your screen will tell you that the disk in the drive you've chosen will be erased. *Make sure the disk in that drive is really blank or of no other use to you.* If you're using the internal drive, remove the *pfs:File* disk! If it is needed again, the program will ask you to reinsert it. If you decide that this isn't really what you want to do, you can press the *esc* key. It's *File*'s bailout back to the main menu from any level you're in.

Since *pfs:File* is a simple program, only one database can be created on each disk. When the disk has been formatted, an almost blank screen will appear. You then design the questions or prompts you'll use to specify what information you want.

To create a fieldname, just enter the word or words you want to use to describe the contents of the field. Immediately after the last character in the fieldname, place a colon. *File* sees this and knows that the fieldname stops there.

With some databases, you also need to describe a field length. Without it, the program wouldn't know how much information to accept for any given field. *File* doesn't need to know. If you wanted to, you could use one fieldname and fill the rest of the screen page (at the appropriate time) with information. *File* works just as well with a screenful of text as it does with a relatively small field. It determines the length of any field, at the time you use the CREATE option, by looking for the colon and counting the spaces to the next fieldname.

You can put up to one hundred items on a screen "page" and can even gain access to as many as thirty additional screen pages by using *control-N*. (*Control-P* brings you back to the previous page.) When you're done, use *control-C* to save the input form or *esc* to abandon it and return to the main menu. If you're not quite sure your form will work, you can try it out and change it later.

Entering information is done through ADD, and it's as simple as filling in the blanks and pressing *control-C* when you've filled in all of the data required by the form.

Some database programs let you assign special parameters to each field. You can define any of them as *required,* in which case information *must* be entered into it. You can also restrict the entered data in each field to either letters or numbers.

File doesn't use tricks like that; it is the simplest of simple database programs. You can enter anything anywhere you want, though you will be prevented from writing over fieldnames.

Other features allow you to find information contained in your file by using any one, or more than one, of the fields to specify the item you're searching for. It can be done with the complete information in a field, or by specifying a partial amount of the data. You can also specify search criteria that will return records containing data greater than, less than, or not equal to the tests you supply. If you want to change the information in the record once you've recalled it, you may.

If you want a printed copy of your data, you can use the same options you used in SEARCH/UPDATE to select which items are to be printed. Additionally, you can specify which field will be used to sort the file and whether the information in each record is printed on one line, on more than one line, or with a mixture of both. However, the printing option under *File* is primitive. The real report-writing features are found in another *pfs* program called *Report.*

Report is also menu driven. It allows you to set up and save complex report formats that can then be used with *File* or printed directly from *Report.*

The program lets you change the fieldnames as they'll appear on the report. In this way, if you've used lengthy descriptions to explain the information, they can be significantly shortened to allow more horizontal space for printing.

You can also specify up to three derived columns. These could be the result of adding two of the numeric fields or multiplying a numeric field by a constant number (if, for instance, you want to show what dollar amount of your income is devoted to income taxes). The derived field is not contained in the original file; it's created and used for the report only.

Taken together, these two programs form the essence of a very handy database system. There are several that are more complicated, such as *DB Master* from Stoneware and *NPL* from DeskTop Software. But for many simple applications the *pfs* series will be more than enough.

VisiDex

Part of the attraction of the Apple //c is its portability. Where you go, it can go. But what happens when you get there? Often there are commitments that you must meet and schedules that you must follow. In the noncomputer world, there is a system for keeping track of such things. It packs a calendar and a little address book into a small 4-by-6 vinyl portfolio.

VisiDex (from VisiCorp) is an electronic scheduler and note keeper. It works differently from *pfs:File* in that you don't need fieldnames. *VisiDex* uses the entire screen in free form. When you've finished entering the information, you can then go back and mark words in the text as keywords. When you want to recall information, you just enter the keyword you're looking for and the applicable screens appear.

When you begin the program, you see a blank screen. You gain access to Help and other available commands by using a command key, the slash (/), or a combination of letters in conjunction with the *control* key. To set up your computerized calendar, you need only begin typing.

On the blank area of the screen, in whatever format you feel most comfortable with, you enter the appointments you'll have on a given day. If you have a long appointment description that will allow only one entry on the screen, don't worry about it. When you're done with the description, press the slash key. Several options will appear at the top of the screen. You'll press "C" for Calendar, followed by "P" for Put.

The program will then ask in what month and day you want the entry stored. It will then prompt you with a WARNING, followed by 00. At this point you can set an alarm feature by substituting a number between 01 and 15 for the 00 default. This will automatically notify you the specified number of days in advance that your appointment or scheduled event is coming due. The reminder will reappear any time you use the disk during that period.

If there are any regularly scheduled events on your calendar, you can respond "yes" to the next question, REPEAT PERIODICALLY? You may tell it to repeat the alarm weekly on the day you've selected (when you tell *VisiDex* the date of the appointment, it knows what day it falls on), monthly by the date, or monthly by the weekday. If the next day you use that disk falls within the warning range, your appointments that have come due will be displayed, one screen at a time, before you're allowed to do anything else.

If you have, or suspect you have, additional appointments outside of the warning period, you can call up a copy of the calendar onto the screen:

```
              MAY          1996

SUN    MON   TUES   WED    THU   FRI    SAT

             [ 1]     2     3     4      5
  6      7   [ 8]  [ 9]    10    11     12
 13     14   [15]    16    17    18     19
 20     21   [22]    23    24    25     26
 27     28   [29]    30    31
```

This display would indicate that a regularly scheduled appointment occurs every Tuesday and that you have an additional commitment scheduled for Wednesday, the ninth. If you were unclear about what this last appointment was, and it hadn't showed up among your reminders, you could then call up any text screen associated with that date. The dialogue you entered would refresh your memory.

There are some problems with this program. Although you could install an internal clock in most of the Apple // series, there are no slots for the purpose in the Apple //c. If *VisiDex* does not find a clock in your machine, it will give you the opportunity to set the date manually. For any of the reminders to work, you must do this every time you use the program. If you forget, you won't be told of anything pending.

Also, *VisiDex* is a product of an older technology. It deals with a 40-column screen only. Previous Apple // series computers had optional 80-column cards available, so it was possible that your computer wouldn't have one. Your Apple //c is different. Taking advantage of its 80-column display capability would give you a larger memo area. Some of the VisiCorp products are in the process of being upgraded to take advantage of the Apple //c, but it remains to be seen if this is one of them.

Juggling Numbers

To do something like this is simple:

$$\begin{array}{r} 12 \\ 21 \\ 133 \\ +\ 255 \\ \hline 421 \end{array}$$

It's compound addition and easy enough to do just by adding the columns and carrying where necessary. Even this:

12	23	42
21	11	22
133	136	133
+ 255	+ 225	+ 155
421	395	352

is not so difficult that it can't be done without the assistance of a calculator. But what if the first column of numbers represented the income from four divisions of a company for the first fiscal quarter? And what if the other two columns represented income from successive quarters? What if you had to use this information to determine the profitability of the company over the next two years?

What if? That's what spreadsheets are all about. With a calculator and a large sheet of paper anyone can do a large amount of columnar math. But picture a sheet of paper wide enough to handle 255 columns of 9-digit numbers and long enough to accommodate 128 rows. Even if you take the time to fill up one-third of a sheet that size, what happens if someone walks along and says "What if we change the number in the 45th column, 20th row?" Even that can be done, as long as the relationships between the numbers are simple. If it's just a matter of addition, it just means adding up one row of numbers, and maybe one column, too. But what if . . .

There are so many complex relationships that *could* be arranged where a change in one number would ripple through the entire sheet. Given the propensity of people to be curious, there is a very great likelihood that "just one change" will blossom into dozens.

This is where your computer thrives. It eats complex numeric relationships and spits out answers faster than the fastest calculator driven by the most experienced hands. But it can't do it alone. As with any other operation you want it to perform, you'll need a program to direct and manage the work.

The Spreadsheet Goes Electronic

There are quite a few programs to handle your numeric needs. They tend to boil down to a rather simple format:

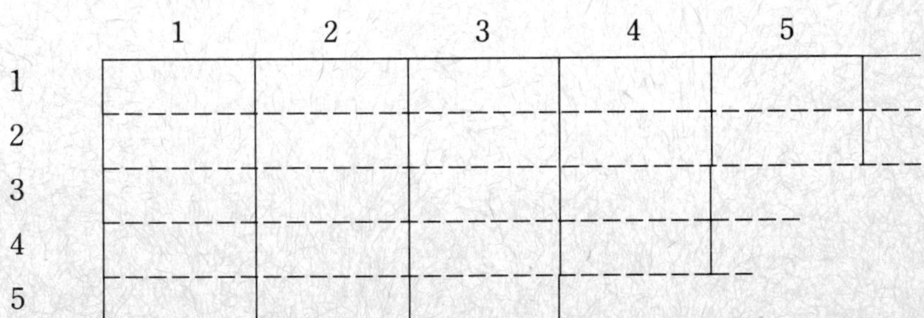

If you've read the chapters on Applesoft, you'll recognize the structure. It's a matrix. That's how spreadsheets handle numbers. The coordinates 1,3 in the matrix refer to a box, called a cell, which, in this case, is in the first column, the third row down from the top.

To use the matrix, and therefore the spreadsheet, you can fill the cells with any of three possible types of information.

Alphanumeric	Alphanumeric data is equivalent to using strings in BASIC. You can use these for titling at the top of the sheet, or as column and/or row labels. They are not processed by the program, and if by misfortune they are included in any calculations, their value is counted as zero. Handling of these types is limited to left, right, or center justification within a cell.
Numeric	These can be either integers or real numbers, and usually you are allowed to specify which type you prefer them to remain. With some programs, real numbers can only be displayed to a maximum of three decimal places although their working value remains the actual numeric quantity. Most spreadsheets permit either value to be augmented with dollar signs, commas, or parentheses (to indicate negative values) as the need requires, and as you choose.
Formulas	Formulas can be rather varied in most of the available spreadsheet programs. They can range from the standard simple mathematic operations, through predefined math functions such as average, mean, sine, cosine, and the like, to complex relationships and interdependencies among values contained in various cells.

It's actually the last of these that has made spreadsheet programs so popular. You can take the value found in one cell, whether it's one you entered or one the computer has figured out from a computation involving other numbers, and formulate a second value in another cell relative to any of a multitude of relationships. You literally have the ability to program each cell independently or interdependently of the others.

The actual tools each program allows you to facilitate your actions can vary, but in format they have mostly become standardized. As an example, if you had numeric values in one of the columns, perhaps four rows long, to add those values, most programs follow a format close to this:

```
SUM(startcolumn,startrow..endcolumn,endrow)
```

The particulars might vary. For instance, some use two dots to indicate a range; others use a colon. Some require brackets around the column and row values, others don't. Averaging a column of numbers would be:

AVG(startcolumn, startrow..endcolumn, endrow)

Simple math functions are done by asking the program to multiply or divide one column-and-row specified cell by another or by a literal value that you enter.

The magic "what if" answers are easy to get. All you do is substitute new values for the old and the program redoes the computations for you.

Juggling the Features

There are two outstanding packages currently on the market for the Apple. *VisiCalc*, the grandfather of them all, and *Multiplan*, a newer contender. Others may offer the particular functions you need, but these two have stood the test of time.

VisiCalc is the spreadsheet program that "made" the Apple //. It's generally agreed that without it the computer would have never taken off as well as it did. Over the years, VisiCorp has revised it often to keep it up-to-date. The newer *Multiplan* is made by the same Microsoft that invented and virtually "owns" the microcomputer BASIC language.

Though the features they offer differ somewhat, you are unlikely to use even half of them in even the most complex spreadsheet you'll develop. In terms of visual presentation, *VisiCalc* appears clear and clean. The screen you're presented with is uncluttered and neatly delineated. *Multiplan* crowds the screen a bit, but that's because it offers a constant display of the commands you have available. There are other differences, but for the average person's use, the programs are fundamentally equivalent.

Prepackaged *templates* that have the mathematical relationships between the cells already set up for common uses (preparing your income tax, for example) can save hours of work and are available in a wide variety of applications for both packages. One reason to choose one spreadsheet over another might be the availability of a template you need. Another reason might be the availability of spreadsheet designs already prepared by friends or colleagues. These can be saved to disk and read into your machine, but the two programs store them in very different formats.

Just one note. The way the Apple //c deals with the character display on the screen is just a little different from the way the earlier models did it. Some of the spreadsheet programs bypassed the Apple's official programming routines for writing characters to the screen and used their own. By doing that they picked up some speed in the way they moved the columns and rows around.

Unfortunately, the conditions under which the homebrew methods worked no longer exist in the Apple //c, which means the programs don't run quite right. Make sure, *before* you purchase any of them, that they specifically state that they are Apple //c compatible. The phrase "for the Apple //e" does *not* guarantee it will work on your computer.

An Oddball Number Cruncher

TK!Solver is from Software Arts, the people who originally wrote *VisiCalc*. It's not a spreadsheet; it's designed to let you set up complex equations, then enter data and let the computer solve them. For some users, it's handier than a spreadsheet, because it lets you enter equations in a more logical way. The program comes complete with a huge library of mathematical formulas, and additional libraries for such special uses as mechanical engineering are also available.

AppleWorks—Putting It All Together

As we've seen with the *pfs* software, some programs are designed to share information with others in the same series. Such programs offer "integration" only at a rudimentary level. Every time you decide you want to handle the information in a different way, you have to exit one program and call up another one.

AppleWorks is different. Apple's contribution to integrated software was originally designed for the Apple /// and brought over under ProDOS. This program combines the functions of a word processor, database, and spreadsheet in one package. The important point is that they are not

```
Disk: Drive 1                    ADD FILES                  Escape: Main Menu
------------------------------------------------------------------------------
   Main Menu
     Add Files

          Get files from:

       1. The current disk: Drive 1
       2. A different disk

          Make a new file for the:

       3. Word Processor
       4. Data Base
       5. Spreadsheet

------------------------------------------------------------------------------
Type number, or use arrows, then press Return _                    55K Avail.
```

An* AppleWorks *menu.

On-screen "file folders" are common sights with this program.

individual programs that must be called from separate menus. With *AppleWorks,* all three functions are available simultaneously.

When you boot the disk, you see a screen representation of a file folder. On this video folder is the main operating menu. Through it you wander among the various functions. Just call in whatever file you want to work with and you're ready to start.

Once you're working, you can pull in information from the database or spreadsheet, keep it in a small holding area in memory, and transfer it to any other portion of the program. It's easy, for example, to take a financial report generated by the spreadsheet or an analysis of information from the database, and cut and paste them into a document prepared with the word processor. The final output then becomes a professional-looking report.

The word processor features on-screen display of the document format, with full printer enhancement features available. The spreadsheet allows a 127-column by 999-row screen page (quite sizable compared to most) and supports all standard mathematics functions as well as the use of formulas. While it is not as powerful as some, it should meet most lower-level needs.

The database portion is a version of an earlier Apple filing program. Since all the information about one record is presented in a single screen line, it's not as versatile as *pfs:File,* for example, in generating screen reports. However, you can zoom in to change details or see data not designated for display.

You may want to investigate using a high-capacity hard disk in conjunction with this versatile program (see chapter 19 for further details).

Communications

There are some obvious reasons why the portable //c marks the first serial modem port Apple has ever built into an Apple // model. Although there are telephones at every turn in the road, it is not always possible or desirable to talk over them. Some things, like long reports, can't easily be dictated over the phone. More important, some very useful information services and databases are electronic-only, and you need a modem-equipped computer to use them. Or you might want to share your programs with your friends. If you all live nearby, it's easy enough to swap disks, but if you're worlds apart, you can use your modems to swap information.

Your computer and modem alone can handle the job, but just barely. Unless you're some kind of masochist, you'll want *communications* software. Using it, your computer becomes an extension of the information services like The Source and CompuServe, large computer systems that allow you access to their equipment over the phone lines. With them, you can search through large databases of information or scan the press releases from UPI, "chat" with friends, or send electronic mail that can be hand-delivered in paper form at the other end of the country in just four hours.

Typical Features Found on Many of the Telecommunications Networks (The Source, CompuServe, Dow Jones, etc.)

Database Services
- Restaurant & Hotel Information
- Airline Schedules and Fares
- Historical Financial Quotes
- Movie Reviews

Bulletin Boards
- Apple User Groups
- Special-Interest Groups
- Classified Advertising
- Personal Interaction

Mainframe Programming
- BASIC
- Pascal
- FORTRAN
- COBOL

News Services
- UPI, Reuters
- Dow Jones Stock Prices (10-minute delay)

Shop-at-Home Services
On-Line Encyclopedias
Games
Electronic Mail

Apple Access //

Apple's adventure into telecommunications software is called *Access //*. It's another immigrant from the Apple /// brought over to take advantage of the ProDOS operating system. It was tailored to the Apple //c environment and provides you with complete control over the serial communications port and all the parameters under which it operates.

The program is menu driven. Even while you're using your computer as a terminal, you can shift in and out of the menus as you need them. And since some telecommunications services require special terminals, *Access //* will let you use your computer as a plain old Apple, or emulate the snazzy Digital Equipment Corporation VT100 or VT52 terminals, the most popular models around.

Access // lets you save to disk all of the dialogue that occurs on your screen and any information transferred to or from your machine. You can also transmit (*upload*) and receive (*download*) files using two different protocols. The popular Christensen protocol (also known as XMODEM) incorporates error checking to assure that the material sent is the same as material received, no matter how hard the phone lines try to garble the information. The "standard" protocol comes in handy when the machine at the other end of the line isn't equipped with the XMODEM capabilities.

ASCII Express

Some features aren't available in *Access //*. For example, given the right modem and the right software, your computer can respond to incoming calls from other computers without your being present. *ASCII Express: The Professional* provides this feature. With your Apple //c on the road, and perhaps another Apple at home, this can help keep you in touch.

ASCII Express also lets you create keyboard macros—strings of up to twelve characters that can be sent with two keystrokes. If a computer you are communicating with requires lengthy codes or expressions to reach some of its functions, you can define them as macros, shorten the number of keys you need to press to access those features, and thus decrease your bill for access time.

ASCII Express also comes equipped with its own editor, which allows you to create or modify text files before you send them. That's useful if you're using an information system that will allow you to leave messages.

Terminal emulation is wide ranging but tricky with *ASCII Express.* It comes equipped to look like a DEC VT52. Changes are possible, but they're not exactly simple. The program comes with a free on-line demonstration of the CompuServe information system, as well as an application to subscribe to its services.

Many similar programs are available. Each has a few features the others don't and lacks some the others include. Before you purchase a communications program, analyze the type of communication you want to do. For most of the low-level communications and some file-transfer operations, a program like *Access //* will work very well. More sophisticated procedures will require more advanced programs such as *ASCII Express.*

Terms Used in Telecommunications

Download	The act of transferring files or programs from a remote system.
Full Duplex	Characters typed at the keyboard are received by the remote computer and transmitted back to you, showing up on the screen. If echo is on and the remote system is FULL DUPLEX, all characters you type will appear twice.
Half Duplex	Characters typed at the keyboard are displayed on the screen by your computer. On the Apple //c this is equivalent to turning the echo on.
Off-line	Also called local mode. Words typed at the keyboard are only interpreted locally (not sent to the remote computer). Also may refer to being disconnected from another computer system.
On-line	Being actually in communication, where what you type is received on the other end and vice versa. Also may simply refer to being connected to another computer system.
Telecommunications	Using computers to communicate over the phone lines.
Terminal	A noncomputerized device consisting of a keyboard, a screen, and sufficient electronics to operate them and a serial port. Most communications programs allow your computer to look like at least one of a variety of these while retaining its own ability to perform disk fuctions, which terminals lack.
Upload	The act of transferring files or programs to a remote system.

19

Graphics, Games, and Goodies: Of Mice and Arcades and a Flat-Screen Future

Apple's success with the Macintosh computer has led to special developments for the Apple //c. Foremost is the technology of the mouse, most ballyhooed of the new "pointing devices."

What's a Mouse?

The reason behind using a mouse is to reduce your dependence on the keyboard. Typically, programs have had you choose among options by asking you to select letters or numbers from a menu list. But on a computer screen there is a limited amount of space to explain what the menu options are. In some cases, you're forced to run a program with the keyboard under one hand and the manual in the other until you learn what all the options are and what they mean.

Apple's new approach incorporates *icons*—pictorial representations of functions or choices. By using a picture as shorthand, the choices can be more descriptive and make more sense without the need for verbose explanations.

The mouse itself is a device just a little larger than the palm of your hand. On the top is a wide, squarish button-type switch. It plugs into the nine-pin D-type joystick/mouse port on the back of the Apple //c.

Inside the mouse is a round rubber ball, visible from and extending through its underside. As you move the mouse along a flat surface, the ball moves as well. Two small rotating wheels inside the mouse rest on this

The Apple //c mouse.

ball. As it moves, they do, too. They, in turn, are read by an optical sensor which transmits the movement information into signals the Apple //c can understand and sends the information down the mouse's 4-foot wire "tail" into the computer. It provides very accurate details regarding the mouse's movements.

Good Mousekeeping

There's very little maintenance needed for the mouse, provided you take some reasonable precautions. The surface you use it on should be relatively smooth and flat. Dust, crumbs, and ashes will all adversely affect the mouse's performance, so keep the area as clean as possible. A nicely polished table may well seem the perfect place for your Apple //c's mouse, but the movement of the rubber ball may mar a fine surface. If you put a piece of paper on it, you should be able to use the mouse without damaging it or the table.

Periodically you might want to clean the ball. You do that by removing it from the mouse. Turning the black circular retaining ring counterclockwise (from the engraved "I" toward the engraved "O"), it will come away from the mouse's body. Cup the underside of the mouse with the palm of your hand and turn it right-side up. The rubber ball will fall gently into your hand and can then be cleaned with plain water. Do *not* use a solvent; the ball may melt. Putting the mouse back together is just the reverse of disassembly.

Mousehold Words: Rodential Terminology

On-Screen:

Icon	The pictorial representation of an option or feature displayed on the screen. For example, a procedure to erase material from the screen might be represented as an eraser, while one that puts things onto the screen might be a pencil or a paintbrush or some other writing implement.
Pull-Down Menu	Menus appearing at the top of a mouse-oriented screen. Usually, they are described by single words. The mouse can be used to select the menu and then "pull down" the options available from it.
Pointer	The physical representation of the mouse on your screen. Usually it appears as a cross hair or some symbol representing the function that has been selected.

On-Mouse:

Clicking	The action of pressing down upon and releasing the mouse's button. It is a short-duration activity, down-up, done as if you were pressing the *reset* switch on the Apple //c itself.
Dragging	Moving the mouse while its button is pressed. For example, to select a menu option from the top of the *MousePaint* screen, you would move the pointer to the word describing the menu you want. When you press the mouse's button, a pull-down menu will appear. You drag to the option on the menu and release the button when the pointer is over your desired selection.

(continued)

Moving	Moving the mouse, in any direction, without performing any other function.
Pressing	A one-directional activity that describes only the pressing down of the mouse's button. You are not expected to release the button again until some action has been performed.

Using the Mouse—MousePaint

Graphics have always been a strong point on the Apple computer, yet Apple has never really supplied its own graphics-handling package—until now. It's called *MousePaint,* and it's distributed free of charge with the mouse.

Although *MousePaint* is not as extensive as Macintosh's *MacPaint,* the first screen you are presented with when you boot *MousePaint* looks very much like it. Across the top of the screen is a row of "pull-down" menus represented by single words that stand for the functions available within the program: FILE, EDIT, AIDS, and FONT.

By moving the mouse to any of the words and pressing its button, you see the appropriate menu for each option. Along the left edge of the screen are icons for the various graphics tools available. These include the hand, the editor's box, the pencil, a large letter *A* for placing alphanumeric

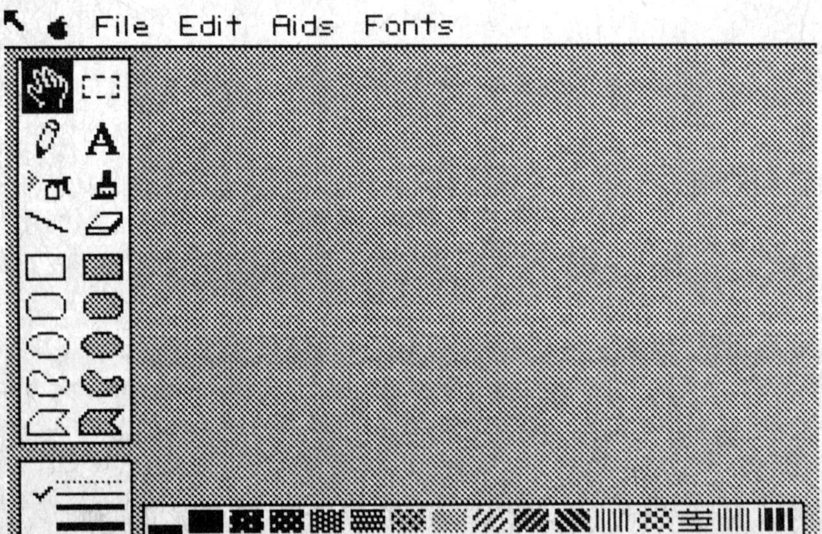

The main **MousePaint** *screen.*

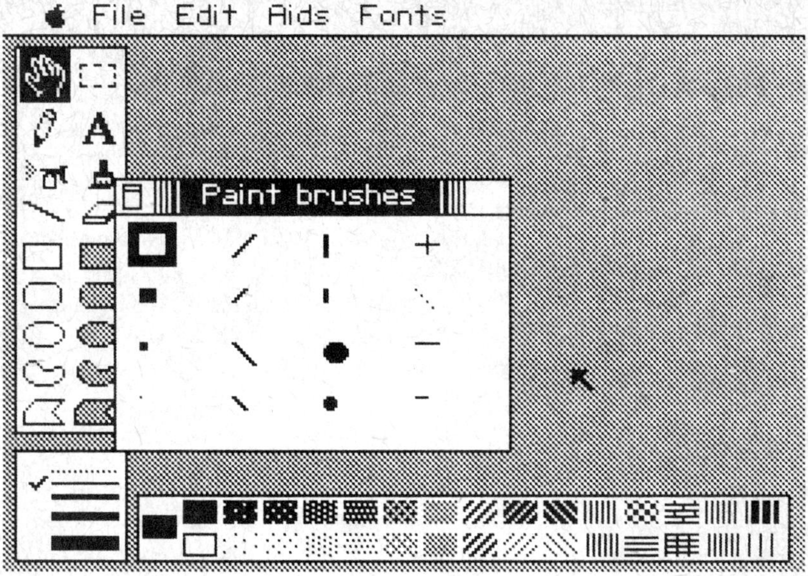

"Paint brushes" available from **MousePaint.**

characters in the graphic area, the spray can, the brush, the straight-edge, and the eraser. Just below these are a variety of predefined shapes (in either open or filled-in versions) that can be used on the screen. The final dimensions of any shape will depend on your use of the mouse.

At the bottom left of the screen are five lines of varying thicknesses. By selecting any of these, you modify the width of the drawing line used on the screen. Immediately to their right is a palette of patterns and colors used to fill shapes and draw with.

It's not the best of all graphics-handling programs: certainly Penguin's *Graphics Magician* is as good if not slightly better. But at this writing, *MousePaint* is the only one that uses the mouse and the only one with provisions for printing on Apple's own Imagewriter printer.

You can cut and paste graphic images by enclosing them in an editor's box and selecting either the cut or copy function from the Edit menu. Unfortunately, anything stored this way is erased if you select *font* to place characters on the screen.

The paintbrush is another sore point. As the icon implies, it will let you paint on the screen. However, at least in the initial release version, no matter which color you select from the palette, the brush always paints in black.

But all in all the software is excellent. It comes free with the mouse, and the mouse itself should prove to be a major implement in the future development of the Apple //c.

Using the Mouse from BASIC

You can access the mouse from Applesoft with some simple programming. It's done like this:

```
10 PRINT CHR$(4);"PR#4":PRINT CHR$(1)
20 PRINT CHR$(4);"PR#0"
```

Your Apple //c imagines that the mouse is connected via slot number 4. Line 10 opens that slot, after which you send CHR$(1) out to the mouse. That's its initialization character. It sets the mouse's position-counter to zero so it imagines that all of its movements are from start.

Now you get some information from the mouse:

```
30 PRINT CHR$(4);"IN#4"
40 INPUT"";X,Y,C
```

Line 30 is obvious: It takes all further input from the device connected in slot 4, in this case the mouse. Line 40 gets the mouse's information. The actual variable names are not important—what they do tell you is the current horizontal (you've used X to hold this value) and vertical (you've used Y for it) position of the mouse. The third value, C, in this case, tells you whether or not the mouse's button has been depressed.

The range of values for the X and Y coordinates are 0 to 1,023, while the button value works as shown below:

Has the Mouse's Button Been Pressed? (Values Passed to BASIC)

Value	Currently	Previous
1	Pressed	Pressed
2	Pressed	Released
3	Released	Pressed
4	Released	Released

At first, those values may make no sense to you. Here's the explanation.

The first time you run the program, the mouse's button has not been pressed previously (and even if it has, the CHR$(1) reset that) and, if you don't touch it, it is not now being pressed. Therefore, the value you'd expect to see is 4.

If you quickly press and release the button so that it all happens before your program has a chance to get those values more than once, you'd expect the value to be 2 (it wasn't pressed before, but it is now). The very next time your program reads the mouse, the value will change to 3 because the button *was* pressed but isn't now. If you hold the button down through successive readings of the mouse, the value of the third variable will then be 1 because the button was pressed during both of the last two reads.

What can you do with it? How about a graphics application? Your Apple //c's hi-res screen is 280 × 192 dots (0–279 across and 0–191 top to bottom). Let's use some simple math:

280/1024 = .273   192/1024 = .188

Every one position your mouse moves horizontally is equivalent to moving .273 positions in the same direction on the screen. Likewise, each vertical movement is .188 of one vertical movement on the screen. Using HPLOT and these ratios, you can make yourself a very nice drawing program (just remember to use PRINT CHR$(4);"PR#0" when you want to do something on the screen).

If all you'd like to do is verify that the values actually change in the way described, add the following lines to the program:

```
50 PRINT CHR$(4);"PR#0"
60 PRINT X,Y,C
70 GOTO 30
```

This will, of course, put the program into an endless loop that always goes to line 30. You'll have to use the *control-C* interrupt to get out of it.

Advanced Mouse Knowledge

The third variable, which you've called C, actually has two functions. As you've seen, it will tell you the previous two conditions of the button. It can also be either positive or negative.

If, when you input it, its value is negative, it's also telling you that a key has been pressed on the keyboard. The sign of the number will remain negative after that until and unless you reset it. If you do that by reinitializing the mouse, you'll reset everything, which could be disastrous for any program you've written. So there must be another way out of it.

And there is. The mouse uses memory location –16368. When a key is pressed, it puts a nonzero value in there and continues to check that spot so it can keep the variable value in the correct state. You can use a BASIC command called POKE to reset that value to zero by doing the following:

```
POKE -16368,0
```

The POKE command directly alters the value of the memory location you've selected. In this case, you've placed zero there, which resets the mouse's third value to a positive number; *which* number depends on the status of the button.

During your graphics program, you could check for use of the keyboard and switch over to a menu of features. Keep in mind, though, that as the subheading of this section suggests, this kind of work involves advanced procedures beyond the scope of this book. But if you're up to it, the potential is there.

The //c at Play: Games

If you mention that you play games on your computer, some misguided souls will look upon you with scorn for abusing a sophisticated piece of electronic equipment. Others will nod knowingly—to them microcomputers are of no other use. No matter which camp you find yourself in, you should know this: The Apple // series has always had color and graphics, and that makes it a first-rate game machine.

There are three basic types of games available for your Apple //c: arcade, fantasy, and adventure. Simulations are often classified as a fourth type, but there's some question about whether the "games" in this category are actually games at all. Educational programs that masquerade as games are also widely available. They attract attention and impart knowledge while letting the user enjoy the experience.

There's no way I can provide an exhaustive list: games for the Apple now number in the many hundreds. But I can give you an introduction to some stellar examples of the various types. I'll include some games that have already become classics and newer products on their way to stardom. Any of them should prove enjoyable.

Arcadian Dreams

Video arcade machines can be found almost anywhere you look. The vast majority have been shoot-'em-ups of one type or another that pit your skill of avoidance and defense against hostile forces bent on your destruction. You survive by the speed of your reflexes and your ability to avoid the attacks and mount your offensive. Variations include maze games like *Pac-Man* and climbing games like *Donkey Kong*. As they come to the Apple, most of the arcade graphics survive.

One reminder: You won't be able to use older Apple // model joysticks on the Apple //c—the old-model sixteen-pin connectors just won't mate with the nine-pin connector on your machine. Apple and others supply the new model, but watch out: other computer brands and a few video games use joysticks that have similar-looking connectors, but they won't work with the //c, either.

Keep your eyes open and make sure that any you buy say they are Apple //c compatible. A good joystick can, at times, be your only friend in the world.

The arcade classics are easy to name. And, with minor exception, they always seem to come from the same companies. Let's look at a few.

Alien Rain

This is the successor to the original Space Invaders. It's a fast-paced alien attack where the attackers circle and dive at you while dropping bombs. You have to do your best to avoid them and fire your own missiles. The faster-paced version of this game, *Alien Typhoon,* has been known to drive people over the edge with its speed. Broderbund makes both.

Apple Panic

This is a cross between *Donkey Kong* and *Burger Time,* released way back at the end of 1981. It's still an excellent time passer as you run up and down ladders and dig holes you hope strange creatures will fall into. From Broderbund.

Epoch

Another blaster action game, but this time with extremely good graphic sequences and music atypical of the usual arcade sounds. Originally released in late 1981 by Sirius Software.

Lode Runner

You can search for the stolen gold by climbing, digging, and jumping through 150 different scenarios. If that's not enough, you can design your own setups. Late 1983, from Broderbund.

Miner 2049er

Underground appears to be the way to go, and the mine definitely needs shoring up. But watch out for the mutants. The game is superb. 1983 from Micro Lab.

Pinball Construction Set

If you're tired of all the rest, you can use this to design and implement your own action games. It's a 1983 game from Software Arts and Bill Budge, the author of *MousePaint.*

Zaxxon

One of the few games which uses 3-D graphics makes you guide your fighter jet through innumerable exploding missiles and firing turrets until finally you face the awful machine Zaxxon. From Datasoft, late in 1983.

Adventure Games

These games face you with a challenge and a quest. You start with a small handful of words that the program understands. You must deduce others as you map your way through a world (not necessarily *the* world). On your journey you can collect items that will help you—but only if you use them in the right combination. Some of these games have graphics. Many do not. You use no joysticks or paddles—only your mind and your wits.

Adventure

The original version of this, *Colossal Cave,* is the granddaddy of all adventure games. This one is from Microsoft and leads you through the underground in search of treasure. Watch out for the dwarf, and if you get into the lower levels make sure you have some change for the vending machine.

Dark Crystal

An adaptation of the movie, with hi-res graphics and some twists and surprises that will keep you going even if you've seen the flick. Just don't cut yourself on the stone. From Sierra On-Line.

Zork I, II, and/or III

These three adventures form the Underground Empire trilogy. The command interpreter, the section of the program that understands the commands you enter, is probably the best of the bunch. This one is from Infocom, the company that's the acknowledged leader in text adventures. Their games do not include graphics; they just keep getting better and better. More recent Infocom games include *Deadline* and *The Witness,* two detective mysteries.

Fantasy

As the name implies, these games involve unreality carried to the extreme. You create the characters you use. You can even assume their identity. All the while you wander through the world acquiring experience and, hopefully, a few dollars. In many cases, overcoming your adversaries is the path to greater glory.

Beneath Apple Manor

The beginning of the fantasy games for the Apple computer, liberally peppered with hi-res graphics. It was first released very early in the Apple's history and has been revamped in the last year or so. From Quality Software.

Ultima I, II, and III

Wander across worlds and time while you fight foes, get horses, ships, armor, and, perhaps, a spacecraft or two. These are independent but visually related games increasing in complexity. With hi-res graphics and some sound from California Pacific, Sierra On-Line, and Origin Systems, depending on which one you want.

Simulations

In an ideal simulation, you could step from the game into similar real-life situations, and perhaps have acquired enough experience to handle yourself well. These aren't million-dollar flight simulators complete with fog and rain, but they're awfully impressive for the price.

Castle Wolfenstein

An old one from 1981, but definitely a classic. It combines strategy with fantasy and adventure as you try to escape from a German fortress. It will help if you can understand German: you'll actually hear the language coming out of your machine's speaker. From Muse.

Flight Simulator II

The original *Flight Simulator,* A2-FS1, was a cassette-based program that offered practically flicker-free graphics—quite an acccomplishment for the late 1970s on any computer. A2-FS2, the new version, is even better. You sit in the cockpit of a single-engined plane before a full panel of instruments. And you fly. You have a choice of airports, flying conditions, and much more. You can even select at which altitude your plane will stall. Every possible control and condition has been recreated. If you'd like, just declare war and you can jump into a biplane and fight the Red Baron. This one is sold by SubLogic, where rumor has it that there may soon (or already) be an interactive version allowing several Apple //c's to connect up via the serial ports and fly interactively.

Sargon III

The Spracklens (Kathe and Dan) are at it again. They provided the original Apple chess game, with hi-res graphics, in *Sargon I.* Then they increased the level of play with *Sargon II,* and now comes *Sargon III.* The opening book is better, the end game is better, and the response time, long a bane to computer chess players, is fantastic. The graphics are still the same—terrific. From Hayden.

Education

The Apple // series is by far the leader in the educational computing world. If you visit any school with a computing program, chances are that the kids will be using Apples. Hundreds of educational programs have been developed on Apple // machines. The excellent book *Turn Your Kid into a Computer Genius* (Dutton) by Carole Houze Gerber gives an extensive rundown on the best programs available.

Of the two programs mentioned here, the first was redone to include one of the Apple //c's features; the other was written with the Apple //c specifically in mind.

MasterType

The whole world is tired of computer-based typing tutors; they have been around since the first keyboard appeared. But if you don't know how to type, it's a different story.

And you *don't* know how to type on your Apple //c. This excellent hands-on typing tutorial is one of the only typing programs that also includes practice on the Dvorak keyboard, the "other" keyboard hiding inside the Apple //c. Just be careful if your high scores make you decide to pry up those keycaps! From Scarborough.

Fact and Fiction Tool Kit

Younger children have a harder time of things than adults. Computer games are usually aimed at the older population and those that aren't are often boringly repetitive. Adults have some relief with programs like Budge's *Pinball Construction Kit,* but children can get little escape from suffering through the same stupid screen faces time after time. Until now.

Fact and Fiction Tool Kit is incredible. It's a *MacPaint* for juniors and as simple as breathing to operate. Using either a joystick or the Apple //c's mouse, children can wander through the tools available selecting icons of trees, animals, and objects or draw their own images. To highlight the story they're drawing, they can add text to the graphics and create a complete storybook.

This is one of the first programs to use the double-hi-res graphics available from the 80-column video electronics—in full color. It's also one of the few programs that supports the Apple //c's mouse.

Also included on the disk, though somewhat overshadowed by the *Tool Kit,* is a file system that introduces the youngster (in body and mind) to the concepts and practices of collecting and saving information. Just think how you felt the first time you heard the word database—wouldn't it have been nice to be prepared? From Scholastic; recommended for those eight and over.

Coming Attractions

Even after releasing two brand-new machines in 1984, Apple Computer is not sitting still. The company is working on new ways of increasing your computer's productivity and versatility. Here are some of the things that should be introduced in the very near future.

Flat Screen

No one can be expected to carry a monitor around on a regular basis, and TV sets are just no good for 80-column displays. One way the Apple //c can become even more portable is by getting a portable display.

And Apple is currently working on just that: an 80-column-by-24-row display device that uses an LCD (liquid crystal display) screen. The screen itself is from Sharp and will plug into the video expansion port of the Apple //c. It's about 1 inch thick and perhaps 11 inches wide by 5 inches high. It's small and light enough to rest on top of the Apple //c's case and will fit in its carryall bag.

Apple promises this for the end of 1984, but do be aware that quality-control problems have long plagued the LCD industry. Apparently there are few effective quality-assurance techniques that don't risk damage to the LCD in the testing process.

Although there are currently no ads for the device or even mention of it beyond the initial information release, it may well arrive near the promised delivery date and could be a boon to users who travel. If there are difficulties in manufacturing, be patient.

Hard Disks

Although the //c is portable, there will come a time when you'll want to set it down somewhere for a while. Perhaps you'll want to keep it in one place and get another to tote around. In any case, when you have tasks involving large amounts of data, floppy disks will be ineffective. They just can't hold enough information for a good-sized database.

Though DOS was never meant to handle large quantities of data, ProDOS solves that problem for you. And Apple is not that far away with a physical solution. Very soon, Apple's well-proven Profile hard disk will be marketed for the Apple //c. It currently has the capability to hold five million characters of information, but an upgrade is in the works to bring capacity up to ten million. Quark, Inc., has also announced a ten megabyte hard disk exclusively for the Apple //c which will be available in the last quarter of 1984.

While neither size hard disk weighs very much, using one is likely to keep your machine nearby for the duration of the project. Because of their delicate nature, hard disks are generally not portable devices.

Color Plotter

Apple markets a multipen color plotter. It's a print output device that uses special pens. Where the printing element of a standard printer may print a section of a letter or a whole letter each time, a plotter works one dot at a time—but it works very fast. It is also very precise, and it is perfect for technical drawing.

Using this method, a screen of graphics can be printed, dot by dot, color for color in most cases, in any of a number of different sizes under software control. Drawings done to scale will remain in scale, and this precision makes the plotter a valuable, and expensive, tool.

Apple's plotter will work with the Apple // series, and therefore should work with your Apple //c. The only modifications to the driver software would possibly be for the double-hi-res graphics, and that should not be a major task. Look for its availability for the Apple //c shortly.

20

Apple Info: Where to Find It

Once you buy an Apple, you're not cut adrift and left to fend for yourself. Thousands of Apple users and fanatics across the country are willing to help you get more and more out of your machine. All you need to know is where to look.

User Groups

Perhaps the best source of information on Apple computers, or products available at a discount, or help with problems you might be having is your local Apple user group. Everyone there, no matter what their current level of expertise, started where you are starting now. And they remember that.

User groups welcome new members warmly. Chances are that if you run into a problem, no matter what it is, someone in the user group has had a similar experience and knows exactly what to do about it. User groups offer public domain software that's absolutely free. And subsidiary special-interest groups (known as SIGs) pinpoint your personal interests, be they graphics or financial analysis. Membership is rarely more than $25, and it's almost always worth many times more than that.

Listing every user group in the world would take more space than is currently available, and just the list for North America is quite sizable. Your Apple dealer will usually know how you can contact your local user group. If your dealer can't help, you might contact:

International Apple Core
908 George Street
Santa Clara, CA 95050

They maintain a current list. You might also look into joining IAC itself. They offer discounts on much software, as well as access to information and recources not ordinarily available.

Information Systems and Bulletin Boards

The following is a list of the major information systems that can be accessed via your computer and modem. Many offer Apple bulletin boards and other services of interest to //c owners, all for a sometimes stiff hourly fee. The phone numbers listed are subscriber information numbers where full details on the systems can be obtained.

BRS and BRS After Dark
(800) 833-4707
(800) 553-5566 (in NY)

CompuServe
(800) 848-8199
(614) 457-0802 (in OH)

DIALOG
(800) 227-1927
(800) 982-5838 (in CA)

Dow Jones News/Retrieval
(800) 257-5114
(609) 452-1511 (in NJ)

Delphi
(800) 544-4005
(617) 491-3393 (in MA)

The Source
(800) 336-3366
(703) 821-8888 (in VA)

Many individuals and clubs offer their own electronic bulletin boards full of free information and software. Unfortunately, their numbers have a tendency to change almost daily. Any list included here would be outdated before the book was published and useless soon after that.

Fortunately, many of the information systems maintain lists of current active bulletin boards. On The Source it can be found under PUBLIC 112 (an address in a bulletin board called PUBLIC). On CompuServe look under MAUG XA4. The information is also available directly at The People's Message System, (619) 561-7277. You'll have to introduce yourself to the system by entering your name and vital statistics, but after that a menu will come up on screen to help you along. You might also want to subscribe to the *On-line Computer Telephone Directory,* a quarterly publication. Write for information to:

OLCTD
P.O. Box 10005
Kansas City, MO 64111

Magazines for Apple Users

A+
The Independent Guide to Apple Computing
P.O. Box 2965
Boulder, CO 80322

Highly readable stories cover applications aspects of Apple computing with emphasis on practical use of the machine in today's world. Includes a large review selection for new products. Monthly.

Apple Orchard
P.O. Box 6502
Cupertino, CA 95015

A publication of the International Apple Core, it's a good source for user-group information and applications reviews. Bimonthly.

Byte
70 Main Street
Peterborough, NH 03458

Not for the new user. It examines the theoretical and high-level applications approaches to computing on all computers. Most issues contain at least one Apple-oriented article or feature. Monthly.

Call-A.P.P.L.E.
21246 68th Avenue So.
Kent, WA 98032

A primarily technical approach to hardware and software on the Apple computer from "the largest Apple User Group in the World." It focuses on projects for the intermediate to advanced user. Monthly.

COMPUTE!
P.O. Box 914
Farmingdale, NY 11737

This is an all-purpose general-duty magazine that is not Apple-specific but often contains useful articles relating to practical applications and innovative software for the Apple computer. Monthly.

Creative Computing
39 E. Hanover
Morris Plains, NJ 07950

A lively publication not specifically aimed at the Apple owner, but often containing informative and entertaining articles on products and applications. Hints and tips on Apple use are available in each issue in the "Apple Cart" column. Monthly.

inCider
P.O. Box 911
Farmingdale, NY 11737

A magazine for the computer enthusiast who might not want to devote his or her life to the machine, but needs to know the fundamentals involved in using it. Covers a broad spectrum of Apple applications. Monthly.

Nibble
Box 325
Lincoln, MA 10773

Primarily aimed at the new programmer. There are some interesting articles and program tips in every issue. Monthly.

Peelings II
P.O. Box 625
Holmes, PA 19043

Features evaluations of hardware and software. Bimonthly.

Softalk
Box 7039
No. Hollywood, CA 91605

Focuses on Apple products, users, and applications with some emphasis on the people and companies behind the scenes of Apple-oriented products. Monthly.

Appendix A

Apple //c Facts

The Central Processor Chip

Type: 65C02 [CMOS 6502]
Address Bus: 16-bit
Data Bus: 8-bit
Address Space: 65536 (2^{16}) bytes
Operating Voltage: +5V
Clock Rate: 1.023 MHz
8-Bit Operations/Second: up to 500,000
I/O: memory mapped

Main Integrated Chips

CPU: 65C02 [CMOS 6502]
RAM: bank-switched; 64K main RAM + 64K auxiliary RAM (which cannot be used at the same time as the main RAM); 48K usable
ROMs:
- Keyboard encoder
- Display character generator
- Firmware:
  - Monitor (screen clearing and updating, key code retrieving and storage)
  - Applesoft BASIC interpreter
  - Enhanced video software
  - Misc. I/O software

Custom integrated circuits:
- Memory Management Unit (MMU)—memory addressing control logic

Input/Output Unit (IOU)—built-in I/O feature control logic
Timing Generator (TMG)—Generates system and I/O signals from 14 MHz main clock
General Logic Unit (GLU)—misc. logic function
Integrated Woz Machine (IWM)—Apple Disk II controller card logic on single chip

Back Panel (left to right)

9-pin D-type miniature connector:	joystick, mouse, other pointing devices
5-pin DIN connector (port #2):	modem, serial I/O
15-pin D-type connector:	video expansion
RCA phono jack:	video monitor
19-pin D-type connector:	external disk drive
5-pin DIN connector (port #1):	serial printer, serial I/O
7-pin DIN connector:	power input

Keyboard Features

Number of keys: 63
Available ASCII codes: 128
Automatic repeat: All characters
Rollover: 2-key buffer

Function keys:	*reset*
Cursor-moving keys:	←
	→
	↑
	↓
	delete
	tab
	return
Modifier keys:	*esc*
	shift
	control
	caps lock

Key combinations:
control + *reset* = warm start (no system reinitialization)
control + + *reset* = forced cold start
control + Letter keys (et al.) = ASCII control characters

Keyboard switch:
  Up position — standard Sholes layout
  Down position — Dvorak simplified layout

Video Features

Text display modes:	40-column text 80-column text
Graphics display modes:	Low-resolution color High-resolution color Double-high-resolution color
Maximum characters:	24 lines × 80 columns (1,920 on one screen)
Character set:	96 ASCII characters
Display formats:	Normal Inverse Flashing *MouseText* (icons)
Graphics specifications:	
Low-resolution	16 colors 40 horizontal × 48 vertical dots
High-resolution	6 colors color—140 horizontal × 192 vertical mono — 280 horizontal × 192 vertical
Double-high-resolution	16 colors color—140 horizontal × 192 vertical mono — 560 horizontal × 192 vertical
Color signal:	NTSC-compatible composite
Color outputs:	RCA phono jack (for video monitor) 15-pin D-connector (for external video modulator via DB-15 connector)

Audio Features

Internal speaker:	mounted on bottom plate
Beep signal:	1 kHz tone, duration 0.1 sec
Volume control:	500-ohm variable resistor, located on left side of case
External connections:	3.5 mm miniphone jack (stereo or mono), insertion of phone jack disconnects internal speaker

Recommended Operating Conditions

Temperature:	10° to 40° C (50° to 104° F)	
Relative Humidity:	20% to 95%	
Power:	105 to 129 AC volts, 60 Hz	
Maximum Input Power Consumption:		25 W
Supply Voltage:		+15 V DC (nominal)
Supply Current:		1.2 A (nominal)

Appendix B

The Keys to the Keyboard

Three Ways to Reset the System

1. Cold Start—(turning off/on switch *on*)—clears display, initiates disk controller firmware start-up routine, loads operating system in internal drive. (Pressing *control* + *reset* before start-up is completed will continue start-up without using disk, then pass control to Applesoft BASIC.)
2. Warm Start—(pressing *control* + *reset after* completion of cold start) —transfers control to active program. At power-up, active program is Applesoft BASIC. If DOS or ProDOS are active, this restarts appropriate BASIC interpreter.
3. Forced Cold Start—(holding *control* + ⌘ , then pressing *reset*)—stops active program. Use this rather than off/on switch to stop one program and start up //c with another program.

ESC Codes

"exits" = exits from ESC mode after performing action
"stays" = remains in ESC mode after performing action

ESC @	—clears window and moves cursor to upper left-hand corner; exits
ESC A (ESC a)	—moves cursor one space right; exits
ESC B (ESC b)	—moves cursor one space left; exits
ESC C (ESC c)	—moves cursor one line down; exits
ESC D (ESC d)	—moves cursor one line up; exits
ESC E (ESC e)	—clears to end of line; exits
ESC F (ESC f)	—clears to bottom of window; exits

ESC I (ESC i) ESC ↑	—moves cursor one line up; stays
ESC J (ESC j) ESC ←	—moves cursor one space left; stays
ESC K (ESC k) ESC →	—moves cursor one space right; stays
ESC M (ESC m) ESC ↓	—moves cursor one line down; stays
ESC 4	—switches to 40-column mode; exits
ESC 8	—switches to 80-column mode; exits
ESC CONTROL-D	—disables control characters; leaves only carriage return, linefeed, bell, backspace; exits
ESC CONTROL-E	—enables control characters; exits
ESC CONTROL-Q	—deactivates enhanced video firmware; exits

Books

Dunn, Seamus, and Valerie Morgan. *The Apple Personal Computer for Beginners.* Englewood Cliffs, NJ: Prentice-Hall International, 1982.

Graff, Louis, and Larry Joel Goldstein. *Applesoft Basic for the Apple // and //e.* Bowie, MD: Robert J. Brady, 1984.

Hartnell, T., and Rohan Cook. *How to Program the Apple //e.* New York: Ballantine Books, 1983.

Luehrmann, Arthur, and Herbert Peckham. *Computer Literacy Survival Kit.* New York: McGraw-Hill, 1983.

Poole, Lon, Martin McNiff, and Steve Cook. *The Apple // User's Guide.* Berkeley, CA: Osborne/McGraw-Hill, 1983.

Rugg, Tom, and Phil Feldman. *32 Basic Programs for the Apple Computer.* Beaverton, OR: dilithium Press, 1981.

Sanders, William B. *The Elementary Apple.* Chatsworth, CA: Datamost, 1982.

Scanlon, Leo J. *Apple // Assembly Language Exercises.* New York: John Wiley & Sons, 1981.

Swift's Educational Software Directory: Apple // Edition. Austin, TX: Sterling Swift Publishing. Annual.

VanLove's Apple Software Directory, 1984 edition. Overland Park, KS: Advanced Software Technology, Inc., 1984.

Index

ABOUT THE AUTHOR

BILL O'BRIEN is a widely published writer and a recognized expert on Apple computers. He is a contributing editor to *A+* magazine, the author of a long-running monthly column in *inCider* magazine, and has written for *Creative Computing, Microcomputing,* and *80 Micro*. He's had hands-on experience with every type of Apple computer ever made and has owned an Apple // since its infancy.